AFTER "THE YEAR EIGHTY"

AFTER "THE YEAR EIGHTY"

THE DEMISE OF FRANCISCAN POWER
IN SPANISH NEW MEXICO

Jim Norris

University of New Mexico Press
Albuquerque

Published in cooperation with the
Academy of American Franciscan History

Library of Congress Cataloging-in-Publication Data

Norris, Jim, 1949–
    After "the year eighty" : the demise of Franciscan power in Spanish
New Mexico / Jim Norris. — 1st ed.
        p.   cm.
Includes bibliographical references and index.
    ISBN 0-8263-2211-5 (alk. paper)
1. Franciscans—New Mexico—History—18th century. 2. New Mexico—
Church history—18th century. I. Title.
BX 3609.N6 N67 2000
    271'.30789'09033—dc21
00-008468

TO MY PARENTS, BILL AND JUSTINE NORRIS

Contents

Maps

Acknowledgments

THIS BOOK was helped immeasurably by numerous individuals and institutions to whom I owe my gratitude. Richard E. Greenleaf, my mentor at Tulane University, encouraged and directed the inception of the project. Eleanor B. Adams and John L. Kessell offered important advice and insight during the initial research stages. The work was further enhanced by scholars who read all or parts of the manuscript and freely contributed their expertise: Robert H. Jackson, Ricki Janicek, Eric Palladini Jr., F. Todd Smith, David J. Weber, and Gertrude M. Yeager. I also would like to thank my colleagues at North Dakota State University for their enthusiastic support.

Many librarians, archivists, and support staff aided my research. I would especially like to thank those at the Center for Southwest Research, University of New Mexico; New Mexico State Library (Southwest Collection); John Carter Brown Library (Brown University); Nettie Lee Benson Latin American Library (University of Texas at Austin); Howard-Tilton Memorial Library (Latin American Library, Tulane University); and the libraries at the University of Arkansas at Monticello and North Dakota State University. In Mexico City, the librarians and staff at the Biblioteca Nacional, México (Archivo Franciscano), the Instituto Nacional de Antropología e Historia (Fondo Franciscano), and the Archivo General de la Nación were gracious, understanding, and helpful on my behalf.

During the course of writing this manuscript, I received financial assistance from several sources. These included the Tinker-Mellon Foundation, John Carter Brown Library, University of Arkansas at Monticello, the Roger Thayer Stone Center for Latin American Studies (Tulane University), and the Graduate School of Tulane University.

Writing After "The Year Eighty" took almost a decade, and many people provided support in ways that are difficult to categorize. I would be remiss if I did not express my warm appreciation to John Allen, Marcy Brekken, B. J. Elzinga, Bill Holm, Letha Kerl, John Kerl, George Mariz, Geoff Skews, Arnita

Skews, Cliff Tramel, Leonard Vader, Catharine Vader, and Virginia Vader. Claire Strom helped polish the final draft of the text and notes and offered invaluable support and encouragement in the final stages. Jan Jenkins, my dear friend and former colleague, did yeoman duty with her editorial scalpel and kept me on track throughout this work. And finally, this book might never have happened without my knowing Julia Kerl.

I would like to thank the staff at the University of New Mexico Press, especially my editor, David V. Holtby.

Of course, any errors are solely my responsibility.

(A slightly revised version of chapter 7, "The Struggle Over Diocesan Control," appeared in the *New Mexico Historical Review* as "The Struggle Over Diocesan Control in New Mexico, 1715–1737," in April 1995.)

AFTER "THE YEAR EIGHTY"

Introduction

I N THE SPRING of 1723, after a long, difficult, and dangerous 1,200-mile journey from Mexico City, Fray Antonio Gabaldón arrived in what the Spanish
called the Kingdom of New Mexico. The physical environment of his new
home was not so different from his familiar world of central Mexico. Except for
the massive bison found on the plains of New Mexico, most of the flora and
fauna of the region were similar, if not the same, to what Gabaldón already
knew. Nor was the altitude of the frontier colony something that required great
adjustment as both central Mexico and New Mexico often exceed 7,000 feet
above sea level. Extensive mountain ranges and solitary volcanic peaks were
also nothing odd to the new missionary.[1,2]

Climatic elements, however, were a different matter. Fray Antonio had just
missed the ice, snow, and freezing temperatures of winter, although he would
endure those often enough during his tenure in New Mexico. Likewise, the frequent days of 90- to 100-degree summer temperatures would also be a hardship
with which he would have to contend. Typically, the temperature extremes of
the Kingdom were about twenty degrees hotter or colder than the more moderate environs around Puebla and Mexico City.

Perhaps the greatest environmental adversity Gabaldón would face was the
physical isolation endemic to New Mexico. He was now about 1,200 miles from
his home and family in Puebla. Supply caravans routinely took six months to
traverse the distance from central Mexico to New Mexico, and couriers on
horseback required one to three months to make the journey. Thus, personal
letters and official correspondence usually entailed long periods of waiting for
replies. If a communication necessitated the attention of officials in Spain, a
New Mexico resident might wait up to three years for a response. Some of Gabaldón's fellow friars in New Mexico received permission to return briefly to
their home regions. However, there is no record that Fray Antonio enjoyed that
respite during his thirty-seven years in the Kingdom. A brother, Juan Manuel
Gabaldón, did join Fray Antonio in New Mexico by 1731. Juan became a
lawyer, married, and fathered eleven children in New Mexico by 1759. Only

two other friars were known to have relatives follow them to the frontier during this era.[3]

Isolation within New Mexico was a problem for the Franciscans as well. Like most missionary priests, Gabaldón was usually assigned to serve a mission alone. Though many missions were within ten miles of one another, traveling alone, usually on foot, subject to attack by Comanches or other raiding natives, and exposed to hazardous weather extremes made these relatively short journeys to visit a fellow friar difficult and perilous excursions. To his credit, Gabaldón was never singled out for reprimand for leaving his assigned station without permission, but many of his brethren were. A sense of loneliness among these friars likely contributed to this dereliction of their duties.

Gabaldón's background was typical of many Franciscan missionaries in New Mexico. He was born in Puebla in May 1700, the son of Don Antonio Ruíz Gabaldón and Doña Michaela Rendón de Córdova. Titles before each parent's name indicate a family of some social importance in Puebla, at least from the middle sector of Spanish society. His father was deceased at the time Antonio applied to enter the Order of St. Francis; hence, the father's occupation was not noted, although he was said to have been a native of Castilla. The paternal grandparents were referred to as Don and Doña, and the grandfather was reputed to have held minor government posts in Spain. Gabaldón's mother was a native of Puebla, as were the maternal grandparents, of which only the grandmother was addressed respectfully with Doña. Her husband secured his livelihood from the slaughter and sale of pork in Puebla. Thus, Fray Antonio conformed to the average social profile of Franciscans in New Spain during the eighteenth century: *criollo* (a Spaniard born in the New World), from the middle sector of colonial society, and a native of one of the urban centers of central Mexico.

His early career as a Franciscan, however, was not quite so normal. True, as did most friars, he entered the Order while in his teens. Gabaldón had just turned sixteen when he applied at the Franciscan convent of San Francisco de Puebla for admission and was accepted in June 1716. His novitiate was a little more than a year, as he made his profession of faith on 1 October 1717, which was also about standard. Gabaldón was only twenty-three, however, when he arrived in New Mexico. This was one year less than the Franciscans' established minimum of twenty-four years of age for ordination to the priesthood. Very young missionaries were extremely rare because the administration of the sacraments of faith, a crucial spiritual duty for a missionary, required a fully ordained priest. No official explanation is extant that might shed light on this anomaly in Gabaldón's professional career.

Like many of his contemporaries, Fray Antonio served in numerous different missions and was moved about frequently during his years in New Mexico. His assignments included at least one stay in each of the Pueblo missions of Pecos, Galisteo, Nambé, San Ildefonso, Zía, Santa Clara, Cochití, and Taos. Furthermore, Gabaldón served in the missions around El Paso for about three years. He closed his tenure in New Mexico as the priest for the Spanish villa of Santa Cruz de la Cañada. Of the nine different sites where he labored, the average length of each stay was about two and a half years, which was also the norm among eighteenth-century New Mexico missionaries.

Gabaldón's performance as a missionary priest appears to have been unremarkable; there were no great achievements, but also no noteworthy problems or scandals. He served as the secretary to the *custos* (local prelate or superior of the Franciscans in New Mexico) for two years, 1728 to 1730. He was also the secretary for Fray Juan Miguel Menchero's *visita* (inspection) in 1730–1731. In 1736, Gabaldón was cited for his obedient and loyal service of more than ten years in the Kingdom. As the priest at Santa Cruz de la Cañada, he was responsible for most of the construction of the church buildings in the 1740s.[4] Citizens of Truchas in 1762 asserted that Fray Antonio had attended to their needs well when he was the missionary at Santa Cruz de la Cañada, despite his having to travel over twelve miles of arduous terrain to reach their community.[5] On the other hand, Fray Antonio did not play an active role in the last major effort to expand the missionary field in the 1740s, nor was he ever acclaimed for his mastery of native languages. He was never selected as custos or vice-custos, nor was he appointed *comisario* (local representative) of the Holy Office (Inquisition), as one might expect of a respected veteran friar in New Mexico. His name did not receive mention in any of the great controversies of the era, nor did his superiors ever reprimand Gabaldón. Hence, Fray Antonio was likely a steady, obedient, loyal, but unspectacular Franciscan missionary.

Like so many of his fellow New Mexico friars, Fray Antonio's active career as a Franciscan priest ended without fanfare. His name last appears on official Franciscan rosters (at provincial headquarters in Mexico City) for New Mexico in 1760. A local New Mexico roster dated 1759, however, has a notation next to Gabaldón's name: "has died."[6] Whichever document is accurate, there is no further mention of him in extant Franciscan records for New Spain. Of course, he was at least sixty years of age by then with almost four decades of service in the rigorous environment of the Kingdom. That he had labored so long was a credit to his stamina, if nothing else. Most friars who served in New Mexico remained past age fifty, and very few of those continued to be active as priests once they left.

Gabaldón's origins and experiences as a Franciscan missionary are not the only factors that make him a representative figure of the Order's history in New Mexico during the 1692–1776 period. His arrival in 1723 came at a time when the mission operation was still understaffed, a situation that was chronic after the reconquest of the region following the Pueblo revolt in 1680. For about three decades there had been only half-hearted attempts to restore the missionary program to pre-1680 levels. Shortly after Fray Antonio's appearance in the colony, the number of friars stationed there began to rise, and by 1736, the Franciscan contingent was nearly equal to that of 1680. Consequently, in the 1730s and 1740s, the Franciscans were able to undertake their only sustained effort to reform and expand the mission system during the eighteenth century.

Changes in the Franciscans' autonomy over the spiritual life of the Kingdom coincided with Gabaldón's time, too. Prior to the 1720s, the Diocese of Durango, which claimed jurisdiction over New Mexico, had been unable to exert its dominion over the territory. During that decade, however, the government ruled favorably for the episcopate in this longstanding dispute. Fray Antonio witnessed Bishop Benito Crespo's visita in New Mexico in 1730, the first ever undertaken by a Durango prelate. While the Franciscans vigorously protested the extension of episcopal authority, they were unable to halt the erosion of their religious authority in the colony. Gabaldón was also present in 1737 for the subsequent inspection by Bishop Martín de Elizacoechea and just missed Bishop Pedro Tamarón y Romeral's visita in 1760.

This change in policy regarding the prerogatives of the Diocese of Durango over the Franciscans is indicative of another important development that paralleled Gabaldón's years in New Mexico: the decline of the Order's local political power and influence. Between 1692 and 1723, their political stature had already ebbed, primarily because of the friars' dependence on the state for protection from both the Puebloan people and non-mission natives such as hostile Apaches, as well as increased control by New Mexico's governors over the Kingdom's fiscal affairs. Because of turmoil within the office of the governor, however, more significant limitations on the Franciscans' political position had not occurred. Beginning in 1720s, the government (from local officials on up to the Crown) maintained a steady effort to augment civil authority at the expense of the Franciscans. By the time Governor Tomás Vélez Cachupín closed his first term in 1754, the friars were virtually impotent in their dealings with the local government officials. Hence, Fray Antonio was also party to the Franciscans' political collapse.

Fray Antonio's experiences and those of other friars reveal the decline of Franciscan power in New Mexico in the 1692–1776 period. Steady, if underachieving evangelical friars, working in isolation in an arduous environment, were not up to the demands of spreading Spanish Catholicism and civilization on New Spain's far northern frontier. To the Franciscans, hostile institutions and officials in Santa Fe, Durango, Mexico City, and at the court in Spain sought to limit and reduce the Order's once-prodigious spiritual, economic, and political influence in the Kingdom. For most of this period the friars were on the defensive, from both the secular hierarchy of the Church and the royal government. In that atmosphere, the heretofore exalted Franciscan position in New Mexico slowly withered away.

* * *

The breakdown of Franciscan hegemony in New Mexico did not occur in one fell swoop, but was an evolutionary process that began with the Pueblo revolt in 1680 and continued throughout most of the eighteenth century. Four different, though often related, developments were most responsible for the Franciscans' decline. The first determinant factor was the legacy of *el año ochenta* (the year eighty), as the Franciscans often referred to the Puebloan revolt. The Puebloans had demonstrated their capacity to rebel and, consequently, when the friars returned to the missions, the priests were more dependent on the state's military protection and less willing to insist on the native people's strict adherence to the tenets of Catholicism. Second, the powers of local civil officials were expanded, as the superior government in Mexico City and Madrid altered the raison d'être of New Mexico from that of primarily a mission field to a region important to the defense of northern New Spain. This change was caused by growing French activity in the area and increased Indian resistance. Therefore, civil and military matters reigned supreme in the higher councils of government. Third, the Franciscans' religious authority deteriorated as the Inquisition placed restrictions on the Order's use of those powers, and the Diocese of Durango increasingly extended its jurisdiction over New Mexico. The latter development was a prolonged process that diverted attention and consumed much of the Order's energy for over two decades. And finally, weaknesses within the Franciscan operation played a prominent role in its own demise. Decisions on how missionaries were trained, deployed, and maintained in the Kingdom led to fundamental shortcomings in the evangelical process. Thus, the propagation of the Catholic faith dwindled in the colony, along with the Franciscans' prestige and stature.

The purpose of this book is to examine how the demise of Franciscan authority occurred. The emphasis will be on the Order of St. Francis itself: how the missionary operation functioned and the nature of its relationship with other rival forces. The Franciscans' interactions with other colonial elements—local government officials, the superior government in Mexico City and Spain, the Diocese of Durango, native people, Spanish residents—will be developed only in regard to the struggle over power in the Kingdom. Consequently, the social, cultural, and economic factors of the Franciscans' interplay with Indian and Spaniard will not be of primary concern herein.

It should be noted that the Kingdom of New Mexico encompassed mission areas in what is today New Mexico, Arizona, Texas, and northeast Mexico. The

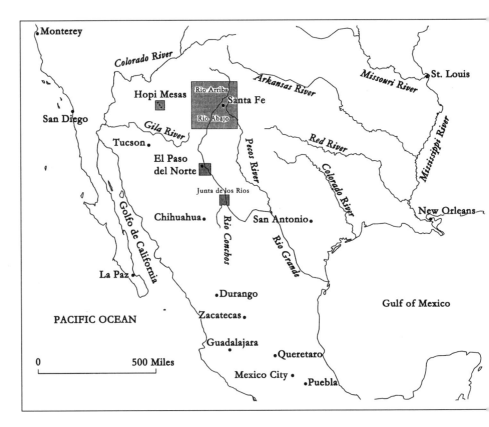

Map 1. The Custody of Saint Paul (see shaded areas)

missions in Texas were located east of the Río Grande near El Paso, and those
in Mexico in present-day Ciudad Juárez and near the confluence of the Río
Grande and Río Conchos (Junta de los Ríos). Essentially, there were three mission districts: Santa Fe (northern and central New Mexico, and northern Arizona), El Paso (environs of El Paso and southern New Mexico), and Junta de
los Ríos. Furthermore, the Santa Fe district was partitioned into two zones: Río
Arriba (from the mission-pueblo of Cochití northward) and Río Abajo (south
from Cochití to near present-day Socorro). This book will focus primarily on
the Santa Fe district, where the greatest number of friars and missions were
maintained and the centers of local government and the Order were situated.
Events in El Paso and Junta de los Ríos will only be discussed in regard to developments in the Santa Fe district. Therefore, a generic use of "New Mexico"
will be understood to refer to the Santa Fe mission district, unless the inclusion
of El Paso and Junta de los Ríos is specifically stated.

CHAPTER 2

The Franciscans in New Mexico to 1692

UNTIL THE Pueblo rebellion in 1680, the missionary effort of the Order of St. Francis in the Kingdom of New Mexico had produced an institution that was at least equal to, if not greater than, the local colonial government in power and influence. At their zenith in the seventeenth century, the Franciscans maintained over forty missions, and as many as seventy friars labored in the colony. Control over the Puebloan people meant that the Order held significant dominion over the region's primary labor force, and the missions' agricultural and livestock production was unsurpassed. As the only representatives of the Catholic Church in New Mexico, the Franciscans held sway in the spiritual and moral affairs of the Kingdom and enjoyed virtual immunity from the secular hierarchy of the Church. Using as their primary weapon the powers of the Inquisition, the friars jealously protected their own positions and privileges, and often used their inquisitorial bludgeon to expand their power at the expense of local civil officials. Acrimonious struggles with colonial political figures, however, seriously eroded Spanish control over the native population and were one of the primary causes of the Pueblo revolt. That catastrophic event for the Spanish marked the beginning of the breakdown of the Franciscans' position in New Mexico.

* * *

The Franciscans' missionary effort in New Mexico actually began with the friars who accompanied the expedition of Francisco Vásquez de Coronado in 1540 to the region. When that force abandoned its effort in 1542, Fray Juan de Padilla remained behind to initiate the conversion of the Puebloans. Padilla soon became the Franciscans' first martyr in New Mexico. Three friars were part of the Rodríguez-Chamuscada expedition in 1581–1582. Again, the endeavor proved fatal to the missionaries. Fray Juan de Santa María was killed by natives during the incursion, and the other two—Fray Agustín Rodríguez and Fray Francisco López—who remained behind to administer to the Puebloans, were slain before a relief force arrived a year later.[1]

A permanent missionary presence was established finally with the conquest and settlement of New Mexico in 1598 by Don Juan de Oñate. This expedition contained ten Franciscans (eight priests and two lay brothers) supervised by Fray Alonso Martínez. There were three reasons for such a large contingent of friars. Part of the Crown's Ordinances of 1573, which contained sweeping changes for Spanish expansionist policy in the New World, dictated that expeditions of discovery and settlement employ more pacific and persuasive means to bring native people under the government's control. Hence, Oñate's contract with the royal government to settle New Mexico stipulated that at least six friars be part of the expedition. Second, another part of the Ordinances delineated separate missionary spheres for the different mendicant bodies active in New Spain. The Franciscans' zone included the area that would become the Kingdom of New Mexico. And finally, in central Mexico where the number of Franciscan missions was largest, a wave of mission secularization after 1570 meant that the friars either open new mission fields or abandon that line of spiritual activity. The Franciscans chose the former.[2]

The grant of the Puebloan people to the Franciscans in September 1598 by Oñate marked the inauguration of the Order's mission system in the Kingdom. The early years, however, were not fruitful ones for the Spanish. New Mexico did not contain valuable minerals, as had been hoped, and the economic potential of the area as a whole did not seem promising. Governor Oñate and his military forces were frequently absent from the colony, vainly searching for gold and silver. The settlers and missionaries often lacked military protection as a result of Oñate's forays and soon the Puebloans became reluctant hosts to the Spanish. Finally, in 1601, most of the settlers and all but three of the friars abandoned New Mexico.[3]

During the next seven years, the government vacillated on what should be done with the colony. In 1608, however, the Franciscans claimed in reports to royal officials that the missionaries that had remained in the Kingdom had baptized over 7,000 Puebloans. Though this figure was inflated significantly, it did offer the Spanish Crown a motive to continue the effort to settle New Mexico. In 1609, Philip III designated the region a royal colony and a new expedition marched north with more settlers, nine additional Franciscans, and a newly appointed governor, Don Pedro de Peralta.[4]

From that point the missionary effort grew remarkably quickly. Between 1609 and 1625, another sixteen friars were posted to New Mexico and at least fourteen missions established. The number of missionaries was augmented significantly in the following decade, and by the late 1630s there were over fifty friars and thirty missions in an area that encompassed central and northern New

Mexico and the Hopi villages of northern Arizona. In 1643, the Franciscans established their first mission among the Suma people to the south around El Paso del Norte (hereafter El Paso). By the 1650s, approximately seventy missionaries in the Kingdom labored in forty-three missions, although the number of friars declined somewhat in the years preceding the Pueblo revolt.[5]

The rapid expansion of the missionary field did not occur without a great human toll. The Puebloan people's interlocking social, religious, economic, and political systems were disrupted, radically modified, or eliminated. Labor requirements and disease reduced their population from perhaps as many as 60,000 in 1598, to about 17,000 at the time of the great rebellion. As they were forced to congregate into missions or fled from the Spanish, the Puebloans abandoned over two-thirds of their villages. The Puebloan people's efforts to retain their religion and social customs were met by torture, enslavement, and often death inflicted by Spanish civil and military authorities as well as the friars.[6]

Puebloan resistance and the difficult environment of frontier life imposed a high human cost on the Franciscans, too. The number of martyred friars rose steadily. Three died at the hands of the Hopi in 1632–1633. Seven years later, another was slain during an uprising at Taos. Apaches killed Fray Pedro de Avila y Ayala. Several others were suspected of having been poisoned by their mission neophytes. In all, perhaps as many as twenty-five friars died as a result of native hostility prior to the rebellion in 1680. No definitive figure can be ascertained of the number that succumbed to natural causes.[7]

* * *

The friars that served in New Mexico were members of a branch of the Order of St. Francis referred to as *observantes ultramontanas*, a designation derived from both an ideological and geographic division within the Order. Throughout the fifteenth century, the Franciscans were consumed by an internal conflict between the "observants" and another group of friars known as the *conventuales*. The main point of controversy centered on a strict interpretation of the rule of poverty, to which the observants adhered. In 1517 Pope Leo X ruled in favor of the observants and decreed that the leadership of the Order from that date forward would be selected only from among the observants. Spain had long been a bastion of the observant friars, and as a result of Leo X's decision, all conventual houses in Spain were closed. It should also be noted that the observants had a reputation for zealous evangelicalism. Observant friars had accompanied Columbus's second voyage in 1493, and were the first missionaries to work in Hispaniola, Cuba, Jamaica, Colombia, and Mexico.

Geographically, the Order was composed of *cismontana* (Italy, Austria, and eastward) and *ultramontana* (Spain, Portugal, England, and northern Europe) friars.[8]

The spiritual and administrative leader of the Franciscans was known as the General, or Vicar, who resided in Rome. Directly accountable to the pontiff, the General served a six-year term and was elected by the *capítulo*, the supreme legislative body of the Order. The capítulo was composed of two elected friars from each Franciscan province.[9]

For the Franciscans serving in the New World, the chain of command originated in Spain. In 1572 the Spanish monarchy ordered the creation of a Franciscan Commissary General of the Indies. The Commissary General of the Indies' responsibilities included the coordination of Franciscan activities in the New World, determination of policy concerning the Order, recruitment and assignment of friars to the colonies, and representation of the Franciscans at the Spanish court.

Directly responsible to the Commissary General of the Indies were officials in the New World, also known as commissary generals. During the seventeenth century, there were two of these local commissary generals: one each for the viceroyalties of New Spain and Perú. Their duties involved setting mission policies, local recruitment, training and management of friars, and the overall supervision of the Franciscan provinces in their respective regions.[10]

The New Mexico missions were part of the Franciscan Provincia del Santo Evangelio (Province of the Holy Gospel) headquartered in Mexico City. This was the oldest Franciscan province in colonial Mexico, created in 1534, and all subsequent provinces on the mainland of New Spain were at one time part of Santo Evangelio. Headed by a commissary provincial, during the seventeenth century its territory included the region around Mexico City and Puebla, extending north and eastward to the mission fields of Tampico and New Mexico. Santo Evangelio was responsible for most facets of the New Mexico missionization operation.[11]

In the Franciscan institutional hierarchy, New Mexico was known as the Custodia de San Pablo del Nuevo México (Custody of Saint Paul of New Mexico). The custodial designation was made sometime prior to 1616. As defined by France V. Scholes, a custody was a "semi-independent area, autonomous and self-governing in local affairs, but still subject to the general control of the province of which it formed a part." The Custody of Saint Paul had its own chapter, *difinitorio* (advisory council), and prelate (the custos). A custody was usually a transitional phase prior to a region's promotion to provincial status, but this custody never attained that status. The elevation to a separate province was considered often during the 1600s, but because of the absence of schools and other training facilities, the poor financial condition of New Mexico, and the danger posed by hostile natives, the Franciscan structure in the Kingdom remained a custody.[12]

The custos, or prelate, of the Custody of Saint Paul was elected by the provincial chapter of Santo Evangelio. During the seventeenth century, this Franciscan official was usually not in New Mexico at the time of his selection but was dispatched to the Kingdom from central Mexico. In the 1600s, the custos generally served a three-year term, although tenure in the post varied greatly. His duties included the direct supervision of the friars and their mission activities, service as the local ecclesiastical judge, and representation of the Order in its dealings with the local civil government. These were, at least, the official duties of a custos.[13]

A custos also held two other powerful positions during most of the seventeenth century. One of these was as the commissary of the Inquisition, which was established in 1626 in New Mexico. The custos was given this office in order to provide the Church with more leverage in relation to the Kingdom's civil authorities. As the representative of the Holy Office, the custos enjoyed immense power in promoting religious orthodoxy over Spanish residents and in protecting the powers and privileges of the Franciscans in the colony.[14]

The other special authority invested in the office of the custos was through the broad "quasi-episcopal" power that had been granted to the mendicant orders. These special prerogatives had been awarded primarily in a series of papal bulls, especially the *Exponi nobis fecisti* (also known as *Ominimoda*) issued by Pope Adrian VI in 1522, which generally authorized the regular orders in New Spain to perform any religious rites or sacraments in the absence of the secular clergy in order to facilitate the conversion of native people. While the Council of Trent and the Mexican Council of 1565 moved to return these rights to episcopal control, Pope Pius V allowed the mendicants to continue offering most sacraments if there were no secular priests available or if bishops were located at great distances (generally more than a two-day ride). Therefore, the custos retained vast episcopal powers in New Mexico throughout the seventeenth century, despite the fact that the Diocese of Durango claimed jurisdiction over the region (see chapter 6).[15]

In addition to the custos, another minor body of religious authority in the Kingdom was the difinitorio. The members of this group were elected locally by the friars, though the number of members in the 1600s is unclear. A document from 1672 indicates that at the time the difinitorio was composed of four friars and the custos. Its principal duties seem to have been in acting as a unified voice for the friars in their relations with other institutions and in assigning priests to mission sites.[16]

The Franciscan Order did not function in a void, however, free from government oversight. Through a number of papal bulls issued between 1493 and

1508, the papacy gave wide powers to the Spanish monarchy over Church matters that came to be known as the Patronato Real (Royal Patronage). These bulls, most notably *Inter cetera* (Alexander VI, 1493) and *Universalis ecclesiae* (Jules II, 1508), acknowledged the right of the Spanish Crown to control all religious appointments, to select the sites for parishes and missions, and to oversee most other Church affairs. In exchange, the monarchy was to promote the propagation of Catholicism in the New World, including financial support. In theory, then, the Spanish monarchy retained ultimate sovereignty over virtually all Church activities.[17]

In an empire so vast, however, this was practically impossible. Thus, the Spanish kings invested some royal officials with vice-patron authority to make the Patronato Real more effective. In New Spain, the viceregal office was granted such vice-patron powers, but through bewildering and often contradictory royal decrees and opinions, so were other agencies and officials. For seventeenth-century New Mexico, the viceroys of New Spain, the *audiencias* of Mexico and Guadalajara, as well as various governors all claimed vice-patron rights at one time.[18]

The net effect was that none of these administrators enforced to the letter the intent of the Patronato Real. Fighting among themselves for control, governors and audiencia judges were no match for the unified Franciscans. The viceroys generally managed the purse strings for the missions and certainly held sway over most of the larger issues concerning New Mexico, but in the day-to-day operations the Franciscans piloted their own ship. The friars jealously guarded this freedom from political control, which consequently became a source of endless conflicts with the local civil authority throughout most of the 1600s.

※　※　※

The consensus among scholars of this epoch is that the Franciscans viewed their evangelical effort to the native people as the most important factor in the settlement of New Mexico. Whether, as John L. Kessell described, the Franciscans insisted that the Kingdom serve as "a vineyard for the Lord" or, as Ramón A. Gutiérrez maintained, the friars were religious "fanatics" whose primary goal was creation of a utopian "theocracy," it is clear the missionaries deemed their work as paramount. In the region's isolation, the Franciscans were free from competition from other religious orders and the secular clergy, and the Diocese of Durango was unable to establish episcopal jurisdiction. The only institution that might interfere with the Franciscans' activities within the colony was the local government authority, especially the governor.[19]

The Spanish government envisioned that governors and missionaries would work closely together, or at least that was the intention inherent in the instructions in 1609 to the first royal governor, Don Pedro de Peralta. In addition to duties to protect and promote the welfare of the Spanish inhabitants, Governor Peralta was to ensure the congregation of native people in missions, attend to other Franciscan requirements that would promote the spread of Catholicism, and to consult closely with the Franciscans in pertinent regional affairs. If the implication was that Peralta and his successors were to function in relative harmony with the Franciscans, the Crown was sorely disappointed. Governors and Franciscans engaged in endless, severe disputes throughout much of the seventeenth century.[20]

New Mexico's governors in this era have been characterized generally as an unsavory lot. Appointed to terms of usually three years, which they often purchased, they had little time to profit from their posts or to consolidate their authority. As Scholes has often noted, the governors' primary goal seemed to be to enrich themselves. Governors habitually violated royal decrees that forbade them from engaging in trade, exploited the Puebloans for goods and labor, and carried out slave raids against non-mission natives. These officials frequently and capriciously appointed or removed district officers (*alcaldes mayores*) to further their own financial ambitions. This action, however, usually created an opposition cadre of those out of office that would often ally itself with the Franciscans. And finally, some governors were also violent, immoral, and contemptuous toward the Catholic Church.[21]

The limitations of this study do not allow for a detailed recapitulation of the conflicts between Franciscans and governors that were endemic to the 1600s. Generally, their disputes centered on control over the Puebloan people within the missions, ecclesiastical jurisdiction and privileges, some governors' lack of support to mission activities, and the personal behavior of royal officials as Catholics. Excommunication of governors by the Franciscans was virtually the norm, and some were imprisoned in the colony through the custos's powers as ecclesiastical judge. One governor, Don Luís de Rosas (1637–1642), was murdered, likely with the tacit approval of some friars. Through the club of Inquisitional authority, the Franciscans had four governors and several alcaldes mayores hauled to Mexico City for trial before the tribunal of the Holy Office. Governors, for their part, undermined mission operations and encouraged Puebloan disobedience to the friars. One custos was incarcerated briefly by a governor. Though there were brief respites, church and state acrimony characterized their relations from 1609 until the mid-1660s, with the Franciscans usually victorious.[22]

Besides their political superiority, the Franciscans were an economic force in the Kingdom. The Pueblo missions included landholdings that measured from two to six leagues in diameter. On these tracts crops such as corn and wheat grew, and livestock, mainly cattle and sheep, grazed. While no accurate figure exists for the amount that was produced in the 1600s, it must have been substantial compared with the non-mission population. No concrete evidence exists that friars individually profited from mission goods; however, the Franciscans stored surpluses and distributed them throughout the colony during lean periods. The Spanish residents' dependence on Franciscan charity of this kind must have enhanced the Order's influence.

A mission supply service, which the Franciscans operated from 1631 to 1664 and, again, from 1674 to 1680, was another powerful economic tool. Up to 1680, it has been estimated that the Spanish government spent over one million pesos on the New Mexico missions. To organize the delivery of supplies and to free the viceregal office from the onus of direct fiscal management of the missions, the Crown provided sums of money directly to the Order, which the Franciscans used to dispatch a supply caravan to New Mexico every three years. Each ordained missionary priest was allotted 450 pesos, and each lay brother, 300 pesos. To outfit a new missionary, the government provided 850 pesos. In addition, about 374 pesos were disbursed for each wagon with sixteen mules. With between forty to seventy Franciscans to be provisioned, and about one wagon for every two friars, the mission supply caravans were massive convoys.[23]

The importance of the mission supply service to New Mexico transcended the monies spent. It was the only regularly scheduled transportation system to and from the colony. Furthermore, the caravans were large enough to offer a measure of security from hostile natives for travelers, goods, and all manner of correspondence. Perhaps more significantly, once the wagons were unloaded in the Kingdom they could be employed to haul back whatever exports existed to New Spain's commercial centers. The mission supply service represented a useful means of Franciscan economic influence and prestige.[24]

From what is known of seventeenth-century New Mexico, the Franciscans likely dominated the colony's social and cultural affairs. Being the only clergy in the region, the friars directed the rhythms and rites of Catholic life for both Indians and Spaniards. The missionary priests sanctioned and performed baptisms, marriages, burials, and all other rituals associated with Catholicism. Under Franciscan auspices, the numerous religious festivals and public ceremonies occurred. Furthermore, in a territory noted for its ignorance and superstition, the friars were the most educated and intellectual group. They served frequently as scribes for the local illiterate people in official and private matters. In countless other aspects that have perhaps escaped notice, the Franciscans could claim dominion over the inhabitants of the Kingdom.[25]

*   *   *

Several factors and developments caused the Pueblo revolt in 1680. Between 1667 and 1672, a severe drought in the region resulted in crop failures that led to a period of starvation. The economic life of the colony was disrupted further by the Order's decision to cease the mission supply service in 1664. This proved to be an absolutely disastrous move and, in 1674, the Franciscans reinstated the supply trains, but serious short-term economic damage had already been done. Beginning in the early 1670s, Apache raids became more numerous and destructive. This danger curtailed many colonial activities, especially agricultural and livestock operations, and also forced the Franciscans to abandon several missions east of the Sandía and Manzano mountains.[26]

Trouble was also brewing within the missions. Since the middle of the century, Franciscan influence among the Puebloans waned as the novelty of Christianity passed and traditional Puebloan social and cultural mores reemerged. Some evidence suggests that friars arriving in the Kingdom after 1650 were less capable and committed than their predecessors. Certainly some were unfit for the habit and were "relentless troublemakers." Many missionaries devoted too much time and effort in defense of their influence and prestige during the conflicts with the governors, to the detriment of their mission responsibilities. When the Puebloans attempted to worship their traditional deities in order to alleviate the droughts, the friars dealt sternly and harshly with this perceived heresy.[27]

The long and bitter conflicts between the Franciscans and local officials also had weakened the Spanish in the Pueblo people's eyes. The two institutions seemed to recognize their peril as the church and state relationship improved after 1667. The Holy Office in Mexico City ordered a relaxation of Inquisitorial activities in the colony and, in 1668, temporarily ended the pattern of the custos concurrently holding the post of commissary of the Inquisition. For their part, the governors became more congenial in their support of mission operations and in restoring discipline among the Puebloans.[28]

It was all for naught, though. In a well-organized and unified uprising, the Puebloan people launched a revolt against the Spanish on 10 August 1680. After a brief resistance in Santa Fe led by Governor Antonio de Otermín, the Spanish population fled south to El Paso, where they arrived in early September. The Spanish suffered tremendous losses; about four hundred of the approximately 2,300 colonists died at the hands of the Puebloans.[29]

The Puebloan people's fury was directed particularly at the Franciscans and the symbols of Christian religion. Of the thirty-two missionaries active in northern and central New Mexico in August 1680, twenty-one were killed. Hence, the Pueblo revolt was the bloodiest single event in the Franciscans' long history in New Spain. In addition, the Puebloans attempted to level mission churches, and they despoiled Bibles, crucifixes, vestments, and other religious articles. In some cases, the Puebloans installed *kivas* (religious and ceremonial chambers) inside the churches. The Puebloan people's rage toward Christianity was a most acute personal blow to the Franciscans.[30]

Except for a few brief forays launched from El Paso, the Spanish remained outside the region for twelve years. Many of the settlers left for other locales. Most of the surviving friars were reassigned to other areas since few of the same missionaries remained available when the reconquest began in 1692. The Order did expand and solidify the mission effort around El Paso during those years, and in 1683–1684, the initial move to open the Junta de los Ríos mission district occurred. The missions established there would be part of the Custody of Saint Paul throughout most of the eighteenth century, albeit with little permanent success.[31]

*   *   *

"El año ochenta," as Franciscan documents often referred to the Pueblo revolt over the following decades, marked a turning point in the historical development of colonial New Mexico. When the Spanish returned in 1692, the purpose of the territory's existence would be fundamentally altered, as would Spanish-Puebloan relations. For the Franciscans, their position in the Kingdom was never the same. The Pueblo rebellion had disrupted the mission operation and, most certainly, provided a powerful, psychological blow to the friars that would resonate throughout the eighteenth century. The virtual dominion the Franciscans previously enjoyed, however, was not totally eliminated in this one violent stroke but gradually eroded during the first half of the 1700s. In that regard, "the year eighty" represented only the beginning of the end of Franciscan hegemony in the Kingdom of New Mexico.

CHAPTER 3

The Friars

B EFORE BEGINNING the narrative and analysis of the Franciscan decline in New Mexico, it will prove helpful to know something about the friars who served there between 1692 and 1776. One hypothesis that has been offered to explain the decline of the Franciscans in eighteenth-century New Mexico is that the friars serving in the Kingdom were less capable than their pre-1680 brethren. While this claim cannot be definitively addressed, biographical knowledge of the missionaries is important to fully comprehend what happened to the New Mexico missionary effort after the reconquest. Who were the Franciscan priests and from where did they come? What were their social class antecedents? How did they become friars and what training did they receive? What were the career patterns for those who toiled in New Mexico? Within the answers to these questions are clues that will help explain why the Franciscan position eroded in the Kingdom during the 1700s.[1]

* * *

While traditionally two terms have been used to describe the nationality of Spaniards in the New World—*peninsulares* (Spaniards born on the Iberian Peninsula) and criollos (Spaniards born in the New World)—the Franciscan province of Santo Evangelio employed a unique three-part classification to identify its personnel. One group was identified as *gachupines*, friars who were born and entered the Order in Spain. A second category was that of *hijos de provincia* (sons of the province), priests who were born in Spain, but who took up the habit in New Spain under the auspices of Santo Evangelio. Criollos were Franciscans who were born and inducted into the Order in the New World.[2]

Between 1692 and 1776, at least 134 ordained Franciscan priests served in New Mexico. Of this number, the designations utilized by Santo Evangelio can be ascertained for 113 friars. The criollos formed the largest group with seventy-one friars, or fifty-three percent of the total known to have worked in the colony. Sixty-nine criollos were born in Mexico, while Fray Francisco de

Corvera (Corbera) was from the Philippines and Fray Francisco Xavier Dávila
Saavedra came from Florida. Hijos de provincia were the second most numerous faction with twenty-five priests (nineteen percent), and gachupines comprised the smallest segment with seventeen friars (thirteen percent).[3]

The preponderance of criollos serving in New Mexico is generally consistent
with the trends noted by Francisco Morales in his study of seventeenth-century
Franciscans throughout New Spain. Morales discovered that during the 1600s
the number of criollo Franciscans continuously grew at a greater proportional
rate than the others, and the nature of that difference became especially notable toward the end of the seventeenth century. Furthermore, in a report from
1703, Morales found that criollos comprised over three-fourths of all Franciscans in New Spain. Therefore, that a majority of criollos would serve with the
Order in New Mexico during the 1700s does not appear to be unusual.[4]

Very little in the places of origin of the post-1692 friars prepared them for life
on the northern frontier. Among the criollos, most were natives of Mexico City
and Puebla. Indeed, out of seventy-one friars born in the New World, thirty-
eight originated in these relatively large urban centers. Another nine criollos
were born in nearby communities such as Toluca and Tlaxcala. Hence, about
two-thirds of the criollos were native to the central region of Mexico. Only two
friars' place of origin might have offered an environment that could have prepared them for frontier New Mexico: Dávila Saavedra (noted above from
Florida) and Fray Antonio de Miranda, who was from Sombrerete, northwest
of Zacatecas. Gachupines and hijos de provincia most often came from Andalucía and the Basque provinces of northwest Spain. One friar, Fray Cristóbal
Alonso Barroso, was born in Lisbon, Portugal.[5]

The social class of the Franciscans in this study period defies clear character-
ization. The most reliable records regarding the friars' family backgrounds are
in the purity of blood statements *(informaciones de limpieza de sangre)*. These
documents were part of the anti-Jewish policies in fifteenth-century Spain that
culminated in the expulsion of the Jews in 1492. The Church immediately
thereafter was concerned that those Jews who renounced their faith *(conver-
sos)* were not true Catholics. To be certain that priests were not tainted by Jew-
ish (or Moorish) blood, the Franciscans, along with other mendicant orders,
legislated in 1525 a provision for determining the purity of blood of novices. In
the New World, purity of blood statements were also tools to exclude those of
non-Spanish lineage, especially mestizos. The informaciones included details
concerning a candidate's background as well as that of his parents and grandparents.[6]

Unfortunately for scholars, few of these documents survive for friars in eighteenth-century New Spain. The most likely reason for this development is
found in royal decrees issued in 1696 and 1697, which declared that mestizos

and Indians would be admitted henceforth into the mendicant orders. While the Franciscans officially protested these orders, they had actually already begun to accept mestizos within the Order. In fact, Morales discovered that mestizos constituted about five percent of the friars during the 1600s. If mestizos were to be allowed in the Order, the necessity of purity of blood statements was reduced and could have served as an embarrassment to priests of mixed-blood heritage. Hence, only seven informaciones exist for the post-1692 friars of New Mexico, and five of these predate the royal decree of 1696.[7]

From a variety of other documents, though, evidence suggests that the New Mexico friars of this era came from the middle strata of Spanish society. Not one was identified from the higher ranks of the nobility. Ten friars' families were involved with artisan occupations (tailors, jewelers, carpenters, blacksmiths, etc.). Seventeen other families were in agriculture, minor government or military officials, or from the professional classes (doctors, lawyers, and educators). A broader determinant of social class origins, however, can be discerned from titles of respect associated with their parents, such as Don, Doña, and Señor. The use of these titles in eighteenth-century Spanish colonial society is identified with individuals from at least the middle sector. Thirty of the friars in this study (out of fifty-one that are known) had at least one parent referred to with these respectful nomenclatures. One friar, Fray José de Arvisu (Arbizu), was an orphan and raised by the Church.[8]

That most of the New Mexico missionaries originated from the middle ranks of colonial society is not surprising. Again, Morales found that by 1650 the largest number of New Spain Franciscans came from artisan families. While this group varied greatly in wealth and social status, artisan families could usually provide their sons with two important criteria for admission into the Order: basic literacy skills and freedom from debt. A religious occupation was viewed also as an acceptable step up in colonial society. As noted previously, the majority of criollo friars were from Mexico City and Puebla, both centers of colonial manufacturing with large numbers of artisans. It is reasonable to conclude that a New Mexico missionary was likely to originate from the middle strata of the colonial social hierarchy.[9]

* * *

The Franciscan Constitution of Barcelona (1451) established the minimum admission requirements into the Order and it remained in effect through the latter half of the eighteenth century. To take up the habit, novices had to be at least sixteen years of age, in good health, of legitimate birth, literate, free of debt, and to willingly accept their vows. A one-year novitiate was required prior to the profession of faith, although some young men accepted in the Order at age fourteen underwent a two-year novitiate. The novitiate period was a time spent in prayer and meditation, religious education, and manual labor for the *convento* (convent) to which they belonged.[10]

Discounting the seventeen gachupín friars, out of ninety-six criollos and hijos de provincia, at least seventy-six of the New Mexico missionaries served their novitiate and professed their faith in either Mexico City or Puebla. Thirty-four men began at San Francisco de México (Mexico City), the oldest institution for the preparation of novices in Mexico (founded in 1527). The second largest group, twenty-seven friars, entered at San Francisco de Puebla. Three took the habit at San Cosmé de México (Mexico City), a relatively new convento opened in 1667 to prepare novices for lives strictly devoted to the conventual routine. One Franciscan began at San Diego de México (Mexico City), and eleven are identified as entering the Order in Mexico City without the convento being specified. One friar, Fray Agustín de Iniesta, had difficulty finishing his novitiate at one convento. The son of a criollo artisan family from Zinacantepec (near Toluca), Iniesta started his year of preparation at San Francisco de México in January 1732 at age twenty-one. For unstated reasons Iniesta then went to San Cosmé, but when that did not work out he was passed over to San Francisco de Llagos in Puebla in September 1733, where he eventually made his profession of faith.[11]

The New Mexico Franciscans usually chose to enter the Order at an early age. The age at profession of faith is known for seventy-two individuals. The youngest was sixteen, the Order's minimum age, and the oldest was forty-two-year-old Jacinto González. Fray Jacinto, an hijo de provincia, had been a resident of Oaxaca for about twenty years where he was stated to have been a lawyer before entering the Order of St. Francis at San Francisco de Puebla in 1729. Of those whose age is known at the time or profession of faiths, thirty-four friars (forty-seven percent) professed before turning eighteen, and forty-nine (sixty-eight percent) were not yet twenty. The average age was 19.2 years.[12]

Interestingly, criollos made their decision at a noticeably earlier age than those born in Spain. Eighty percent of the criollos professed while still teenagers, with an average age of 18.3 years. On the other hand, hijos de provincia were more likely to be at least twenty (sixty-two percent), and their average age was 22.3 years. This four-year differential can best be explained by career expectations. Because criollos would be more aware of what opportunities colonial society offered at an earlier age, the advantages of a religious career were readily apparent. Those who came from Spain were probably seeking social and economic advancement, and the ability of the Church to satisfy their aspirations would not be realized until other career options proved unlikely or impossible. The average age that gachupines professed was 22.0 years, but because the sample consists of only five individuals, it is too small to have great significance.

The education and training of friars between their profession of faith and ordination, at age twenty-four, occurred at San Francisco de México and San Francisco de Puebla. At these conventos, the young men were instructed in reading, writing, Latin, theology, and the administration of the sacraments. There does not appear to be any set number of years the Order established for training. Some who entered at more advanced ages were in New Mexico as ordained missionary priests in only a few years. Probably the time devoted to preparation was based on the educational capability a friar brought with him into the Order. Since they could not be effective as missionaries until ordained at twenty-four, and assuming an average age at profession of faith of 19.2, it is reasonable to assume most Franciscans spent four to five years at these conventos.[13]

Three Franciscans, however, did arrive in New Mexico before their ordination. Fray Antonio Gabaldón, as noted previously (chapter 1), was twenty-three when he arrived in the Kingdom. Fray Rafael Benavides, a criollo, was only twenty-two when he appeared in the colony in 1771. The most unique exception, though, was Fray Juan Álvarez. Álvarez, a criollo from Mexico City, began his novitiate at San Diego de México in September 1679, but was dispatched to New Mexico in 1680 before he professed. Indeed, Álvarez professed his faith in El Paso in 1681, the only friar known to do so in this study period. Even more unusual, that same year Álvarez was designated *cura parroco interino* (provisional parish priest) and ecclesiastical judge; he was a mere eighteen years of age! Other than, perhaps, the exigency required by the Pueblo rebellion, there is no extant explanation for this anomaly.[14]

At some point, either before or after his ordination, a Franciscan was designated as a missionary priest and usually enrolled in the missionary training school at Santiago de Tlatelolco, just outside of Mexico City. In theory, all missionaries were volunteers, although an individual's decision was likely influenced by the needs of the Order. At Santiago de Tlatelolco, the neophyte missionary continued his studies in theology and administration of the sacraments, but preaching skills were also honed and he received instruction in native languages. Because of the multiplicity of native languages in New Spain, a shortage of qualified instructors, and the existence of few native grammar texts, the trainees were only able to study three native tongues: Nahuatl, Otomí, and Tarascán, the primary languages of central Mexico. This deficiency in linguistic education would have an enormous influence on the missionary programs in New Mexico, as will be noted later.[15]

The preparation of missionaries obviously had its shortcomings, and a reform effort began in New Spain in the late 1660s with the introduction of the first of the Colegios de Misioneros de Propaganda Fide. The Sacred Congregation of the Propagation of the Faith was created in Rome in 1622 to promote better, more specialized instruction for missionaries. The Propaganda Fide first appeared in New Spain in 1683 when the Colegio de Misioneros de Propaganda Fide de la Santa Cruz de Querétaro opened. Other Propaganda Fide institutions were established later for New Spain in Guatemala, Zacatecas, and Mexico City.[16]

The Propaganda Fide schools endeavored to upgrade the quality of Franciscan missionaries. Preaching skills, native languages, and evangelical fervor were especially stressed by the Propaganda Fide. In the first decades, however, several problems were obvious with these colegios. Virtually all early members were peninsular Spaniards, and distrust or animosity often marked their relations with other Franciscans in New Spain. Compounding those difficulties was the fact that initially the Propaganda Fide was only responsible to the Commissary General of New Spain, not to the local provinces in which they were located. Finally, while a Propaganda Fide friar might have been touted as a sort of supermissionary, in reality most were devoid of New World experience and, consequently, their early operations were unspectacular.[17]

The Propaganda Fide has only a little bearing on the Franciscan missionary effort in New Mexico. Eight friars from the school in Querétaro were assigned temporarily to the Custody of Saint Paul to assist in opening the missions during the reconquest. Most were pulled out of the colony by 1696, and none remained after 1700. Another friar, Fray Carlos José Delgado, came to New Spain as part of the Propaganda Fide in Querétaro in 1708. Within two years, however, Delgado had left the Propaganda Fide and was serving in New Mexico, permanently billeted to the Custody of Saint Paul. As far as it can be determined, no other member of the Propaganda Fide labored in New Mexico through 1776.[18]

*   *   *

Franciscans typically began their careers in New Mexico at a mature age. The ages of these friars can be definitely established for seventy-three individuals. The youngest, as noted above, was Juan Álvarez, and the eldest was sixty-two-year-old Fray Manuel José de Sopeña (criollo) who served briefly around 1750. The average age was 34.9 years and, in fact, forty-seven (about fifty-seven percent) were between thirty and forty-nine. Five missionaries were over fifty (about seven percent), and the remaining friars were less than thirty.[19]

Considering an ordination age of twenty-four and, perhaps, two to three years at Santiago de Tlatelolco, most friars then should have had some professional experience when they came to New Mexico. Only fourteen seem to have served in a missionary capacity, however, usually in the Custody of Tampico, Santo Evangelio's other primary mission field. The others had no previous exposure to frontier mission conditions. Most had simply been engaged in duties within the conventos in Mexico City and Puebla where they taught, served as notaries, conducted investigations of applicants to the Order, and performed other routine tasks. The remainder came to the Kingdom direct from the missionary training facility.[20]

The missionaries who arrived in New Mexico after 1692 could expect to remain there for a relatively lengthy period. Of the 121 missionaries whose tenure is known, forty-five priests (about thirty-five percent) were in the Kingdom for ten years or less. That number included, though, the eight on temporary assignment from Querétaro and several who died. Otherwise, eighty-three Franciscans were there more than ten years, and of those, forty-five (thirty-five percent) labored two decades or more. Two friars were active for at least forty years: Fray Juan José Pérez de Mirabal (hijo de provincia) and Fray Andrés Varo (gachupín). Altogether, the average number of years of service in New Mexico was 17.4.[21]

It is not clear whether Franciscans were expected to remain continuously in the field once they were in the Kingdom or if there was a policy that provided for periodic leaves to visit their homes or to rest from the rigors of the frontier. About a dozen friars appear in documents on some business for the Order in Mexico City or Puebla during their tenure in New Mexico. A few others were noted as recuperating from illness in Mexico City, Puebla, and Chihuahua. It is difficult to imagine laboring for decades in the wilds of New Mexico without the chance to see their families; the documents, however, are mute on any formal leave policy. Certainly those friars whose families and friends were in Spain would find it most difficult to return for a short time.

When one considers, then, about seventeen years in New Mexico with an average age of about thirty-five when first in the colony, many friars must have been over fifty when they finally left this missionary field. Indeed, out of 134 Franciscans, a minimum of fifty-one (thirty-eight percent) were fifty years or older; at least twenty-eight were sexagenarians. Two missionaries were known to be over eighty when they ended their terms in the Kingdom: the former lawyer from Oaxaca, Jacinto González (about eighty-two), and Andrés Varo (about eighty-five). At a time when life expectancies were less than fifty years and knowing the arduous conditions of frontier life, that these men lived and worked so long was quite a feat.[22]

Mortality rates among New Mexico's missionaries between 1692 and 1776 seem to be relatively low. Twenty-one died while active in the colony, which represents only about sixteen percent, although several others seem to have expired very soon after leaving the region. Six met their end in a violent manner, five in the Pueblo uprising of 1696 (see chapter 4). The evidence is inconclusive, but three others may have died at the hands of the Puebloans. The remaining twelve apparently succumbed to natural causes.

The Franciscans in the Kingdom during this era usually served in many different missions and were moved about frequently. The careers of sixty-six missionaries can be reconstructed fairly well, and it appears that on average a friar could expect to be billeted to five separate mission sites, often with more than one term at each. The typical tenure of each posting was about 2.5 years. There was no established policy concerning the assignment of missions. Some managed to remain at a site for very lengthy periods, such as Fray Juan de Tagle (hijo de provincia), who was based continuously for twenty-five years at San Ildefonso in the early eighteenth century. Although no official explanation has appeared as to why the friars were rotated in this manner, the likely causes were the perpetual shortages of personnel and the desire to achieve a suitable match between a friar and the mission population. Nonetheless, as will be seen, the revolving door standard among the friars had serious negative consequences on the mission programs.[23]

Unlike the pre-1680 Franciscans who often were assigned in pairs to a mission, those who served in the eighteenth century in most instances labored alone. Some effort was made to keep two missionaries at the same time at Taos and Zuñi, the most remote and historically dangerous assignments, but that goal was rarely achieved at Zuñi. In fact, after the relatively lengthy solo tenures of Fray Juan de Garaicoechea and Fray Francisco de Irazábal during the first two decades of the 1700s, Zuñi was one of the most difficult places to keep even a single missionary. The Zuñi people had a reputation for being especially difficult neophytes, and it was the most isolated mission, over twenty-five leagues from the next closest site at Acoma. At minimum, twenty-one different friars performed religious services at Zuñi at some point during this period, although often those efforts were made as an extension of duties from missionaries assigned to Acoma and/or Laguna.[24]

The highest position within the Custody of Saint Paul that a Franciscan could realistically aspire to was custos. Twenty-one different friars are known to have served as custos during this era, with virtually all holding the office more than once. Most were in New Mexico at the time of their selection, and their tenure seems to have run two to three years each. Being the most numerous segment of Franciscans, ten of the prelates were criollos. On a proportional basis, however, the custos was most likely to be a hijo de provincia (six) or a gachupín (four). The nationality of one custos is unknown.

Service in New Mexico was not a springboard for advancement into the upper echelons of the Order. Only three friars are known to have achieved higher office after they left the colony. Fray José de Arranegui (hijo de provincia) served in the Kingdom in the first decade of the eighteenth century. He was later selected as Santo Evangelio's *procurador general* (supply officer or agent) around 1713. Fray Antonio de Miranda (criollo) and Fray Jacobo de Castro (hijo de provincia) both went on to become provincial secretaries for Santo Evangelio. Miranda held that position between 1745 and 1748, and Castro held it in the early 1770s. No other New Mexico veteran appeared to make similar advances.[25]

The upper hierarchy of the Franciscans was a rather closed world. A cursory examination of the eighteenth-century Franciscan rosters reveals that the same individuals appear over and over again in the more powerful and coveted positions in Mexico City and Puebla. Perhaps the missionaries in New Mexico did not desire to move up or were not qualified for leadership roles. Other factors, however, might explain why an infinitesimally small number of the Kingdom's friars were promoted. Certainly, life in the metropolitan centers was more comfortable and stimulating than in frontier missions. It would have been easy for a process of self-perpetuation to be tacitly agreed to among those in the upper hierarchy. Class and social connections, too, might have been factors. The rather less-than-exalted origins of the New Mexico friars has already been noted.

Another important reason that likely affected the New Mexico friars was the *alternativa* system. The alternativa was an agreement reached in the 1600s by the mendicant orders to quell incessant disputes between peninsular and criollo priests over the higher positions. Since these posts were elective, the more numerous criollos had begun to garner most of the desirable offices. The alternativa represented a compromise by which upper-level positions were parceled out equally. In Santo Evangelio, then, criollos, hijos de provincia, and gachupines all received the same number of higher offices. This would have the net effect of creating a logjam among the more numerous criollos wishing to advance.[26]

By and large, New Mexico's friars seem to have devoted most of their professional careers, once in the Kingdom, to the Custody of Saint Paul. Not only did they endure extensive tenures until advanced ages with little possibility to move up, but they also rarely appear on extant rosters of Santo Evangelio or in any other province after they left New Mexico. Only sixteen missionaries are known to have continued actively as missionary priests or in other professional capacities after they left the Kingdom. Most of these, again, were likely to have labored in the Custody of Tampico.

* * *

How do the background and career patterns of the Franciscans who served in eighteenth-century New Mexico compare with their brethren who served in other frontier mission districts in New Spain? Unfortunately, empirical studies such as this have not been duplicated for other frontier Franciscan mission regions. There exists, however, information that allows us to gain some perspec-

tive as to whether the friars' experiences in the Custody of Saint Paul were typical or not. Through Francisco Morales's study of seventeenth-century Franciscans in New Spain, it is known that being a criollo from the middle sector of
colonial society was the norm.

There appears to be considerable continuity between the Franciscans who
served in the colony up to the Pueblo rebellion in 1680 and the missionaries of
this study period. Gachupín friars formed a greater percentage in the early seventeenth century, but apparently, criollos formed the largest contingent from
about 1650 to 1680. These earlier Franciscans, too, seem to have served fairly
long tenures in the colony and were also often transferred about from mission
to mission. No extant evidence suggests that these friars were any more likely
to have previous frontier mission experience or to be promoted into the upper
ranks of the Order.[27]

There are at least three important differences between the pre-1680 New
Mexico Franciscans and those that served between 1692 and 1776. As noted in
the previous chapter, the province usually selected the earlier prelates from friars present in central Mexico who were then dispatched to the Kingdom. This
implies greater control over the custody by the leadership of Santo Evangelio.
Secondly, the mortality rates of the earlier group were much higher than those
of the eighteenth century. Without including those slain in 1680, perhaps another twenty-five earned the martyr's mantle (chapter 2) compared with at most
nine in the 1692–1776 period. Indeed, the total killed in this earlier group ex-
ceeds the entire number who expired from all causes in New Mexico after the
reconquest. Finally, as seen previously, Franciscans before 1680 were more
likely to be assigned in pairs to a mission.

Robert H. Jackson, in his recent study of the Franciscan missionary district in
Alta California, provides some data that are useful in placing the friars of eighteenth-century New Mexico in perspective. Although the Alta California missions were not established until 1769 and were managed by the Propaganda
Fide colegio in Mexico City, two career pattern points are noteworthy. According to Jackson, the California friars also tended to serve long periods in the
field. A typical missionary of California was there for sixteen years, slightly less
than the 17.4 years of those in New Mexico. Jackson also discovered that thirty-
five percent of the California friars remained over twenty years, the exact proportion of those in New Mexico. Conversely, the mortality rates in Alta
California were much higher than in New Mexico after 1692, with about forty-
five percent dying there, compared to about sixteen percent in the current
study group. In fact, it appears that the mortality numbers in California would
be much closer to that of pre-1680 New Mexico.[28]

The Franciscans in post-reconquest New Mexico differ in significant ways
with another mission region in New Spain: Guatemala. Adriann C. Van Oss

noted in his very fine study of missionary activity in Guatemala that friars were assigned to a mission site an average of three and one-half years, a year longer than those of this study period in New Mexico. In addition, missionary priests in Guatemala usually were posted to a mission in pairs or threesomes. Finally, the Franciscans in Guatemala apparently were offered better linguistic training. Each Franciscan province, according to Van Oss, provided apprentice language programs for its friars. Language skills were further enhanced through a policy of having new priests assigned to missions with veterans who already had some degree of fluency. Consequently, Van Oss found that Franciscans in Guatemala were more often proficient in the language of their neophytes, a trait not shared by missionary priests in New Mexico, as will be seen later.[29]

*   *   *

A picture can be drawn of the typical missionary priest of New Mexico in the 1692–1776 era. He was most likely to be a criollo from an urban area of central Mexico. This friar probably came from a family of moderate means, certainly not from the upper class of colonial society. He likely took his vows to the Order as a teenager and received whatever training was available at facilities in Mexico City and Puebla. Though he arrived in New Mexico at a mature age, his background, training, and previous service in the Order did not prepare him well for work in an isolated, frontier mission environment. Our typical Franciscan remained in the Kingdom for most of the remainder of his life, but he was often moved about from one mission site to another where he, alone, was expected to convert and civilize the native people. His chances for upward career mobility were remote. Surprisingly, despite long years of toil and the dangers inherent in this occupational milieu, this Franciscan was likely to live to a relatively advanced age and leave the Kingdom alive. His professional career most often did not extend past service in New Mexico, and once departed he disappeared into historical obscurity. In this career pattern, as will be seen, are significant keys to explain the decline of the Franciscan position in New Mexico during the eighteenth century.

CHAPTER 4

Reconquest and Rebellion

THE 1692–1696 PERIOD was an extremely chaotic and dangerous time in the Kingdom of New Mexico for the Spanish. While Don Diego de Vargas, the new governor and captain general, proclaimed his initial campaign of 1692 a triumph in overcoming Puebloan resistance, the Spanish did not achieve permanent occupation of the region until 1694. Even then, Spanish control was tenuous at best. Several Puebloan groups refused to return to the missions, and those that did were often openly hostile to Spanish authority. Rumors of Puebloan conspiracies to rebel again periodically swept through the Kingdom and, indeed, another major insurrection erupted in the summer of 1696. It took Vargas and his army almost six months to restore peace to the region after that rebellion.

In this charged atmosphere, it was abundantly clear that the security of the Spanish colonists rested on the military expertise of Vargas and his soldiers. Among the Franciscans struggling to renew the missionary programs to the Puebloans, this pattern of dependency was especially evident. It was quickly obvious to these friars that the implementation of the evangelical program, and their very lives, were linked to that of Vargas and the presidial force. The result was that from the very beginning of the new era in New Mexico a standard of dependency was established in which the Franciscans relied extensively upon the civil and military arms of the Spanish empire.

* * *

When Don Diego de Vargas arrived in El Paso in February 1691 to assume his post as governor and captain general, over a decade had passed since the Pueblo revolt. During that interim, the settlers and friars had languished in that small, dusty villa near the Río Grande. Many former residents of the Kingdom had simply given up and moved on to try their fortunes elsewhere. Over half of the surviving Franciscans had been posted to other religious assignments away from New Mexico. True, the missions around El Paso were stabilized and expanded, and a new mission field for the Custody of Saint Paul was opened to the south at La Junta de los Ríos. Otherwise, the Franciscans' evangelical effort in the region was at a standstill.

This unhappy situation for the Spanish was not a result of governmental indifference. In fact, His Majesty's officials were most anxious for the Puebloans to be pacified and the Kingdom reoccupied. The Pueblo revolt had only been the first in a series of native uprisings that jeopardized the entire northern frontier and threatened the security of New Spain's principal mining regions. More importantly, by the mid-1680s, the Spanish were aware of French efforts to colonize Texas. Although the French threat proved not to be dire, the Spanish government believed that its European rival posed a real menace to the frontier and those same beleaguered mining zones. During the ten years after the Pueblo revolt, royal officials constantly urged the various New Mexico governors to reoccupy the Kingdom. Because of a lack of resources and, sometimes, will, all attempts to restore the colony had proved futile.[1]

Don Diego de Vargas, however, appeared to be a more apt individual for the task at hand. Born to a renowned Spanish family in 1643, Vargas came to New Spain in 1673 primarily to win acclaim and, by extension, to restore his family's declining fortunes. Prior to his selection as governor of New Mexico, he had held two other appointments as alcalde mayor. The first of these was at Teutila, south of Mexico City, and the other, the mining district of Tlalpujahua, northwest of the capital. Vargas proved a capable and energetic administrator in both posts, and his nomination by the viceregal government to restore Spanish control over New Mexico reflected confidence in his political and military skills. Certainly his new position offered Vargas the twin opportunities to win fame and financial rewards. If he was successful, his family's economic ship might be righted and, perhaps, he could go home to Spain.[2]

While Vargas's familial concerns and his personal ambitions were driving forces during his tenure in New Mexico, he also exhibited a relatively deep commitment to the Catholic faith and respect for the Church's representatives. This was consistent with his family's history; the Vargas clan had long enjoyed a reputation for their contributions and support of the Church through the erection of altars, chapels, and dowries. An examination of his personal and official letters reveals a man to whom references to his Creator were the staples of everyday life. "May God grant . . .," "May God keep . . .," and "May God watch . . ." were liberally sprinkled throughout his correspondence. Vargas was no shrinking violet when it came to trumpeting his victories, but at the same time, he was often effusive in crediting divine intervention for his successes. Throughout the reconquest Vargas constantly took the time and care to ensure that the native population was offered the sacraments. In several letters, he offered his concern for the Puebloans' souls as a significant motive for reestablishment of Spanish control. In a report to the viceroy in August 1691 Vargas

noted, "Three things are at risk if there is a delay in their [the natives'] reduction and conquest. First, if they die in apostasy as the devil's slaves, they are
damned. Second, in their wickedness as apostates, they become evil and make
their reduction impossible. Third, because they are so new to our holy faith,
scarcely reduced, most are in danger of being lost." Political and military concerns dominated Vargas, but he was a more pious man than most governors
who preceded him. His relationship with the Franciscans never eroded to the
level of petty bickering, personal slanders, and obstructionist actions so characteristic of church and state affairs before 1680. In many ways then, Vargas was
an anachronism to that sixteenth-century triad of "Gold, God, and Glory.[3]

Nonetheless, Vargas's main goal was the subjugation of New Mexico, and he
would brook no interference from the Franciscans when it came to that over-
riding task. Two incidents with the Franciscans in El Paso during 1692 attest to
his priorities. Apparently, Vargas got on well with the Fray Francisco de Vargas
(no relation), who was custos when he arrived in El Paso. A problem, however,
soon surfaced with one of Fray Francisco's successors. Fray Joaquín de Hinojosa became the interim prelate upon the sudden death of the new custos, Fray
Diego de Mendoza. Hinojosa, a criollo, had been in the custody since the mid-
1680s, primarily at La Junta de los Ríos. His personality seems to have been
somewhat prickly, and he soon clashed with the new governor in the more serious of the two disputes.[4]

The first problem centered on the Franciscan missions around El Paso.
While some of these had been maintained since the mid-1640s, no formal act
of possession had ever been made that legally gave these sites to the Order to
operate. When Hinojosa pointed this out to Governor Vargas, Vargas moved
quickly to rectify the oversight. Through the elaborate ritual, Vargas conferred
on the Franciscans the mission churches, conventos, and other related buildings, but to Hinojosa's chagrin, refused to establish land boundaries. Vargas
stated that the reason he refused to delineate mission land holdings was the
fact that it had been customary for land in El Paso to be used in common,
since its quality was poor and the settlement was vulnerable to native raids.
Unsaid, but perhaps equally important, was the fact that if the missions'
boundaries were clearly established, then it would it easier for the villa's residents to get land titles, too, and thus shrink the pool of Spaniards willing to return north. Whatever Vargas's true motives were, he refused to back down in
the face of Hinojosa's angry tirades.[5]

The second episode also took place during Hinojosa's brief tenure. The apostolic notary, Fray Francisco de Corvera (Corbera), consistent with his duties,
began to interrogate some of the soldiers and prospective colonists as to the nature of their religious beliefs. Vargas became quite agitated over this matter because, he claimed, the Franciscans had not sought his prior permission to

conduct these inquiries. Again, Vargas likely feared the loss of sorely needed per-sonnel. He claimed he held rights of "vice-patron" in this affair, and he refused to allow Corvera to continue the questioning. The Franciscans threatened to censure Vargas, but he disarmed them by pledging his personal fidelity to the Church. Vargas, however, maintained his ban on the friars' investigations of the Spaniards in El Paso. Relations soon improved between Vargas and the mission-aries when the reconquest began and Hinojosa was replaced as custos.[6]

✻   ✻   ✻

On 21 August 1692, almost twelve years after the Pueblo rebellion, Vargas began the first phase of the reconquest of New Mexico. A detailed narrative of that effort is beyond the parameters of this study but, generally, the expedition was a whirlwind event in which Vargas treated the Puebloan people in a rela-tively benign manner. Essentially, the Spanish went quickly from village to vil-lage, and at each Vargas announced to the Puebloans that as the Spanish had returned to the region, they should submit once again to His Majesty's author-ity. In the bargain, the native people would be dealt with in a lenient fashion. These methods, in Vargas's opinion, resulted in the resounding success of the campaign as the formerly rebellious Puebloans acquiesced to his entreaties, and no significant violence occurred. Vargas and his command were back in El Paso before the year ended.[7]

Three relatively untried Franciscans were part of this expeditionary force: Fray Francisco de Corvera, Fray Cristóbal Alonso Barroso, and Fray Miguel Muñiz de Luna. Corvera, the apostolic notary who had clashed with the gov-ernor earlier, was from Manila, Philippines. He had only professed his faith in 1684 and seems to have come directly from Mexico City in 1691. Barroso was from Lisbon, Portugal, and had entered the Order in 1685 in Mexico City. Muñiz de Luna, a criollo from Puebla, arrived in El Paso in 1691. He also had professed in 1684, and was but twenty-six years of age. None of these three fri-ars had much experience either as missionaries or in frontier conditions.[8]

Despite their lack of knowledge of local conditions, these Franciscans con-tributed an important, though largely symbolic, role in the campaign. As part of the Spaniards' show of reestablishing dominion over the native people, Var-gas encouraged the Puebloans to accept Catholic sacraments such as absolu-tion and baptism. In fact, the three friars baptized over 2,200 Puebloan people, according to Vargas's reports on the expedition, with the governor himself standing as godfather in many instances for the children receiving baptism. Vargas commended the missionaries' efforts, and especially noted the zeal dis-played by Barroso and Corvera in the face of Puebloan hostility at Santa Fe.[9]

Almost ten months passed before the Spanish launched the resettlement stage of the reconquest. Much of that time was devoted to recruiting settlers and soldiers. In November 1692, the government in Mexico City agreed to finance the campaign and Vargas was authorized to enlist colonists and a presidial force of one hundred soldiers. The latter provision marked an important change for the Kingdom and revealed the new defensive purpose the Spanish envisioned. Previously, New Mexico had been without a presidial unit as the defense of the colony was left mainly to the Spanish inhabitants. Now the government intended to station a permanent, professional military force in the Kingdom.[10]

While Vargas and some of his officers dashed about the northern frontier enlisting settlers and soldiers in places such as Durango, Parral, Sombrerete, and Zacatecas, a Franciscan played a key part in arranging a contingent of settlers from Mexico City. Vargas tapped two New Mexico veterans to oversee recruitment in the viceregal capital: Fray Francisco Farfán and Captain Cristóbal Velasco. Farfán was a dependable, resourceful friar. He had immigrated as a child with his family to Mexico City from Cádiz. His father was employed as a night watchman in the capital when Farfán joined the Order in 1661. Fray Francisco was in Santa Fe at the time of the Pueblo revolt. During that Spanish debacle, Governor Otermín entrusted Farfán with four soldiers to break out of the beleaguered villa and establish contact with the other Spaniards already fleeing to the south. Farfán remained in El Paso after those events, and he now held the office of procurador for the Custody of Saint Paul.[11]

Farfán did yeoman duty for the resettlement effort throughout 1693. He managed the provisioning of religious and personal supplies for ten new missionaries. With Velasco, Farfán signed up over two hundred new colonists for New Mexico and contracted for their supplies. When the local commercial transporters demanded more money than the viceregal government allocated for these settlers, Farfán handled the negotiations by which the Franciscans assumed the cost of moving these families for about twenty-five percent less than the private company had demanded. And finally, when Velasco later abandoned the entire enterprise, it was Farfán who shepherded these settlers north to New Mexico.[12]

* * *

Before Farfán's group and other parties of settlers arrived in El Paso, however, Governor Vargas had already begun the second stage of the reconquest. Innumerable problems in gathering personnel and provisions had caused long delays in the expedition's departure. Therefore, by October 1693 Vargas had to move or accept idly waiting in El Paso until the next spring. Although perilously close to winter's onslaught, Vargas opted for launching the campaign. The governor's force in El Paso numbered over 1,200, including soldiers, settlers, and native auxiliaries. Vargas assumed that number would be sufficient, based upon the lack of resistance he encountered during the initial expedition. Thus, on 4 October 1693, the feast day of St. Francis, the Spaniards crossed the Río Grande toward the north. One of the banners leading the way for the Spanish column was that of Our Lady of the Rosary, La Conquistadora.[13]

Fray Salvador Rodríguez de San Antonio, the new custos, personally led the Franciscan contingent of sixteen missionary priests and two lay brothers. Fray Salvador was in Mexico City when he was chosen by the Order to assume the office of custos, but he was a veteran of the New Mexico missionary field. A criollo from Puebla, San Antonio was previously stationed in the Kingdom from 1664 to about 1677 where he ministered to the Zuñi people's mission for over a decade, and he claimed to still be proficient in those natives' language. The Franciscan group he directed now was considerably less than the number Vargas had requested. The governor believed forty missionaries were needed to help pacify the region; however, the government refused to fund so many, citing the uncertainties of the reconquest.[14]

The Franciscans moving north with the expedition were an inexperienced lot. Five were from the Propaganda Fide college in Querétaro (three others later followed), on temporary assignment to the Custody of Saint Paul. Two of these, Fray José Díez and Fray Francisco de Jesús María Casañas, had been among the original friars from Spain who established the Querétaro facility in 1682. Díez had been active in preaching missions around Querétaro in recent years and, indeed, just previously had been involved in cases of diabolism associated with that evangelical effort. Díez would rise to the position of guardian of the Querétaro institution in 1703, but for now, he was unfamiliar with frontier missionary conditions. Casañas did have some experience, though. In 1690–1691, he took part in the attempt to open a mission field among the Caddo people in east Texas. Casañas's zealousness and inflexibility, however, were partially responsible for the failure of the operation. The other three Propaganda Fide missionaries—Fray Antonio Baamonde (Bahamonde), Fray Domingo de Jesús María, and Fray Gerónimo Prieto—had only come to New Spain in 1692 and were the colegio's most recent graduates.[15]

The remaining ordained missionaries were not much better prepared for the task ahead. Francisco de Corvera and Miguel Muñiz de Luna had, of course, been with the earlier expedition under Vargas. Fray Antonio Carbonel was a gachupín who had been in the Americas a short time. Fray Antonio de Obregón, an hijo de provincia, had only professed in 1689. Fray Juan Daza, a criollo from Mexico City, had been a Franciscan for over thirty years, but there exists no record of prior missionary activities. The only veteran missionary was Fray Juan de Zavaleta (Zabaleta) who had been laboring at Isleta at the time of the 1680 revolt. Of the others—Fray Juan Alpuente, Fray Juan Antonio del Corral, Fray Antonio Sierra, and Fray Diego Zeinos—nothing is known of their previous careers.[16]

These friars were therefore potentially suspect as a group. Most were inexperienced as missionary priests and unfamiliar with the special conditions to be encountered in New Mexico. Apparently, their commitment can be questioned, too. Within a year of the expedition's departure from El Paso, only nine of the sixteen were available to assume their mission posts among the Puebloan people.

Since the expedition left El Paso with winter so near, it was imperative for this stage of the reconquest to proceed as smoothly as Vargas's original campaign. Unfortunately for the Spanish, that did not occur. Throughout much of the northward trek, rain, sleet, and then snow from an earlier-than-expected winter plagued the Spaniards. While some Puebloan groups exhibited a conciliatory position toward the conquerors, most were hostile. Upon arriving outside of Santa Fe where Vargas hoped to shelter the colonists, the governor discovered the former capital fortified and defended by Puebloan warriors. Entreaties by Vargas and the Franciscans failed to persuade them to lay down their arms and surrender the villa. From late November to the end of December, the Spanish huddled in their camp outside of Santa Fe, cold, wet, and hungry. Illness and malnutrition soon stalked the encampment. Several infants perished under these conditions, and among the incapacitated were three grievously sick friars.[17]

In this precarious atmosphere, Governor Vargas stunned the Franciscans when he announced in mid-December his intention to install some friars in missions among the Puebloans. Vargas believed that the natives of Tesuque, Nambé, San Ildefonso, San Juan, San Lázaro, Picurís, Taos, Jémez, Zía, Pecos, and Cochití were ready to receive missionary priests, and he ordered the Franciscans to prepare to assume their duties.[18]

Vargas's plan alarmed the Franciscans. On 18 December, Custos San Antonio wrote Vargas to protest the placement of friars in the missions at that time. The custos noted the rumors that the Puebloans were planning further attacks against the Spanish, and he reminded Vargas of the tragedy that befell the missionaries in "the year eighty." San Antonio insisted that this did not mean that his friars were not capable of performing their duties, but he argued that to install the missionaries at that time was patently dangerous and likely would lead only to unnecessary deaths. All sixteen ordained friars affixed their signatures to San Antonio's letter to Vargas, and the governor quickly rescinded his orders. Perhaps Vargas had become desperate over the stalemate in Santa Fe and believed the installation of missionaries would curb Puebloan hostility. He might have thought that the reopened missions would facilitate the gathering of desperately needed foodstuffs for his hungry colonists. Nonetheless, Vargas's idea was ill conceived and he seemed to realize that. Martyred friars would not speed the reconquest.[19]

Vargas captured Santa Fe two weeks later, but he followed a more cautious schedule in placing Franciscans in the missions. Indeed, almost nine months passed before he deemed the Kingdom pacified enough that the missionaries could assume their primary tasks. During the interim, the friars were in Santa Fe administering to the needs of the expedition and accompanying the army on its campaigns. It was during this period that at least five priests, including Custos San Antonio, departed the region for unspecified reasons. In regards to Fray Salvador, who was at least fifty-four years of age, perhaps the difficult winter had taken its toll. Certainly, he realized by now that the mission program in New Mexico was going to be a long, difficult, and perilous task, and maybe he was no longer up to those demands. Whatever his reasons, San Antonio resigned his office once he reached El Paso and, shortly thereafter, he permanently departed the Kingdom.[20]

* * *

By September 1694, the subjugation of the Puebloans was superficially complete, with only Picurís, Taos, Zuñi, and Acoma, and the Hopi people still defiant of the Spanish. At this time, the Franciscans petitioned Governor Vargas for permission to return to the missions. On 22 September, they drafted a letter to Vargas indicating their readiness: "And thus, all of us, in unanimous agreement, fulfilling our duty of obedience, say that we are ready to assume the said ministries and that we see no objection whatever to being sent to serve in them . . . ; indeed, we are of the opinion that a decision to the contrary might bring certain inconveniences that would be to the discredit of our seraphic order."[21] No doubt, to have further delayed assuming their principal duties would likely have meant severe criticism of their evangelical effort from both the Franciscan hierarchy and the royal government. Only nine ordained priests were available to sign the letter.[22]

Two days later, and more than fourteen years after the Pueblo revolt, Franciscans began to resume their missionary roles to the native people of New Mexico. Fray Diego Zeinos was the first installed, taking over at Pecos on 24 September. Before the month was over, friars were placed at San Felipe, Jémez, Santa Ana, and Zía. The latter two were entrusted to a single missionary, Fray Juan Alpuente. Early in October, the Spanish carried out more installations with a friar each placed at Tesuque and San Ildefonso, while Fray Gerónimo Prieto took responsibility for both Santa Clara and San Juan. Late in October, Fray Antonio de Obregón was assigned to both San Lázaro and San Cristóbal.[23]

In early November, a familiar face arrived in the region to assume the post of custos when Fray Francisco de Vargas appeared in Santa Fe with four additional friars in tow. Fray Francisco, it will be recalled, had been the custos at the time Governor Vargas assumed his offices in 1691. Like the governor, Custos Vargas was a gachupín and previously served in the El Paso district for over ten years. With the new custos and the additional priests, there were now fourteen ordained missionaries in the field. Consequently, the custos made some adjustments in the friars' assignments by reducing those attending to two missions to a single site, and ordering the installation of missionaries to Cochití and Santo Domingo.[24]

Two important developments should be noted concerning the installation of missionaries during 1694. First, when the Spanish placed each friar in a mission site, Governor Vargas and a sizable contingent of soldiers accompanied the Franciscan. This indicated to the natives, of course, the support their priest enjoyed from the military, but to a degree it further symbolized the friars' evolving dependency upon the local civil and military authorities. In addition, Governor Vargas seized the opportunity at the installation ceremony to have each

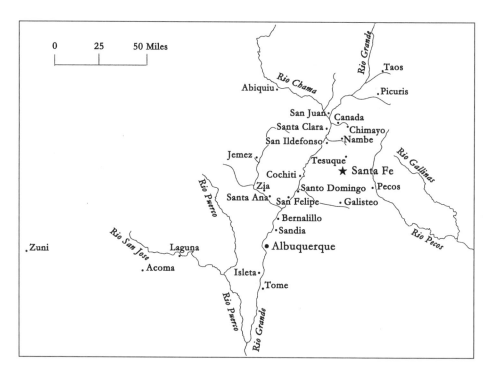

Map 2. The Santa Fe District (Río Arriba and Río Abajo)

Puebloan group elect their tribal officers, who then were confirmed in their posts by the governor. Before 1680, the missionaries often held significant sway over the selection of native leaders; however, these initial officers of this new epoch gained their posts without Franciscan influence. Indeed, for the remainder of the colonial era, with few exceptions, the friars had little say in the Puebloans' political administration.[25]

Throughout this period, as the friars returned to the missions, the relationship between the Franciscans and Governor Vargas was not completely harmonious. Custos Vargas had seemingly worked well with the governor in El Paso, referring to Don Diego in one glowing report as another "Hernán Cortés." Now, in the fall of 1694, the custos was not pleased that the governor had begun the installation process without the prelate's approval of which friar was placed in each mission. Furthermore, Fray Francisco did not believe that his missionaries were receiving adequate military protection. In fact, the custos submitted written protests to the governor over the lack of military support for the mission operation. Governor Vargas, however, ignored the Franciscan's complaints.[26]

In December 1694, with some friars now in the missions almost three months, Custos Vargas dispatched a questionnaire to his priests asking them to evaluate the state of affairs in their respective missions. Specifically, the prelate wanted to know what behaviors and attitudes the Puebloan people were exhibiting, what successes had taken place in winning over the souls of the people, to what degree the Puebloans provided sustenance for the friars, and whether the missionaries believed each mission would ultimately adopt Spanish religious beliefs and customs.

Nine friars' replies to the custos exist, and they generally provide a guardedly optimistic assessment of the mission operation. All nine priests claimed some successes in baptizing children into the faith, although none stated that they had induced adults to accept Catholicism. Some older natives, ill or near death, had accepted the sacrament of extreme unction. Six friars had performed marriage ceremonies with Diego Zeinos at Pecos leading the way with thirteen Catholic-sanctioned unions. Significantly, most of those Puebloans who were married by friars were tribal officers, men who would likely attempt to ingratiate themselves with the Spanish authorities. Six friars claimed that idolatry (the practice of native religion) was still obvious among their flocks with only the missionaries at Santo Domingo, Zía, and Santa Ana avowing that this was not occurring.

Most Franciscans seemed pleased with the level of cooperation they received from the Puebloans. All, except for the Propaganda Fide priest José Díez at Tesuque, attested to the fact that their natives provided them with food and water. For the most part their diet was simple: twelve to fifteen tortillas a day. Another Queretaran, Gerónimo Prieto at San Juan, petulantly complained that his neophytes refused to augment his meals with fresh corn, though he knew they had some. All of the missionaries, except for Díez, noted that chapels were being erected and their conventos prepared. In some missions, the construction of new churches was in progress. Considering that these men had only been installed a brief time, these achievements were notable.

Poring over these responses to his inquiry, Custos Vargas must have been at least somewhat pleased. While the adult Puebloans appeared reluctant to embrace Catholicism anew, at least they allowed the Franciscans to baptize their children. Furthermore, the native people were evidently cooperating with their priests, at least to some degree. A foreboding observation, however, was also to be found in the friars' answers to the question on whether they were hopeful for the potential success of the mission program goals. All responded that the Puebloan people could be converted to Catholicism, but four missionaries believed (those at Tesuque, San Juan, San Ildefonso, and Santa Clara) that another major Puebloan uprising was a distinct possibility in the foreseeable future.[27]

Through the following year, the missionary operation slowly expanded. At least three other missions reopened, and Governor Vargas established two Spanish settlements, Santa Cruz de Cañada and Bernalillo, which also required the Franciscans' attention. While a few additional friars arrived in the region, the missionaries were still stretched to the limit. Compounding the friars' problems was a growing restlessness on the part of the Puebloan people, which sometimes bordered on the antagonistic. Fearful and isolated, some priests frequently left their missions for the relative safety and security of Santa Fe. On numerous occasions, Custos Vargas petitioned to the governor for the assignment of soldiers to the missions, but he failed to obtain permanent protection for his friars.[28]

Early in the winter of 1695–1696, the situation in New Mexico began to deteriorate. Agricultural production, which had been disrupted during the military campaigns in 1694, declined further that summer. Starvation soon stalked the region, and disease, especially plague and typhus, swept through the colony killing Spaniard and Puebloan alike. Governor Vargas, too, was bedridden for a time, apparently suffering from typhus. More ominously for the Spanish, information began to mount indicating that the Puebloan people were conspiring to launch a new rebellion.[29]

Two weeks before Christmas, Custos Vargas convened the difinitorio into session to consider whether the friars should be evacuated from the missions. Citing the numerous rumors of an imminent Pueblo rebellion and noting the precedent of 1680, the difinitorio recommended that Governor Vargas either provide military protection to the missions or allow the friars to abandon their posts temporarily. While Don Diego was plainly unhappy with the Franciscans' petition, he consented to congregate the missionaries at Zía and provided them with sixteen soldiers to defend that mission. While the feared Pueblo revolt did not take place, by the end of 1695 the Franciscans clearly were becoming alarmed over the inherent dangers of their situation. Therefore, the Franciscans were linking their personal safety to the yoke of the governor and his soldiers.[30]

* * *

In early March 1696, the Franciscans again believed that a Pueblo rebellion would soon occur. According to a letter from Custos Vargas to the governor, the friars had uncovered a plot to murder the lay brother Blas Navarro who was working in the mission at Picurís. In addition, José Díez at Tesuque claimed that some natives had warned him of an impending coordinated Pueblo uprising. Throughout the missions, the custos claimed, there were unmistakable signs of Puebloan hostility: "These miserable Indians must find themselves in contempt of and unwilling to again accept our holy faith and law, and in view of their rebelliousness and the repeated deaths they have committed. For they have already profaned the temples which were built at the request of the reverend father missionaries a year and a half ago, as well as the sacred vessels and the articles of divine worship. And also they have seized the cattle and sheep. . . ." The prelate further reminded Governor Vargas of what had transpired in "the year eighty." At the same time, Custos Vargas called the difinitorio into session and again that council renewed the request for military protection at the missions.[31]

Governor Vargas responded to these developments quickly. First, he noted that the Franciscans seemed always to be confronted with imminent Puebloan revolts, yet none of these dire predictions had ever come to pass. Moreover, the governor pointed out that the presidial garrison was severely depleted from the winter epidemics and was unable to provide blanket protection at all the missions. Don Diego placed the onus on the friars. He requested that the missionaries determine among themselves which missions needed troops and, more specifically, how large a contingent of soldiers each missionary desired.[32]

Dutifully, Fray Francisco polled his friars. At this time there were fifteen Franciscans billeted to the missions in the region, and their replies offer stark evidence of their wish for military protection and, thus, their reliance on the governor. Navarro, the lay brother at Picurís, asked for a squad of twelve soldiers, José Díez at Tesuque desired a like number, and at Taos, Fray Diego de Chavarría, a newcomer to the district, wanted "a very considerable number." Some missionaries wanted to let the custos or governor decide for them. All in all, eleven of the fifteen friars wanted troops garrisoned at their mission. As further evidence of the Franciscans' dependency, all of those who wanted troops stated that they could not provide sustenance for the soldiers and requested that Governor Vargas shoulder that burden as well.[33]

The governor did not have these numbers of soldiers available in the Kingdom, and stated as much in his reply to the custos. To bolster this argument, Governor Vargas included an inventory of military strength in his letter to the prelate. Nonetheless, Don Diego did promise that some detachments would be sent to those missions that appeared to be most threatened and he accepted the responsibility for provisioning those units. Custos Vargas did not feel that the governor's assistance was sufficient, however, and he offered the choice to his priests either to remain in their missions or abandon them, stating that: "[A]nyone [who] does not wish to go [back to the missions], especially since it is realized, as regards these apostates of our holy faith, that little fruit can be obtained from their souls by a minister offering up his life."[34]

At least fourteen friars responded to Fray Francisco's request. All of their replies were sent from the Spanish settlements of Santa Fe, Santa Cruz de Cañada, and Bernalillo, which suggests they must have left their missions at some point in this most recent crisis. Nine respondents unequivocally did not want to return to their missions without military support. Most of these replied very simply, such as Fray Juan Alpuente of Pecos, who wrote that "in conscience I cannot serve there without the said guard." Perhaps more indicative of their fears, however, was the response of Blas Navarro who, after vividly recounting the destruction of a saint's image by the Puebloans, said, "And if they do this to the saints, they will be more likely to do it to me."[35]

Five of the missionaries left the decision to return to their posts up to the custos or expressed a willingness to sacrifice their lives. These friars were Díez at Tesuque, Chavarría at Taos, Antonio Carbonel at Nambé, Pedro de Matha at Zía, and Francisco de Jesús María Casañas at Jémez. Perhaps the most zealous reply was from Casañas, who avowed to the custos: "[F]or I did not come to seek death but rather the lives of these miserable ones. And if His Divine Majesty wishes to grant me the prize [martyrdom], he will do so even if it is in the public square of Mexico." The custos, however, decided to keep the Queretaran and the other friars in the relatively secure Spanish settlements for a time. Yet again, though, the rebellion did not materialize, and the missionaries resumed their duties.[36]

Less than two months later, on 4 June 1696, the Puebloans finally rebelled and attempted to duplicate their success of "the year eighty." The uprising seems to have been organized by a Puebloan of Cochití, Lucas Naranjo, but it was not as well coordinated as the one in 1680. Five Pueblos remained loyal to the Spanish—Pecos, Tesuque, Zía, Santa Ana, and San Felipe—and others merely fled, choosing not to play an active part in the revolt. Thus, the 1696 rebellion could have been more disastrous for the Spanish because inexplicably, despite the rumors and the precedent of 1680, they were caught off guard again. At least twenty-one Spanish soldiers and settlers were slain during the initial uprising.[37]

In addition to those losses, five Franciscans were also killed early in the rebellion. Fray José de Arvisu (Arbizu), the missionary at San Cristóbal, and Fray Antonio Carbonel, who was in the process of traveling to Taos, were killed by a large group of Puebloan warriors. The resident friar of San Ildefonso, Fray Francisco de Corbera, along with Fray Antonio Moreno, who was posted to Nambé, sought shelter in San Ildefonso's convento from the Puebloans. Those two missionaries suffocated when their assailants set fire to the mission buildings. And finally, Francisco de Jesús María Casañas, who had expressed his willingness for the martyr's laurel, was killed at his mission post of Jémez. Like the 1680 revolt, the Puebloans also destroyed churches, images, vestments, and other symbols of the Spaniards' religion.[38]

For the next five months, the mission program was completely inactive as the governor and his forces campaigned to put the rebellion down. Those friars who had survived congregated in the Spanish villas, where they huddled with other refugees. Their religious duties were limited to ministering to the Spaniards or serving as chaplains to the military forces. One friar, Juan Alpuente, was slightly wounded by an arrow during one battle.[39]

With peace generally restored to the Kingdom by November, the governor and custos requested that more missionaries be sent in order to reopen the missions. In addition to the five slain friars, just prior to the rebellion the Propaganda Fide in Querétaro had withdrawn four of its priests—José Díez, Gerónimo Prieto, José García Marín, and Domingo de Jesús María. Consequently, there were only eight ordained Franciscans available in the region. Both Fray Francisco and Don Diego requested at least eight replacements. Governor Vargas's petition included several interesting statements that reveal his assessment of the previous friars' commitment and capabilities, and itemized the attitudes the new missionaries should bring to the Kingdom: "the religious that come should come very much of their own free will and aware of the danger to their lives, because I cannot assure them protection. . . . [T]hey should not fail to have justifiable fear. . . . I do not want them to be making petitions asking for guards for the protection of their lives, either from their very reverend father or in the name of the difinitorio or from other discreet fathers, saying that if not provided they will leave the said missions uninhabited."[40]

* * *

Governor Vargas's warnings and admonitions went to the heart of the Franciscans' problems in New Mexico during the reconquest era. As noted earlier, the initial contingent of eighteen was rather inexperienced as missionary priests. At least nine Franciscans supplemented the original group over the next eighteen months. Three of these were also from the Propaganda Fide institution in Querétaro, and were equally untested as missionaries. Navarro, the lay brother, Fray José García Marín, and Fray Miguel de Trizio had all arrived in Querétaro from Spain in 1692. Of the other six friars, some background information exists for five. Fray José de Arvisu, one of those killed in 1696, had professed in Puebla in 1679 at age sixteen. He was an orphan, raised by the Church but identified by the Order as a criollo. Fray Diego de Chavarría, a criollo, professed in 1679 in Mexico City. He had labored in the El Paso area for at least four years before moving north. Fray Pedro de Matha, hijo de provincia, had only professed his faith in Mexico City in 1688. Fray Antonio Moreno, a criollo killed in 1696, entered the Order at age seventeen in 1682. Fray Diego de Ramírez, a criollo, was the oldest of the replacements. A criollo from Puebla, he had professed in that city in 1658 at age sixteen. Other than his being identified as a criollo, nothing is known of Fray Alonso Jiménez de Cisneros's background. Furthermore, no records exist of prior frontier mission service for any of these friars. Therefore, most of these Franciscans were relatively young and, except for Chavarría, inexperienced.[41]

Despite the enormous strain under which all Spaniards suffered during this era, the Franciscans and Governor Vargas seem to have worked together reasonably well. The friars did balk at being placed in the missions before Santa Fe was even captured, but Don Diego bowed to their protests with little acrimony, as well he should have. Custos Vargas was angered that the governor had already begun installing his priests in the missions, but the friars had requested that, and no heated controversy resulted. Even through all the turmoil leading up to the 1696 revolt, the prelate and the governor conducted their relationship in a civil manner, a most uncommon characteristic in the pre-1680 epoch. As will be noted in the following chapter, Custos Vargas actively lobbied on Governor Vargas's behalf through Don Diego's years of tribulation that followed the reconquest period.

The primary difficulty between the friars and the civil authority in the Kingdom centered on the matter of military protection for the mission priests. While Governor Vargas did the best he could to support the mission operation, considering the forces he had available, this issue illustrated the new relationship that was being forged between Franciscans and the state. With the memory of "the year eighty" still fresh in their minds, their relative inexperience, and continuing evidence of Puebloan hostility, the friars feared for their lives. This was an honest, and very human, reaction. Consequently, the Franciscans believed that their self-preservation and the success of the evangelical enterprise relied on the governor and the soldiers he commanded. For the first time, the Franciscans in the Kingdom of New Mexico were vitally dependent upon the local political authority. This pattern, once established, contributed to the eclipse of Franciscan power and prestige.

CHAPTER 5

A Period of Accommodation

WHILE THE DECADE that followed the rebellion in 1696 was less chaotic, it was by no means a time of tranquillity in New Mexico. Some colonists illegally fled the region because of the poor economic conditions and the continued danger posed by the native inhabitants. Thus, the Spanish population grew very slowly, if at all. Realizing the need to completely pacify the Kingdom and attract more colonists, the local government directed much of its energy and resources to induce all Puebloans into missions and diminish the threat from other native people such as the Apaches and Navajos. The military forces, however, were severely limited by shortages of personnel, mounts, and equipment. Problems within the governor's office also compounded the Spaniards' difficulties. Governor Vargas was replaced in 1697 and even found himself imprisoned for a time in Santa Fe. The government later reappointed Vargas to the office, but he died shortly after his return. An interim governor then assumed the post for almost three years until a permanent replacement arrived in 1707. Local government, in short, was unstable for a considerable portion of the decade.

As for the Franciscan missionaries, these ten years were also difficult. Though back in their missions after the 1696 uprising, the friars still had reason to fear their neophytes as the Spanish uncovered several Puebloan rebellion conspiracies. In addition, shortages in the number of missionaries and inadequate supplies constantly vexed the Franciscans. Indeed, by 1706 the number of ordained missionaries in the region was the same as the total immediately prior to the 1696 rebellion. Despite these dangers and limitations, the mission program doggedly expanded.

In this milieu, governors and friars shied away from potentially inherent conflicts and reached some level of accommodation in order to preserve the Spaniards' fragile position in the colony. Conflicts and controversies did arise, but both sides seemed to realize their need for each other. Certainly, the missionaries were still dependent on the governors in order to expand the mission

44	*Chapter Five*

field and for personal protection. On the other hand, the various governors seemed aware that Franciscans made better allies than foes.

* * *

In July 1697, Pedro Rodríguez Cubero arrived in Santa Fe to replace Vargas as governor of the Kingdom. Rodríguez originally received his appointment in 1692, but because of discrepancies concerning Vargas's term, Rodríguez did not accede to the post until 1697. The new governor was from a family of modest status in Andalucía. After entering the Spanish military as a common soldier in 1674, he had risen steadily through the ranks during his service in the Sicilian campaigns and with the fleet. In 1689, he was promoted to command the La Punta fortress, one of the sites guarding the port of Havaña. Though the governor post in New Mexico was promised in 1692, Rodríguez was also waiting for a similar position to open in what is today Venezuela. Indeed, Rodríguez petitioned the royal government in 1695 to void the New Mexico posting, citing that his health would suffer in the temperature extremes of that region. Rodríguez was a proven military man, exactly what the government believed the Kingdom required. Hence, under the warmth of July skies, the forty-one-year-old Rodríguez assumed his office in Santa Fe.[1]

Whether because of class differences or professional animosities, Rodríguez and Vargas clashed. At first, Vargas refused even to surrender his office, although he soon gave in to the inevitable. Rodríguez then conducted the *residencia*, the formal judicial review mandated by Spanish law that an official made of his predecessor. No charges were brought against Vargas at that time. In September, however, the *cabildo* (municipal council) of Santa Fe, perhaps at Rodríguez's behest, offered several allegations against Vargas. Among the more serious accusations were embezzlement of royal funds, mismanagement of his office causing the famine in 1695 and the Pueblo revolt in 1696, and the illegal executions of native prisoners. Within two weeks of these charges being made, Rodríguez placed Vargas under house arrest and ordered that Don Diego's property be confiscated. Several of the former governor's aides were also charged with crimes. Eventually Rodríguez ordered that Vargas be manacled and visitations be severely restricted. Vargas endured these conditions until the summer of 1700 when he was allowed to go to Mexico City to defend himself.[2]

In this type of acrimonious environment in the pre-1680 epoch, the Franciscans would have embroiled themselves in the controversy in an effort to expand their own power in the Kingdom. The friars' interference often resulted in an increase in their authority, but just as likely in the end created deep fissures among the Spaniards, especially between the clergy and civil officials. In fact, some incidents along this line occurred at the time. When his term as custos expired in 1697, Fray Francisco de Vargas departed New Mexico for Mexico City where he lobbied vigorously on behalf of Don Diego. In addition, some friars visited the former governor during his incarceration in Santa Fe, against the expressed orders of Governor Rodríguez. The governor verbally chastised these priests for their defiance and threatened to banish them from the colony.[3]

There were other indications of tensions between Rodríguez and the Franciscans. In 1699, Fray José García Marín, the last remaining Propaganda Fide priest in New Mexico, complained that the governor had slandered him by publicly stating that Fray José solicited women in the confessional and preached heretical sermons. García called for the Holy Office to investigate this matter, but no records of any subsequent Inquisition inquiry have been uncovered. For his part, Governor Rodríguez complained in a report drafted in 1699 that the friars were meddling unduly in government affairs in the Kingdom, and that the missionaries were failing to master the Puebloan languages of their neophytes.[4]

Despite these incidents, both the Franciscan leaders and Rodríguez worked to keep a potentially difficult situation from becoming worse. To Rodríguez's credit, he did what he could to pacify the Puebloans in order to allow the Franciscans to reopen missions. In a series of military campaigns in 1698–1699, the governor induced holdouts from the Puebloans of Acoma and Zuñi to agree to peace treaties, and missionaries were installed in these sites shortly thereafter. Rodríguez played an important part in congregating some Keres natives who had fled the region during the reconquest in a new village at Laguna. A missionary was placed there in 1699. The governor also attempted, though without success, to subdue the Hopi and renew the mission effort among these people. In addition to these operations, Rodríguez built at his own expense (about 6,000 pesos) a new convento in Santa Fe for the Franciscans.[5]

The Franciscans also seemed to focus their energy on their primary responsibility: the missionary program. Besides initiating evangelical activities among the Puebloans that Governor Rodríguez pacified, the friars mounted at least two efforts to win back the Hopi. In 1699 Fray Juan Álvarez led a small expedition into the Hopi province, but was forced to turn back before making contact with these natives. The following year Fray Juan de Garaicoechea and Fray Antonio Miranda got as far as the Hopi village of Awátovi. At first, these friars enjoyed some success. The missionaries baptized seventy-three Hopi and the Franciscan convento there was rebuilt. The missionary effort collapsed soon thereafter, however, when other Hopi attacked and destroyed Awátovi. Thus, it seems as if both Rodríguez and the friars realized that concentrating on the mission operation was the point of convergence between the civil and spiritual spheres.[6]

The various Franciscan prelates during this period made a determined effort to keep the missionaries out of the Rodríguez-Vargas conflict specifically, and out of government matters in general. Indicative of this strategy were orders drafted to the friars in 1701 by Custos Fray Antonio Guerrero. After noting that past problems in the Kingdom were often the results of friars becoming enmeshed in civil disputes, Guerrero ordered his brothers to avoid being drawn into civil lawsuits or to "secretly" write letters to Mexico City complaining about the governor. If difficulties should arise with civil authorities, Fray Antonio stipulated that friars must bring their complaints to the custos and allow him or the provincial leaders in Mexico City to attend to the dispute. Furthermore, Guerrero admonished the missionaries to stay out of Santa Fe unless they had permission to be there, thereby reducing their chances of being swept up into political conflicts. Other prelates during this era echoed Guerrero's directives.[7]

On a practical level, the Franciscan leadership in New Mexico had to be keenly aware that the security of the friars and success of the mission operation continued to be dependent on the governor's role as head of the presidial forces. Because of the unsettled conditions in the western regions, the Franciscans requested and received a small military garrison at Zuñi. In 1702, the Spanish uncovered a plot involving some Puebloans at Acoma, Laguna, and Zuñi. Apparently, these natives were in league with some Hopi and Navajo bands in the area to rebel and drive the Spanish out of western New Mexico. Some ringleaders later testified that their hostility was mainly directed at the missionary based in Zuñi, Juan de Garaicoechea. The Puebloans claimed that this friar taught them little of Catholicism, yet punished them harshly when they erred in matters of faith. This episode must have reminded the Franciscans of the uncertainty of their hold on the natives and their continued animosity toward the religious. If they needed further evidence of this, the friars soon witnessed it. In 1703, the Zuñi people did rebel, killing three Spanish soldiers stationed there, although they spared the life of Garaicoechea. The Spanish withdrew from Zuñi and briefly suspended the missionary operation there.[8]

Near the conclusion of Rodríguez's term in office, and probably as a result of the still volatile nature of the situation in the Kingdom, the Province of Santo Evangelio moved to bolster the power of the Custody of Saint Paul. As was noted earlier (see chapter 2), until the 1660s, the custos in New Mexico also held the title of comisario of the Inquisition. These duties were taken away at that time to help ease relations between the Franciscans and local government officials and had not been restored. In 1703 Fray Juan Álvarez, who had already served one term as custos (1697–1698), was once again selected as the custody's prelate. In a circular announcing his election, Álvarez included in his titles that of comisario of the Holy Office. Virtually every custos until the mid-1700s also held this office, though those powers were used sparingly, as will be noted later.[9]

* * *

During the summer of 1703, Rodríguez departed New Mexico before his successor, Don Diego de Vargas, arrived in Santa Fe. The viceroy, aware of the bad blood that existed between Rodríguez and Vargas, allowed Rodríguez to forego a residencia that would have been conducted by Don Diego. This meant, however, that New Mexico was without a governor and captain general until Vargas arrived in November. Being spared the judicial review proved to be of small consequence to Rodríguez. Within a year he died in Mexico City, though whether the harsh New Mexican environment he earlier feared contributed to the cause of death is unknown.[10]

Vargas should have been in good spirits as he once more took the reins of government. The government had exonerated Don Diego of the charges made during his residencia and awarded him a new term as governor and captain general. Although somewhat belatedly, a grateful monarchy had rewarded the reconqueror of New Mexico with a title: Marqués de la Nava de Brazinas. Vargas's sense of achievement and honor, however, was to be short-lived. In April 1704, he contracted a fever while campaigning against some Apaches and soon died. Thus, his second term lasted barely six months.[11]

Two incidents from Vargas's brief second administration point to a similarity in the Franciscans' willingness and desire to pursue a relationship based on accommodation with the local government. First, the leadership of the Order clearly aimed to keep the friars out of difficulties that might ensue between Vargas and the cabildo of Santa Fe. In August 1703, after Rodríguez departed and before Vargas appeared, Custos Álvarez relayed instructions from Fray José de la Llana, the Commissary General of New Spain, to the missionaries that they work constructively with the civil officials throughout the Kingdom and that they keep out of all civil disputes. Álvarez also reminded the friars of his earlier injunction that they stay out of Santa Fe unless they had his permission to be there.[12]

The second incident was another example of the dangers yet present regarding their evangelical duties. In December 1704, the Spanish uncovered another native plan to rebel. Centered around the Puebloans of Santa Clara and San Juan in concert with several nearby *rancherías* of Navajos, the Spanish took this intrigue very seriously. Troops were dispatched to the area, and those forces attacked and dispersed the Navajo bands. The Puebloans offered several reasons why they had become involved in this conspiracy with the Navajos. They had been very depressed and were drinking, they admitted, but they further claimed grievances against their mission priest, Fray Pedro de Matha. Fray Pedro, they charged, forced them to drive Spanish-owned livestock to Santa Fe, and he disdained learning their language, speaking only Spanish to them.

The Puebloans mainly blamed the Navajos, however, for instigating the idea of rebellion and, apparently, the Spanish accepted their claim, since no records exist detailing any further proceedings or punishment against these Puebloans.[13]

Don Diego's untimely death threw local government and military affairs into disarray until a new governor arrived. In March 1705, almost a year after Vargas's death, Don Francisco Cuervo y Valdés arrived in Santa Fe to assume the title of interim governor. Cuervo was an experienced government official and military officer on the northern frontier of New Spain. Born to a minor noble family in Asturias, Don Francisco was about seventeen years of age when he came to the New World in 1678. Since then, he had served as an infantry officer in Sonora, acting governor and captain general of Nuevo León, and for five years as governor of Coahuila (1698–1703). He was residing in Zacatecas between assignments when the viceroy, the Duke of Alburquerque, selected him to temporarily fill the vacant position in New Mexico.[14]

The two and a half years of the Cuervo administration were marked by two major problems. The first of these was the poor economic situation in the Kingdom. Almost ten years after the 1696 rebellion, the colony was still economically stagnant and the residents were still unable feed themselves adequately. New Mexico was so far from the trade and manufacturing centers of New Spain that both essential and luxury goods were imported from afar at great expense. Most Spanish colonists either did without, fashioned their own, or went into debt to secure items they required. In addition, agricultural produce was still insufficient because of ongoing hostile native raids, animal predation, and the general scarcity of fertile land. The colonists frequently ran short of food, and during the severe winter of 1705–1706, starvation stalked the region, and even people in Santa Fe died.[15]

The second problem that Governor Cuervo constantly faced came from hostile natives. While not as destructive as they would later become, raiding Apaches and Navajos disrupted most facets of Spanish frontier life. Soon after arriving in New Mexico, Cuervo dispatched punitive expeditions against Apache and Navajo bands in the western and southwestern regions. In 1706 he launched another military campaign northward in what is today Colorado. Later that year Cuervo persuaded the Navajos to agree to a peace treaty; however, that respite proved to be only temporary.[16]

Accommodation continued to rule church and state affairs during this period as the Franciscans and Governor Cuervo enjoyed rather good relations. The friars worked actively to get Cuervo's appointment made permanent. Custos Juan Álvarez and Vice-custos Juan de Tagle penned glowing certifications to Mexico City attesting to the interim governor's abilities. They claimed that Cuervo had strengthened the capabilities of the presidial forces and lauded his campaigns against the Apaches and Navajos. The Franciscan leadership in the Kingdom gratefully noted Cuervo's financial assistance to the mission program in light of the fact that the custody had not received its alms (royal stipend) for several years. Álvarez and Tagle also stated that the governor willingly provided military escorts for missionaries serving in the most isolated areas. Finally, both friars testified that Cuervo set an excellent example in Christian attributes for all in the colony by his "devotion to the Kingdom of Heaven."[17]

Governor Cuervo also contributed to the harmony between the local government and the Franciscans. During his term in office, Cuervo issued orders that all inhabitants in the Kingdom — Spanish, Indian, African, mestizo, and mulatto — must attend church services to ensure the propagation of the faith at the hour so stipulated by the custos. At the request of Custos Álvarez, Cuervo ordered Spaniards to stay out of the mission sites, although this directive proved to be ineffective, as will be noted later. The governor renewed the attempt to pacify the Hopi, but these efforts were as unsuccessful as those of his predecessors. Cuervo tried to improve the defenses of the colony by creating additional settlements. Two new Spanish villas were established — Alburquerque (named after the current viceroy) and Santa María del Grado (this one soon failed) — and Cuervo congregated some Tano natives in a mission called Galisteo. Governor Cuervo also strongly supported the Franciscans' pleas that more missionaries be assigned to the Kingdom. It should be obvious that Cuervo desired a regular appointment as governor, and he probably believed that Franciscan assistance would help achieve this end. Nonetheless, his administration was one of the high-water marks in close ties between the government and the Franciscans in eighteenth-century New Mexico.[18]

One other development during the Cuervo period should be noted. Under orders from the viceroy, the Duke of Alburquerque, the office of *protector de indios* was reactivated in New Mexico. In 1589, Philip II created this position in the New World. Essentially, the protector was to ensure the rights of the native people in civil and criminal cases, and to serve generally as a bridge between the Indian and Spanish worlds. The government designed the office to be secular in nature, though some clergymen did hold the title in New Spain. While little is known of the protectors in pre-1680 New Mexico, evidence exists that the position was only sporadically operative. The office was vacant at the time of the reconquest, however, and remained so until the Duke of Alburquerque's order and appointment of Captain Don Alfonso Rael de Aguilar as protector.[19]

The significance of the recreation of the protector de indios office was twofold. First, it clearly demonstrated the viceroy's plan to promote a more peaceful approach in dealings with the Puebloans and, hopefully, hasten pacification of the region. Second, by renewing this position, the role of civil institutions in native affairs was augmented, and, consequently, that of the

Franciscans weakened. Historically, protectors tended to side with local government in disputes that involved the Catholic Church.[20]

How effectively the protectors filled this dual role in New Mexico seems rather inconsequential as the office became vacant in 1716, and from all indications was not restored until 1763. Furthermore, during that forty-six-year period, the Franciscans appear to have frequently acted as legal advisors and scribes in legal matters involving Puebloans. Generally, it was the friars who served as advocates of the natives in cases where they were being abused. It was obvious, however, that the government intended at least partially to enhance civil authority at the expense of the Franciscans in the Kingdom.[21]

*   *   *

The Franciscans' major problems during this decade were the shortage of ordained missionaries and the material provisions of their faith, with the former being the most acute. Over and over the Franciscan leaders in New Mexico begged for more friars. The need was so great that even the governors of this era added their voices in support for additional missionaries, as noted above.

A glance at the number of friars that comprised the missionary effort during these years reveals the severity of the problem. By the time the rebellion of 1696 had been subdued, there were eight ordained priests left in the Santa Fe district. Over the next ten years, seventeen friars are known to have been posted to the region. During the same period, at least eleven disappeared from the Custody of Saint Paul's rosters. That left a net gain of six friars since 1696. Upon considering that additional mission sites were added at Acoma, Galisteo, Laguna, and Zuñi, as well of the Spanish villa at Alburquerque, the Franciscans were still stretched to the limit.[22]

The often-cited 1706 report authored by Custos Álvarez illuminates the Franciscans' personnel shortage. In the Santa Fe district, Álvarez noted that there were seventeen active mission sites as well as four villas inhabited mainly by Spanish citizens. All required attention from the Franciscans. For these twenty-one locations, the custos had available, including himself, thirteen ordained missionaries and one lay brother, the surgeon José Narváez. Another friar, Fray Domingo Martínez de Araoz, was incapacitated by illness and was being cared for in El Paso. Clearly, the ideal evangelical situation of assigning two priests to each mission was impossible under such circumstances.

Indeed, the custos had to reverse the very concept and frequently assign one friar to two missions. Álvarez, in addition to serving as custos, took care of the missions at Nambé and Tesuque, three leagues apart in distance. Fray Juan de Tagle (vice-custos) was based at San Ildefonso, but also took care of Santa Clara, four leagues away. Fray Juan Muñoz de Castro administered to the missions at Cochití and Santo Domingo, traveling about three leagues between the two. The most difficult posting belonged to Fray Antonio de Miranda. This friar was assigned to Acoma and Laguna, about eight leagues from one another. In all, seven friars were tending to more than one mission apiece, and one of them, Fray Pedro de Matha, had three: Picurís, San Juan, and the Spanish villa of Santa Cruz de Cañada.

The lack of missionaries also meant that some friars were placed in hazardous situations. The Franciscans generally preferred to keep two missionaries each at Zuñi and Taos. These missions were large, relatively isolated, and historically hostile to the Spanish. According to Álvarez's report, however, a single friar administered each at this time. Fray Alonso Jiménez de Cisneros was in charge at Taos, and Fray Juan de Garaicoechea covered Zuñi. To make matters worse, Garaicoechea died at Zuñi within a year of the Álvarez report.[23]

The missionaries in New Mexico were overextended as well as somewhat inexperienced when they arrived in the region. Of the seventeen friars who entered New Mexico in the 1697–1707 period, some background data exists for ten men. At least seven of these were relative newcomers to the evangelical life. Fray Domingo Martínez de Araoz had only professed his faith six years prior to his arrival in the Kingdom in 1705. Fray José de Arranegui professed in 1695 and came to this missionary field in 1700. Fray Cristóbal Alonso Barroso was also without experience when he accompanied Vargas's expedition in 1692 (see chapter 4). He returned to Spain for unspecified reasons in 1693 and did not reappear in New Mexico until 1698. Barroso served only nineteen months, however, before he permanently left the area. Fray Antonio Camargo donned the habit only two years before appearing on Saint Paul's custody roster. Fray Juan de Tagle was but twenty-four years of age when he first set foot in New Mexico and had professed only four years earlier. Fray Juan de la Peña was also twenty-four years old when he began his missionary career here. Fray Antonio Guerrero took his vows in 1692, seven years removed from the start of his time in the Kingdom.[24]

At least three friars were seasoned veterans as frontier missionaries, either in the El Paso or Junta de los Ríos districts. Fray Juan Álvarez had been in the field in El Paso for eighteen years (see chapter 3) before he came north in 1698. When Fray Agustín de Colina was transferred in 1702, he had spent the previous fifteen years between El Paso and Junta de los Ríos. The most experienced, of course, was Fray Francisco Farfán (see chapter 3). Farfán brought about two decades worth of missionary knowledge with him when he renewed his labors there in 1697. Farfán did not remain long, however, as he departed the Custody of Saint Paul for good in 1703 at the age of sixty.[25]

In addition to their personnel shortages and employment of raw recruits, the Franciscans suffered from serious material shortcomings. According to the Álvarez report, the mission field was in dire need of vestments, chalices, crucifixes, and other necessary articles of the faith. Álvarez offered two reasons for this unhappy state of affairs. First, as they had in "el año ochenta," the Puebloans who rebelled in 1696 destroyed large numbers of Catholic religious items. Secondly, Álvarez noted that many years had passed since the mission operation last received its alms. The Franciscans should have been receiving 330 pesos a year for each ordained friar and 230 for each lay brother. Part of these monies were used to supply missionaries with the tools of their trade. The War of the Spanish Succession, which was going on during part of this period, no doubt hampered the disbursement of royal funds to the New World. In the interim, New Mexico's friars were forced to do without or seek assistance from others, such as they had with Governor Cuervo.

Álvarez blamed former governors Rodríguez and Vargas for exacerbating the Franciscans' financial woes. Because of their disputes, Rodríguez and Vargas did not fully appreciate how dreadfully the lack of vestments, crucifixes, and other items hurt the mission program. Álvarez stated bluntly, "I see that although the fathers custodians who were my predecessors asked for succor [from Rodríguez and Vargas], they were not able to attain it because the governors were deeply concerned with nothing save their own lawsuits." In the meantime, the friars carried, or used native porters to tote, the articles of faith with them on their lengthy treks between the missions they administered.[26]

Nonetheless, the effort to convert the native population to Catholicism continued. Though the claim was standard in the 1706 Álvarez report, all mission sites had finished constructing and repairing churches, or were in the process of doing so. Traveling significant distances between missions, carrying the objects of their religion over rough terrain, often in foul weather, the missionaries pursued their calling. Neither the dangers from hostile bands of Apaches and Navajos, nor the recalcitrance of the Puebloans deterred the missionary operation. On the other hand, these adversities no doubt reduced the zeal these Franciscans brought to their vocation, and, perhaps, accelerated the erosion in the New Mexico mission program that would later be evident.[27]

*   *   *

Spanish secular and religious institutions were beset by numerous difficulties in New Mexico during the 1697–1707 period. Economic stagnation, food shortages, and native hostilities dominated the various governors' concerns when they were not absorbed with trying to hold on to their office. Personnel and equipment shortages for the ever-expanding mission field plagued the Franciscans. Puebloan intentions to rebel or more passive means of resistance only made the friars' work more demanding and dangerous.

Although there were some conflicts, the Franciscans and the governors generally strove to accommodate each other. The former continued to be dependent on the local government for personal protection, security of the missions, and financial support. The Franciscan leadership in the region worked diligently to reduce disharmony with the civil authorities by keeping as tight a rein as possible on the friars when it came to secular matters. While the government did expand its position somewhat at the expense of the religious in New Mexico, the governors realized that the success and expansion of the missions helped to cement Spanish control over the area. Furthermore, it is clear that at least Cuervo, and to a lesser degree Rodríguez, came to view the Franciscans as helpful allies in their struggles to hold on to their posts. The period of accommodation was soon to break down, however, and in the church and state conflict to come, the Franciscans' prestige and power in New Mexico would be further weakened.

CHAPTER 6

Conflict

I F THE PRECEDING DECADE was one of accommodation between the Franciscans and the civil authorities in New Mexico, bitter disputes characterized their relationship during the 1707–1715 period. Two primary interrelated problems confronted the governors during this era: improving the military capacity of the presidial forces in the colony and warding off hostile native assaults, especially from the Apaches and Navajos. These Spanish officials responded to the twin challenges by striving to expand their civil authority in an effort to secure New Spain's northern frontier, and, thus, ensure the success of their administrations.

A likely area for the governors to strengthen their authority was over the Puebloan inhabitants of the colony. Not only were the Puebloans an important economic factor in New Mexico, but more importantly, they were potentially a military asset. Since the Spanish first came to New Mexico, control over the Puebloan people had always been a foundation of their power in the region. As previously noted, the governors had already augmented their power regarding the region's native population since the reconquest. Naturally, any gains by the Kingdom's governors came at the expense of the Franciscan missionaries who had traditionally reigned supreme over the Puebloans. Hence, further efforts by the governors to establish greater influence over the Puebloans brought them into direct confrontation with the friars and set the stage for conflict. As would be expected, the Franciscans resisted any reduction in their status in the colony, and in the ensuing controversies the stakes increased for both governors and missionaries. By 1715, when the struggle was prematurely suspended, the contest for power in New Mexico affected virtually all aspects of church and state relations.

* * *

The arrival of Admiral Don José Chacón Medina Salazar y Villaseñor, the Marqués de la Peñuela, as the new governor of New Mexico in July 1707 must

have come as a disappointment to the colony's friars. They had worked diligently to secure a regular appointment for the ad interim Governor Cuervo, an
official with whom they had enjoyed generally good relations. Disappointment,
however, would become an understatement to describe the Franciscans' emotional reactions. The Chacón administration would become one of the most
acrimonious periods in eighteenth-century church and state affairs.

Chacón was thirty-nine years of age when he arrived in the Kingdom. The
son of a noble family from Sevilla, he had received his appointment as governor in March 1705. The royal decree arrived too late for Chacón to sail with the
fleet for the New World that spring, and because of other disruptions associated
with the Spanish War of Succession, over two years passed before he could assume office in Santa Fe. While little is known of his previous positions,
Chacón's family had a long history of government and military service. That
Chacón held the title of admiral and membership in the military Order of Santiago indicates at least a significant military career.[1]

Several unique aspects concerning Chacón's selection as governor attest to
the increasing interest by the monarchy in New Mexican affairs. First, Chacón
was the only hereditary nobleman to hold the office of governor of New Mexico. Diego de Vargas, of course, was awarded a noble title after his first term in
office, and since Chacón technically was Vargas's successor, perhaps the government reasoned that one marqués should follow another in this newly restored and strategically important colony. Second, the Crown selected Chacón
over the recommendation of the viceroy, the Duke of Alburquerque, who fa-
vored Cuervo y Valdés. In the seventeenth century, the government in Spain
often merely rubber-stamped governors chosen by the viceroys of New Spain.
This would not be the case in the 1700s; most New Mexico governors were selected in Spain. Finally, Chacón represented the first Bourbon appointee to
the New Mexico governor's office. It seems reasonable to assume that the new
ruling family of Spain held Chacón's abilities in high esteem.[2]

Clouding the atmosphere of Chacón's first years in office was a conflict with
the man he replaced. Chacón presided over a suit brought against Cuervo by
soldiers of the Santa Fe presidio concerning irregularities in their pay. It seems
that Cuervo, like other governors, had been paying the soldiers in goods rather
than currency, and apparently, these items were of less value than their monetary equivalent. For his part, Cuervo accused Chacón of public slander and
failure to reimburse him for goods that the new governor had commandeered
from Cuervo. These issues were finally settled in Chacón's favor, but not until
1710. Thus, Cuervo remained a disruptive figure in Santa Fe for almost three
years of Chacón's administration.[3]

Besides the problems with Cuervo, one of Chacón's main concerns during
his first years in office was restoring the defensive capacity of the colony. Some

improvements in the presidial forces had occurred under Cuervo; however, severe deficiencies still existed. Since the soldiers' pay was often in arrears, many had become virtually destitute. To alleviate their condition, the soldiers, including officers, often sold or traded their weapons, equipment, and horses to native people, even to hostile Apaches and Navajos. This obviously increased the military capabilities of the raiders while simultaneously weakening the Spanish forces. Chacón issued several *bandos* (decrees) in 1707 and 1708 strictly forbidding this practice and providing harsh punishments, including execution, for those found guilty. The new governor worked to improve discipline within the ranks by ordering banishment from the military for those who disobeyed commands. Finally, Chacón held a colonywide inspection to determine the military preparedness of the region's inhabitants.[4]

The need to sharpen the ability of the colony's military forces reflected fundamental changes occurring among the native people in North America. On the one hand, Chacón's term in office coincided with increasing peaceful coexistence with the Puebloans. His was the first administration during which no Puebloan plots to rebel were uncovered. Indeed, after the 1704 conspiracies discovered at San Juan and Santa Clara noted in the previous chapter, there exists no evidence of any further serious efforts by the Puebloans to free themselves from Spanish domination.

On the other hand, pressure from raiding Apaches and Navajos reached new heights during this period and continued unabated into the 1730s. As native people to the east were displaced by French and English colonization and trade, pressure increased on those to the west. In the case of the Apache people, the Comanches were pushing them west and south from the Great Plains, directly into the Spanish settlements of New Mexico. Together with the renewed hostility of the Navajo people, Chacón had his hands full with marauding native bands. Between 1707 and 1709, destructive as well as lethal attacks took place against the missions at Cochití, Pecos, Santa Clara, and Jémez, and the Spanish settlement at Santa Cruz de la Cañada.[5]

It was in response to this new wave of hostility that Chacón took his first step toward expanding the powers of the governor's office at the expense of the Franciscans. Apparently, the missionaries had become lax in their efforts to extirpate Puebloan religious traditions. This was especially evident in the proliferation of kivas (*estufas*), the spiritual underground ceremonial chambers belonging to various Puebloan religious societies. Chacón accused the friars of not being diligent enough in the eradication of Puebloan religion, and in numerous missions during 1708 and 1709, Chacón ordered the alcaldes mayores, assisted by presidial troops, to destroy the kivas. Though the custos, Fray Juan de la Peña, supported these actions, many of the missionaries were angered by Chacón's measures. They argued that the destruction of the kivas might lead to a resurgence of Puebloan hostility and that Chacón's methods were an illegal intrusion into the Franciscan sphere of authority.[6]

Governor Chacón's campaign to dismantle the kivas was motivated by more concerns than just embarrassing and reducing the Franciscan position. The trend in New Mexico since the reconquest era had been for the Spanish to rely more and more on Puebloan auxiliary forces in military campaigns. This was a remarkable about-face from the pre-1680 period when the Puebloan people were considered too timid to be of military use. Governor Vargas, however, had given arms and mounts to trusted Puebloans during his administration, and the Spaniards' reliance on Puebloan warriors became more common throughout the eighteenth century. Chacón, an admiral and Knight of the Order of Santiago, probably reasoned that if the Puebloans were to be used as military allies, then they should comport themselves as much like Spaniards and Christians as possible.[7]

There was, however, another important area during this early portion of his administration in which Chacón moved to expand the governor's power over the native people. According to Spanish law, New World native people who were deemed not yet fully converted to Catholicism were exempt from the jurisdiction of the Inquisition. After the Holy Office was installed in New Mexico during the 1620s, however, the Inquisition was used against the Puebloans, especially in witchcraft cases. In fact, virtually all known incidences of witchcraft up to 1680, whether Spaniard or Puebloan, were handled by the Franciscan custos who also held the Inquisition office in the Kingdom. Therefore, jurisdiction over witchcraft cases was another area that the Franciscans exploited prior to the Pueblo rebellion in 1680 to expand their power in New Mexico.[8]

In light of this questionable legal practice by the Franciscans and Governor Chacón's low opinion of the friars' efforts to extinguish Puebloan paganism, it is not surprising that when Doña Leonor Domínguez claimed to have been bewitched by three San Juan women, Chacón stepped in and took over the investigation. The proceedings soon revealed that witchcraft was not the real issue in this matter. Doña Leonor's allegations had more to do with her jealousy over her husband's sexual infidelity with these women. Hence, the Puebloan women were soon exonerated through Chacón's investigation, but the governor's role in this affair established a precedent. Throughout the remainder of the colonial era in New Mexico, local government officials, either governors or alcaldes mayores, handled all cases involving accusations of Indian witchcraft. Thus, another element of power was stripped from the Franciscans.[9]

As Richard E. Greenleaf noted in his study of the Holy Office in eighteenth-century New Mexico, the use of Inquisition powers fundamentally changed after the reconquest. In the decades before 1680, the powers of the Holy Office were used by the Franciscans as an instrument to force Puebloan "acculturation" through its attacks on "paganism, idolatry, and religious syncretism," and as a weapon in the friars' struggles with local government authority. When the Inquisition was reintroduced after the reconquest, however, it was a limited tool of social control, used solely against the non-Puebloan population in the Kingdom. The Inquisition was only employed in cases such as bigamy, sexual immorality, blasphemy, and the like. Nor were the powers of the Holy Office ever invoked in the quarrels between church and state, although in some instances the friars did request intercession by the Inquisition in those conflicts.[10]

During the first years of Chacón's administration, the governor certainly displayed a proclivity to expand the powers of his office at the expense of the Franciscans. His moves in these matters drew surprisingly little opposition from the missionaries. Some friars applauded Chacón's destruction of the kivas, which suggests that the missionaries were not united in viewing the governor's actions as a threat to the Franciscan position. Furthermore, it seems that Chacón's relationship with Custos Juan de la Peña was relatively harmonious. In early 1710, however, Peña suddenly became ill and died. His successor was Fray Juan de Tagle, and this prelate would soon exhibit an altogether new attitude toward Chacón's other efforts to expand government authority. The relationship between the Franciscans and Chacón was about to enter a stage of significant and fundamental conflict.[11]

* * *

Fray Juan de Tagle was a native of San Vincente de Barquiera, Spain, and born to a family of some stature, since his parents were addressed as Don and Doña in Spanish records. It is unclear when he came to New Spain, but he professed his vows at twenty years of age to the Order in the convento of San Francisco de México in April 1695. Tagle first appeared in New Mexico in 1699; thus, he was only recently ordained as a missionary priest. His first recorded assignment was to San Ildefonso in 1701, and he remained the mission father there until his time in the colony ended in 1726. Tagle seems to have been at least a competent missionary. That he labored only at San Ildefonso for a quarter of a century suggests some degree of harmony between Tagle and his neophytes. In addition, there are no extant records of any irregularities or complaints associated with his administration of that mission. Tagle had twice previously held the vice-custos office—first, under Fray Juan Álvarez (1704–1706), and most recently under Juan de la Peña. Tagle actively supported Cuervo's efforts to secure a regular appointment as governor (see chapter 5) and had sided with Cuervo in his lawsuit against Chacón. Therefore, a basis for ill feeling already existed between Tagle and Chacón. An examination of Tagle's letters and reports further reveals a friar who was a staunch defender of the Franciscans' rights and privileges in New Mexico.[12]

Even before Tagle assumed the office of custos, some Franciscans in New Mexico were alarmed by the direction of Chacón's administration. A few missionaries had sent secret letters complaining about Chacón to Mexico City, including a charge that the governor was forcing Puebloans to perform personal services without remuneration. In 1710, the provincial of Santo Evangelio responded to these reports by ordering the newly appointed Tagle to direct the friars to stay out of civil affairs in general, and specifically the Chacón-Cuervo lawsuits, or face excommunication for disobedience. Tagle transmitted these directives to his friars, and added his own admonition that problems or complaints with the local government officials must be channeled through the office of custos. Clearly, the Franciscan hierarchy in Mexico City and Tagle wished to maintain a handle on any estrangement that might arise between the friars and Governor Chacón.[13]

The issue that ignited the first major conflict between Chacón and Tagle developed shortly after Tagle became custos. As noted earlier, the disbursement of missionary funds since the reconquest had often been haphazard, and, consequently, the friars had sometimes been forced to rely on the generosity of the governors as had occurred during Cuervo's administration. This situation obviously increased the dependence of the Franciscans on local government. Therefore, the Order raised the question to the Crown of whether the New Mexico friars might engage in commercial activities solely to raise funds when government alms were not provided. In 1710, a royal *cédula* pertaining to this matter arrived in New Mexico. While the monarchy disallowed the Franciscan petition, Chacón interpreted the cédula to state that the Franciscans were forbidden to participate in any type of economic activity at any time, including handling products generated by the inhabitants of the missions.[14]

A precedent had already been established giving the New Mexico governors a virtual monopoly over trade in the region. The current viceroy, the Duque de Alburquerque, had specifically given Governor Cuervo the privilege of procuring all manner of materials, from pickaxes to women's clothing, for the citizens of the colony. Alburquerque extended the same right to Governor Chacón. With the extensive powers of the governors, it is easy to see the inherent economic advantages this opportunity afforded these officials. Since the missions controlled by the Franciscans represented the only other institution in the region that could possibly compete with the governors economically, Chacón's order forbidding mission commerce solidified his monopoly. Furthermore, it left the Franciscans even more dependent on local government.[15]

An additional peril from the governors' trade monopoly was that they could charge exorbitant prices for their goods, and apparently, they did. Custos Tagle made economic exploitation the basis for his opposition to Chacón's ban of mission commerce. In letters to Governor Chacón, the Franciscan hierarchy, and viceregal officials in Mexico City, Tagle charged that the governors (Cuervo and Chacón) had taken undue advantage of the poor Spanish citizens in the Kingdom. While waiting for a response to his letters, however, Tagle decided to act on his own. In collusion with friars and unnamed officials in El Paso, Tagle had Chacón's most recent supply train delayed in that villa.[16]

While Chacón represented many firsts for Spanish government in New Mexico, in one area he was the same as most of his predecessors: he had purchased the office. Chacón had paid 4,000 pesos for the governorship in 1705. Furthermore, he had paid 1,000 pesos for the *media anata* (a royal tax on officials amounting to a half of their first-year salary). What with travel expenses, Chacón had spent well over 5,000 pesos when he arrived in Santa Fe. The supply monopoly over New Mexico was how Chacón recouped most of these expenses as he was paid only 2,000 pesos per year. Since the governor's term in office was to expire in 1712, any difficulties in getting these goods to Santa Fe jeopardized Chacón's investment. The supply train was only delayed briefly, however, and Chacón's interpretation of the limits of mission commerce did not stand. The major result of this dispute was that open acrimony now existed between the governor and the custos.[17]

While the controversy over trade was still raging, a new arena of conflict appeared. The problem centered on Chacón's intention to move some Puebloans of the Tiwa group who were residing in the mission at Taos to Isleta, south of the Spanish villa at Alburquerque. Prior to the rebellion in 1680, the Franciscans operated a mission for Tiwa people at Isleta, but during the reconquest these people dispersed, some fleeing to the Hopi region while other Tiwas scattered among various Puebloan groups. Isleta had only been reopened during Chacón's first years in office, while Juan de la Peña was still custos. With Apache attacks becoming more numerous and severe, the governor believed that Isleta could help secure the southern flank of the colony. The idea to move the Tiwas from Taos to the new mission had been under consideration for some time, and Custos Peña had agreed to their relocation prior to his death.[18]

The problem was that these Tiwas did not want to leave Taos. On two occasions, Spanish soldiers were dispatched to force the Tiwas to move to Isleta, but both times the Tiwas gathered within the mission church at Taos and begged Fray Francisco Bretons (Brotons), their missionary father, to protect them. Not much is known of Bretons except that he was a criollo and had only come to New Mexico in 1707. Taos was his first mission assignment, and he apparently enjoyed a rather benign relationship with his neophytes. He had previously drawn Chacón's ire for tolerating the existence of a large number of kivas at Taos. Now Bretons defended the Tiwas against being relocated. He argued that the Tiwas had labored hard to build homes and plant crops at Taos. The land around Isleta was less fertile, and, because of marauding Apaches, unsafe. Bretons claimed that the original purpose for the Isleta mission to be reopened was to administer to Tiwa people living among the Hopi who could be induced to return to the Christian fold. Finally, raising a larger issue, Bretons claimed that to forcibly evict the Tiwa after they pleaded for sanctuary would violate the Church's traditional immunity from the government in such cases. Convinced by his friar's reasoning and already engaged in battle with Governor Chacón, Tagle decided to block the transfer of the Tiwas to Isleta.[19]

Governor Chacón did not back away from this Franciscan challenge. He replied to their objections by first noting that the soil around Isleta could easily support the Tiwas. Chacón further pointed out that as vice-custos, Tagle had been involved in the initial plans to move the Tiwas from Taos and had offered no reservations at that time. Indeed, Chacón charged that the Franciscans had been clamoring for some time for greater protection for Isleta, and the population increase would help establish that security. Warning that the Tiwas' resistance could set a dangerous precedent, Chacón demanded that Tagle punish Bretons for encouraging the Tiwas. Finally, after stating that this affair did not affect the sanctuary tradition in any way, Chacón sternly warned the Franciscans not to interfere further in the matter. Although this issue was not resolved during Chacón's administration, the Tiwas at Taos were later placed at Isleta.[20]

A more fundamental and explosive issue soon further strained Tagle and Chacón's relationship: what was the governor's authority over the Franciscans under the Patronato Real? This matter came to the forefront in the spring of 1712 when Tagle moved to transfer Fray José López Tello from Santa Fe. López was a native of Mexico City who had professed at San Francisco de México in April 1702. He had arrived in the colony in 1707, probably in the same caravan that brought Chacón. López had been assigned to Santa Fe since arriving in the Kingdom, where he was responsible for the spiritual and educational needs of the capital's Spanish citizens.[21]

At first, Custos Tagle offered only performance deficiencies to explain why López was to be moved from Santa Fe. Tagle charged that López was not preaching on all days when he should and that he was negligent in his educational duties. Tagle also stated that López failed to assist other friars in the vicinity when they needed help or support. The custos soon offered more sensitive reasons, however, for the necessity to relocate López. Apparently, López was providing support to Chacón in the governor's disputes with the Franciscans. First, López had certified, without Tagle's authorization, the disbursement of Franciscan materials from Chacón's supply train once it arrived in Santa Fe from El Paso. Even more damning to Tagle's position, López had advised

Chacón on Tagle and Bretons's claim of Church immunity in the Tiwa relocation conflict. Tagle believed that López was a traitor to Franciscan interests,
and the prelate's suspicions were not without some merit. In a letter he wrote to
the provincial of Santo Evangelio, Fray Luís Morrote (Morote), López por-
trayed Chacón as a very capable governor who had only the best interests at
heart of the missionary program in New Mexico.[22]

Chacón and Tagle soon were at loggerheads over López's transfer. At first,
the governor produced a petition from the citizens in Santa Fe that bemoaned
the removal of such a competent and respected friar. Chacón soon went further, however, by invoking Patronato Real powers over the Franciscans. Citing
several past agreements between the Spanish government and the papacy,
along with numerous royal cédulas pertaining to the Patronato Real, Chacón
stated that his rights in this matter were clear. In addition, Chacón ordered
Tagle not to appoint a replacement friar to Santa Fe for López until higher government officials made a decision on the matter. Tagle countered by claiming
that governors had authority only over *collatores* (priests holding benefices or
parish posts), and since none of those existed in New Mexico, the governor
held no vice-patron rights over the Franciscans. Chacón rejoined that all missionaries in the Kingdom were funded by the Real Hacienda (Royal Treasury),
which, as governor, he administered. Since this was the identical arrangement
under which collatores were supported elsewhere, the governor of New Mexico
must then enjoy the same rights of vice-patron over the Franciscan missionaries. Chacón ominously warned the custos that if he attempted to place another
friar in Santa Fe, the consequences would be serious for Tagle.[23]

At this point, before the conflict escalated further, Chacón's replacement arrived in Santa Fe and the stalemate between Chacón and Tagle ended. While
no definitive ruling on the governor's rights as vice-patron resulted from this
episode, the issues raised in this matter, along with disputes over Franciscan
economic endeavors and relocation of the Tiwas to Isleta, boded ill for the future of church and state relations in New Mexico. Chacón had moved boldly
to expand secular authority over the missions and the friars, and Tagle stridently
tried to rebuff those efforts. The question then became how would Chacón's
successor administer the office of governor in its affairs with the Franciscans?

*   *   *

Don Juan Ignacio Flores Mogollón, the new governor, arrived in Santa Fe to
take up the reins of government in October 1715. Like Chacón, Flores was a native of Sevilla. Flores was a former governor of another northern territory,
Nuevo León, which further attests to the government's interest in New Mexico
that a proven official preside over the region. Flores was a much older man

than Chacón, however, and was apparently not in particularly good health by the time he appeared in the Kingdom. Uncharacteristically, the transfer of power from Chacón to Flores must have occurred with little animosity, as no records exist of any lawsuits growing out of Chacón's residencia.[24]

Interestingly, another important official, the provincial of Santo Evangelio, Fray Luís Morrote, arrived in Santa Fe at the same time as Flores. Whether Morrote came to New Mexico because of the rupture between Chacón and Tagle or simply to inspect Santo Evangelio's northern outpost is unknown. No doubt, once in the colony, Morrote was made aware of the problems that had developed between Chacón and Tagle. Morrote would have been especially worried about the controversy concerning the governor's rights as vice-patron. Any expansion of the government's authority over the Church always provoked a reaction from the clergy. On 12 October, Morrote petitioned Flores to allow Tagle to continue as custos for another term since Tagle "promised to maintain himself" to the tranquillity of the Kingdom. The obsequious nature of Morrote's dealings with Flores suggests further the provincial's worries. By nominating Tagle to continue as custos, however, Morrote assured the Franciscan operation in New Mexico of a strong defender if Governor Flores proved to be an especially assertive administrator. Flores agreed to Morrote's request, and Tagle continued as custos into 1715.[25]

The Franciscans began the Flores period on the defensive, and their position now was threatened further by an Inquisition investigation of one of their own. Fray Francisco Bretons, the missionary of Taos who had resisted the relocation of the Tiwas to Isleta, was charged with solicitation of women in the confessional. The inquiry dragged on for most of Flores's first year in office and only ended in 1713 when Bretons suddenly died from natural causes.[26]

The investigation and subsequent scandal involving Bretons may have had its roots in the Chacón-Tagle disputes. The alleged solicitation occurred in May 1712 when Bretons, along with other friars, was in Santa Fe to assist with the numerous confessions that took place annually when the Edicts of Faith were posted. This event coincided that year with the serious breach in church and state relations over the transfer of the Tiwas to Isleta and the removal of López by Tagle from Santa Fe. The capital was still a rather small settlement, and it is doubtful that Chacón missed Bretons's presence. Because of the number of witnesses who testified in the Inquisition investigation, a large portion of Santa Fe citizens had at least heard rumors of Bretons's solicitation of women. Chacón surely also knew of the matter. Apparently, the charges against Bretons first surfaced in Chihuahua about the time Chacón would have passed through that villa on his return to Mexico City. Since Chacón could assume that Tagle, who was comisario of the Holy Office, would not begin proceedings against

Bretons during their conflicts, it is certainly possible that Chacón initiated the allegations against Bretons as a final jab at his Franciscan opponents. In any event, the Franciscans in the Kingdom were reeling from the previous problems with Chacón and the Bretons scandal as Flores began his term as governor.[27]

Similar to that of his predecessor, escalating attacks by the non-Puebloan natives of the region plagued the administration of Governor Flores. Apache raids continued unabated, and the Navajos, now joined by Utes, also pressured the Spanish. By 1713, these assaults were becoming especially troublesome for the Spanish missions and villas in the territory north and west of Santa Fe.[28]

Governor Flores responded to the deteriorating situation in much the same manner as Chacón. Realizing the importance of the Puebloans to the defense of the colony, Flores pressed for an accelerated pace in acculturating the Franciscans' neophytes. Flores soon came to the conclusion that the friars were too lax in converting and civilizing the Puebloans, and he took an activist posture in eradicating what the Spanish viewed as vestiges of idolatry. Ignoring the missionaries, Flores ordered the alcaldes mayores to destroy any Puebloan kivas that had managed to escape destruction under Chacón.[29]

Flores's moves against Puebloan culture and the ongoing raids by hostile natives finally resulted in a major conflict between the governor and the Franciscans during a *junta de guerra* (council of war) called in 1714. Bringing together the presidial military officers, the alcaldes mayores, and the missionaries, Flores submitted a plan to disarm the Puebloans of their Spanish weapons, to close their trade with the Apaches and Navajos, and to terminate Puebloan customs in dress and body painting. The governor believed that the Puebloans were trading their Spanish firearms and swords with the same natives who were threatening the colony, thus improving the military effectiveness of the Apaches and Navajos. Flores was incensed further by the Puebloans' appearance, which to him was uncivilized and too similar to the enemy Apaches and Navajos.

The Franciscans were not unified in their response to the governor's plan. Some had applauded the destruction of the kivas and now agreed with the proposed campaign against the Puebloans' personal appearance. Most of the missionaries, led by Tagle, however, were vehement in their opposition. The Puebloans needed their Spanish weapons to help defend the missions, these friars argued. Furthermore, many of the Franciscans were worried that attacks on Puebloan culture might lead to a renewal of the rebellions of 1680 and 1696. In the great scheme of missionization, just how important was dress, asked the missionaries? Was Puebloan body painting so very different than Spanish women's use of facial makeup? Flores overrode their objections, banned body painting, and took Spanish weapons away from the Puebloans. Tagle protested these policies to Mexico City, however, and the new viceroy, the Duque de Linares, later rescinded Flores's orders regarding both body painting and possession of Spanish weapons.[30]

Governor Flores seemed to expand his authority at the expense of the Franciscans in another matter as well. In 1715, without specifically invoking any power of vice-patronage, Flores called upon the Franciscans "with all brevity" to assign a missionary to Zuñi. The governor noted that a single friar, Fray Francisco Irazábal, currently administered to Zuñi, Laguna, and Acoma, a mission area that covered about thirty leagues. Zuñi was the westernmost outpost under Spanish control, and, hence, was strategically placed. Flores stated that it required the attention of at least one missionary at all times. Surprisingly, the Franciscans did not resist this intrusion into their domain. Vice-custos Fray Antonio de Miranda avowed to Flores that his "order" would be directly carried out.[31]

Flores's administration was not marked, however, by unrelenting conflict with the Franciscans. Not all of the governor's activities produced hostility from the Franciscans, and, indeed, some coincided with the friars' goals. For instance, Flores issued orders that all Puebloan males were to live with their spouses and provide for their wives in accordance with the holy sacrament of marriage. The governor also addressed a longstanding concern of the Franciscans when he issued a bando stipulating that all Apache captives and slaves held in New Mexico must be baptized and taught the Catholic faith. The treatment of native prisoners in the colony had been a sore point between the friars and Spanish settlers since the reconquest, and, despite Flores's decree, would continue to be an issue, as will be noted later.[32]

Therefore, while Flores pursued policies similar to that of Chacón, the antagonism between Flores and the Franciscans never escalated to the stridency seen during Chacón's term in office. Certainly the friars were less than pleased with some of Flores's measures and let their opposition show, but Custos Tagle's reactions to Flores's policies were comparatively muted. Perhaps when the provincial was in the colony in 1712, Morrote had chastised Tagle. Inexplicably, when Tagle's stewardship ended in 1715, the Franciscan named to replace him was José López Tello, Chacon's former ally.[33]

It is interesting to speculate what might have transpired in church and state relations in New Mexico if Flores had completed his term as governor and a degree of continuity had existed in the process of governors being regularly installed in office. Would the erosion of the Franciscan position have been hastened? Would a pre-1680 style struggle have ensued between them and the local civil authority? It is a moot point, though, because in December 1715,

Flores abruptly resigned when he became embroiled in a dispute with Captain Don Félix Martínez, the commander of the Santa Fe presidio. For the next five years, several claimants would hotly contest the governor's office in New Mexico, and, consequently, the power of local civil authority would be weakened.[34]

* * *

While the 1707–1715 period was often a time of conflict between the governors and the Franciscans, stability and consolidation prevailed within the missionary operation. Only one new mission site was added (Isleta) and the number of friars in the region remained fairly consistent with the levels achieved in the first years of the eighteenth century. During this eight-year span, nine new missionaries arrived in the Santa Fe district for the first time. Five friars left the area, and two, Juan de la Peña and Francisco Bretons, died. A net gain of two Franciscans occurred, although perhaps because of illness or other leaves, that increase was not always evident. A report for 1710 showed fourteen friars present, one more than Álvarez noted in 1706, but a roster for 1715 listed only twelve.[35]

The stagnation in the contingent of missionaries was not for lack of effort to augment their numbers. Without more friars there could be no expansion of the mission system or extension of Spanish control over the region. On at least two occasions, in 1708 and 1712, the Franciscan hierarchy in New Spain formally petitioned the government to increase by thirteen the allotment of friars for New Mexico. The viceregal office in Mexico City endorsed both petitions; no action, however, was taken in Spain. Another ten years would pass before the monarchy approved an increase in the number of missionaries that it would support financially in New Mexico. The failure to post more friars to New Mexico helps to explain an anomaly of the Chacón-Flores period. These were the first governors since the reconquest who would not undertake major campaigns to subdue the Hopi people. Without mission priests to administer to the Hopi, Chacón and Flores probably saw little reason to replant the Spanish flag on the Hopi mesas.[36]

The Franciscans continued to dispatch relatively inexperienced friars to New Mexico during this period. Of the nine new priests who came north during this time, fragments of background material exist for six. The controversial Fray José López Tello was a criollo who only professed his faith five years prior to his arrival in the colony in 1707. Fray Miguel Francisco Cepeda y Arriola entered the colony in 1709. Cepeda was a criollo from Puebla who became a Franciscan in 1704 at the age of thirty-three; hence, he was at least an older friar. Fray Carlos José Delgado came to New Spain in 1708 with the Propaganda Fide in Querétaro. Delgado was born in Andalucía in 1677, where he later joined the

Order. Fray Carlos did not remain with the Propaganda Fide long, however, as he was in New Mexico by 1710. Fray José Antonio Guerrero was the most likely to have been an experienced friar. A criollo from Mexico City, Fray José professed his faith at age sixteen in the capital city in 1694, twenty years before he arrived in the colony.[37]

Besides Delgado, two other Franciscans who had been born in Spain and had professed there arrived in New Mexico during the 1707–1715 period. These were the first gachupines to appear in a decade. Just as the War of the Spanish Succession disrupted the flow of money from Spain for the mission operation, the conflict also had curtailed the travel of Iberian friars to the New World. With the war concluded in Europe, gachupín missionaries now began to trickle into New Mexico. In 1706, Fray Antonio Aparicio and Fray Lucas de Arévalo departed from Spain. By 1709, Arévalo was in New Mexico, and Aparicio was on the Franciscan roster there in 1714. It is doubtful, though, that either gachupín had much, if any, experience as a missionary.[38]

One factor that contributed to the stability of the mission program during these years was that by now a cadre of Franciscans clearly qualified as veterans in the region. As noted previously, friars in New Mexico tended to labor there for lengthy periods, averaging about twenty years. By 1712, only one active missionary, Muñiz de Luna, had achieved that number, but three others had over a decade of service each. Both Tagle and Fray Antonio Camargo were veterans of thirteen years, and Fray Antonio de Miranda had labored as a missionary for at least a dozen years. Five other friars had between five and ten years of experience: López, Bretons, Fray Domingo de Araoz, Fray Francisco de Irazábal, and Fray Juan Mingues. Of thirteen friars in the Santa Fe district in 1712, nine missionary priests had accumulated considerable experience in the mission operation among the Puebloan people.[39]

This seasoned core of missionaries helps to explain the obvious contradiction within the mission operation in New Mexico by 1715. On one level, peace appears to have been attained in the missions, at least on the surface. As noted earlier, a decade had passed since the last plot by the Puebloans to rebel had been reported. Yet, the process by which the Puebloans were to be converted to Catholicism clearly was stalled. These Franciscans were not burning with evangelical zeal to remake the Puebloans into Spanish citizens. Indeed, many friars tacitly allowed Puebloan customs and religious activities to continue, as evidenced by Chacón's and Flores's campaigns to eradicate the kivas. Some missionaries even defended these practices among their neophytes by noting that Puebloan customs were not all that alien to Spanish practices or that to destroy all vestiges of Puebloan tradition could precipitate a new rebellion. One might suspect that fear of revolt, the lesson of "the year eighty," was the friars' real concern. The missions were still understaffed, and almost all mission priests worked alone among their charges. That the Franciscans sought accommodation with their Puebloan neighbors was, perhaps, inevitable.

* * *

No matter what the explanation might be, the Franciscan mission program to convert and civilize the Puebloans was proceeding at a snail's pace. These shortcomings by the friars presented governors Chacón and Flores with an opening to expand civil authority in New Mexico at the expense of the Franciscans' position. As the governors gained more influence and power over the Puebloan people, the friars saw their own status wane. The criticisms leveled by the governors of this period against the missionaries would be echoed again and again by other ambitious and/or assertive administrators of the Kingdom. The clear failure by the Franciscans to carry out their missionary obligations would eventually prove lethal to their position in New Mexico.

Of course, both Chacón and Flores were regularly appointed governors with the full backing of the Spanish government. Neither had problems with rivals for the office. During the preceding Rodríguez and Cuervo administrations, those governors did not enjoy the same luxury. Thus, deficiencies within the Franciscan mission operation were not made into important issues. Since neither Rodríguez nor Cuervo aggressively attempted to expand his own powers, the friars and governors enjoyed relatively good relations. This identical situation now reoccurred between 1715 and 1720 with Flores's sudden resignation. Therefore, the expansion of state hegemony in New Mexico seemed to require, locally at least, two preconditions: fully empowered governors and Franciscan failures to convert and civilize the native population.

Though the conflicts between the Franciscans and governors during the 1707–1715 period did not prove to be decisive, civil authority in the Kingdom had grown at the expense of the Franciscans. In the economic sphere, the governors tightened their grip on the financial affairs of the colony. Chacón and Flores also expanded their control militarily, politically, and socially over the Puebloans. Chacón's aggressive pursuit of a governor's rights as vice-patron over the missionaries had shaken the Franciscans to such a degree that the friars steered away from directly confronting Flores in a similar instance. Although the fierce controversies between church and state in New Mexico would fade for a time, the augmentation of civil authority by Chacón, and, to a lesser extent, by Flores, provided a springboard for future assaults on the Franciscan position.

CHAPTER 7

The Struggle Over Diocesan Control

AFTER Governor Flores resigned in late 1715, New Mexico again entered a period of political instability. As had occurred previously, the Franciscans were granted a short respite in their struggle with civil authority, but they would not be able to enjoy it. In 1715, the bishopric of Durango began a campaign to secure jurisdiction over the kingdom and the friars who labored there.

For over 125 years, a pillar of the Franciscans' power in New Mexico rested on their freedom from episcopal control. Special privileges had been granted the mendicant orders during the sixteenth century in order to facilitate the conversion of the native population in New Spain in the absence of the secular clergy. This state of affairs was reversed in the latter half of the 1500s, when the Council of Trent restored most rights to the bishops and more secular priests appeared in the New World. The regular orders, especially the Franciscans, however, continued to enjoy their unique powers in many frontier regions far removed from the episcopate centers. By the early 1700s, New Mexico represented one of the last bastions free from diocesan control. The friars in the Kingdom administered the sacraments, collected the *diezmo* (tithe) and other special fees, assigned priests to missions or other sites as they saw fit, and excommunicated parishioners at will. Hence, absolute control over the rhythms of the Catholic faith was an indispensable component of the Franciscans' position.[1]

Although the bishopric of Durango claimed jurisdiction over New Mexico, it was not until after 1715 that the diocese began to effectively implement dominion over that region. Three key factors caused this change to occur. First, beginning with the installation of Don Pedro Tapiz y García as bishop of Durango in 1713, three vigorous determined bishops successively administered the See of Durango. Second, the Spanish government's relatively new view of New Mexico as a defensive bastion against rival European states in North America created a climate in which political concerns, not religious activities, became paramount in determining policies for the colony. Finally, the ongoing failures of the Franciscans to convert and civilize the native people left the friars open to criticism that weakened their claim to autonomy. Consequently, by 1737, the bishopric of Durango triumphed in establishing its jurisdiction over New Mexico.

* * *

In 1621, the bishopric of Durango was created by royal order out of territory that had been part of the diocese of Guadalajara. The immense size of the See of Guadalajara, a region that spanned virtually all of northern New Spain, pre-cipitated the creation of the new bishopric, although the bishopric of Guadala-jara fought the reduction in size by claiming the region was too sparsely populated to support two episcopates. As events would prove, Guadalajara's prophecy was correct and financial limitations on the Durango prelate espe-cially shaped its relationship to New Mexico. Nonetheless, in 1622 the papacy issued a bull establishing the new episcopate, and Fray Juan González de Her-mosilla y Salazar was installed as Durango's first bishop.[2]

Even with a smaller territory to administer, the Durango bishopric com-prised an extremely vast area. In present-day geographic units, it included the Mexican states of Durango, Chihuahua, Sonora, Sinaloa, and portions of Coahuila, Zacatecas, Nayarit, and Jalisco. In addition, the See also consisted of all or parts of Arizona, California, and New Mexico. It would be a formidable task today to manage such a territory, but for the bishops of the colonial epoch the difficulties were monumental.[3]

The enormous size of the diocese and uncertain geographic knowledge pro-vided the principal foundations for the controversy between Durango and the Franciscans in New Mexico. According to the cédula of 1621 that established the new bishopric, its territorial jurisdiction included the area east from the villa of Durango to the Río Grande and all regions northward that "continue to the North Sea." The body of water here that the Crown understood the "North Sea" to be remains as unclear today as it was in the early 1600s when knowl-edge of geography still included the notion that California was an island. Nonetheless, to the men who served as the Durango prelate, the New Mexico region clearly was part of their diocese. To the Franciscans, however, the omis-sion of a specific reference in the cédula to the Kingdom of New Mexico or the Custody of Saint Paul obviously exempted them from the Durango bishop's control.[4]

The establishment of any episcopal authority over New Mexico posed a sig-nificant threat to the Franciscan position. Tithes and fees for services collected from the non-Indian population would have to be remitted to Durango. As it was, the tithe was paid to the archbishop of Mexico. Throughout the 1600s, the Franciscans in the colony apparently retained the fees collected for marriages, burials, and other services. A Durango bishop would be able to appoint eccle-siastical judges, notaries, and secretaries who would not owe allegiance to the

Franciscans. Influence in the assignment of friars to missions or churches could fall to the bishops as well. Excommunication, a tool often used by the Franciscans in their battles with local officials, would have to be sanctioned in Durango. Finally, the bishopric of Durango would control decisions regarding the secularization of mission sites. If the Franciscans were to retain their power and influence in New Mexico, it was imperative for them to disallow Durango's claim to jurisdiction over the Custody of Saint Paul.[5]

The Durango prelates made only sporadic and ineffective efforts to establish their hegemony over New Mexico in the 1600s. The first prelate, Bishop Hermosilla (1622–1631), claimed his jurisdiction over the colony and stated his intention to make a *visita* (visit or inspection) to the region, but he died before he managed to undertake that venture. The problem of episcopal authority was put on hold during the 1630s as the Franciscans endeavored to have the Custody of Saint Paul itself elevated to diocesan rank under the authority of bishops who would be Franciscans. The viceregal office in New Spain and court officials in Spain endorsed this plan. The monarchy, however, never approved the change.[6]

With the installation of Bishop Fray Francisco de Evia y Valdez (1640–1654), the diocese once again asserted its claim over New Mexico. Bishop Evia petitioned the government to force the Franciscans to recognize his authority and to comport themselves accordingly. Upon receiving Evia's requests, the government in Spain ordered the viceroy's office in Mexico City to investigate and report on the matter, but apparently nothing occurred at this time. Bishop Evia also stated his plan to inspect the mission program in New Mexico; however, he never carried out this threat.[7]

During the administration of Bishop Don Juan de Gorospe y Aguirre (1662–1671), a petition originated from New Mexico asking that diocesan control be extended over the colony. In 1667, at the close of one of the most bitter confrontations between the friars and the local civil authority in New Mexico, the cabildo of Santa Fe requested Bishop Gorospe to appoint an ecclesiastical judge for the territory in order to protect the citizens from the capricious actions of the Franciscans. The Durango bishopric referred the issue to Mexico City, but again, no definite actions were taken to resolve the jurisdictional dispute.[8]

The last major incident involving diocesan control in the seventeenth century took place during the tenure of Bishop Fray Bartolomé García de Escañuela (1677–1684). Bishop Escañuela, himself a Franciscan, made the first real attempt to visit New Mexico when he entered the Kingdom at El Paso in 1681. The Pueblo rebellion had forced the Spaniards out of New Mexico the previous fall and made it impossible for Escañuela's visita entourage to venture further north. Escañuela did appoint an ecclesiastical judge for El Paso (Fray Juan Álvarez), another first for a Durango prelate. The Franciscans told their

fellow friar that they would accept his dominion if he would be the bishop for-
ever, but given his unlikely immortality, they could not acknowledge the episcopate's jurisdiction over New Mexico. Furthermore, the viceregal authority in
Mexico City confirmed the Franciscans' religious autonomy over the colony
that same year because of the unsettled conditions arising from the Puebloan
insurrection.[9]

For the next three decades, the differences between the bishopric and the
Franciscans hibernated. Bishop Fray Manuel de Herrera (1686–1689) also designated one of the Franciscan missionaries in El Paso as ecclesiastical judge
and pledged to visit the region; however, he never made the journey. Sometime during the 1680s, at least some friars posted to New Mexico began to pass
through Durango to have their assignments registered with the episcopate.
With Spain's precarious control over New Mexico through the 1690s and a
wave of other native rebellions throughout the northern frontier of New Spain,
the Durango prelates possessed little leverage with the government or inclina-
tion to press their case for jurisdiction.[10]

The lack of resolution over the diocesan control issue by 1715, almost a century after the diocese in Durango was created, can be explained by several factors. Certainly an important reason was that no bishop of Durango, except for
Escañuela, was willing to force the issue by actually making a visita to New
Mexico. The relative success of the Franciscan missionary effort until 1680
probably also precluded a favorable ruling for the diocese from the government. It should be further noted that the secular clergy were a distinct minor-
ity throughout northern New Spain; therefore, the government was very
dependent on the efforts of the Franciscans and Jesuits. Most important,
though, was the very nature of seventeenth-century Spanish government that
often found expediency in overlapping and contradictory rules and regulations.
As Eleanor B. Adams has noted concerning the jurisdictional dispute over New
Mexico, if the Crown made a definitive decision there, it might have implica-
tions for similar controversies throughout the empire. Unless a clearly desirable
end would be achieved from settling the matter in favor of the Durango episcopate, the Spanish monarchy would continue to procrastinate.[11]

*   *   *

After almost thirty years of relative quiet, the issue of episcopal jurisdiction
over New Mexico appeared with renewed vigor in 1715. Three primary developments produced an atmosphere now conducive to settling the controversy in
favor of the diocese. For a variety of reasons, the Durango bishops more forcefully pressed their claim of control over New Mexico. Additionally, because of
French intrusions into Texas, the Spanish government began to view the region as more strategically vital and took a keener interest in its affairs. Finally,

shortcomings in the Franciscan missionary operation to the native people placed the Custody of Saint Paul in a vulnerable position with the new Bourbon monarchy.

The reasons why the prelates of Durango pushed the jurisdictional issue more rigorously beginning in 1715 are not exactly obvious. Officially, each bishop maintained that his central motivation was for the good of the empire and the desire to promote the Catholic faith throughout his diocese. These prelates simply pointed out the original boundaries delineated in the cédula of 1621 and their obligation to fulfill the duties of their office. Now that New Mexico had been permanently restored from the Puebloan uprising, they argued, the advantages of episcopal jurisdiction should be extended to the inhabitants of the colony.

Apart from the official motives cited, however, there were likely underlying concerns for the bishops as well. From a close examination of Guillermo Porras Muñoz's financial details on the Durango diocese, it is clear that the episcopate was in difficulty by the second decade of the eighteenth century. The cathedral in Durango underwent major renovations between 1688–1707, which cost the diocese almost 200,000 pesos. Since it lacked sufficient funds to complete the project, the diocese borrowed at least 35,000 pesos. In the 1720s, Bishop Don Benito Crespo y Monroy extended the cathedral improvements at an additional cost of 70,000 pesos. During the first decades of the 1700s, the total income generated by the diocese amounted to only about 45,000 pesos each year. Considering the episcopate's other financial obligations, such as salaries for the bishop and cathedral cabildo (dean, archdeacon, canons, etc.), schools, materials, and legal expenses, the repairs to the cathedral constituted a serious drain on the episcopal coffers.[12]

The poor economic conditions of the region also negatively influenced the prestige of the bishopric. The salaries paid to the members of the cathedral cabildo were among the lowest in New Spain. Consequently, the prelates found it difficult to keep a full staff. During the 1700–1730 period out of twenty-seven cathedral posts, only eighteen were occupied at any one time. Unless the diocese could generate more income, it would continue to suffer personnel shortages. Since the tithe and fees for services comprised the primary sources of revenue, the only immediate and direct way to address these financial shortfalls was to expand the pool from which these monies originated. Porras Muñoz noted that Bishop Crespo, in particular, exhibited a keen interest in augmenting diocese income. One logical place to look for more money, of course, was the disputed region administered by the Custody of Saint Paul. It seems reasonable to conclude that financial issues partially motivated the bishopric of Durango to strive for a settlement of the jurisdictional dispute with the Franciscans.[13]

Bishop Don Pedro Tapiz y García (1713–1722) fired the opening salvos in the diocese of Durango's renewed offensive to assert control over New Mexico. Shortly after his installation, the new bishop set out on an extensive inspection of his diocese as required by Spanish law. The energetic Tapiz undertook at least four of these treks during his nine-year term, journeys that proved to be both financially and physically taxing. Each visita cost the bishopric about 10,000 pesos, and as Bishop Tapiz noted, "the journey was rigorous and [so] laborious that no one who has not done it will believe it." None of these visitas extended into New Mexico, however.[14]

The report Bishop Tapiz submitted to the government after his first inspection established a pattern in his ideas and concerns toward the administration of the diocese. He noted that the territory lacked monetary resources and roads, suffered from a shortage of clergy, and required closer diocesan supervision, since his was the first visita in many years. Tapiz stated most of the churches seen on this visita were either Jesuit or Franciscan missions. The Jesuits, the prelate claimed, had obtained excellent results in converting the native people. The Jesuits' neophytes displayed appropriate knowledge of Catholic doctrine, skills in reading and writing Spanish, and proper behavior during mass. On the other hand, Tapiz found much to criticize regarding the Franciscans. Their missions were dirty and in poor condition, and little progress had been achieved in the effort to Christianize their charges. This latter shortcoming, Tapiz believed, resulted from the Franciscans' inability to speak the indigenous languages and the friars' arrogant manner toward the natives. The bishop also complained that the Franciscans were not conforming to the *arancel* (a fee schedule for religious services) nor remitting these alms to Durango. Clearly more impressed with the Jesuits, Tapiz announced that he planned to merge the diocese's school with a Jesuit facility in Durango, and to turn over its operation solely to the Society of Jesus. While Tapiz did not make the point in his report, this consolidation in education would save the bishopric money.[15]

In his initial inspection report, Bishop Tapiz revealed his preference for the Jesuits (a trait shared by his two immediate successors); his low opinion of the Franciscans became a primary factor in the upcoming jurisdictional conflict. In 1721 in yet another report to Mexico City, Tapiz stated that he had ordered the Jesuits to establish missions among the Hopi people in northern Arizona. The Franciscans, who claimed that region as part of the Custody of Saint Paul, refused to recognize the bishop's authority in this matter. Therefore, Tapiz petitioned the government to uphold his hegemony over New Mexico.[16]

The Hopi province had been part of the New Mexico mission field since the early seventeenth century. After the reconquest in the 1690s, however, all attempts by the Franciscans to once again evangelize among the Hopi had failed. With the high esteem Bishop Tapiz held for the Society of Jesus and the proximity of their missions in southern Arizona to the Hopi, it is not surprising that the prelate would give the task of converting the Hopi to the Jesuits. More important, though, the bishop's intentions threatened both the Franciscans' claim to diocesan immunity as well as the territorial integrity of the Custody of Saint Paul.

Astonishingly, the royal government in Madrid reacted relatively quickly and forcefully to Bishop Tapiz's plan for the Hopi and his request to resolve the jurisdictional stalemate. The government's decisive and rapid response was influenced by the increasing French presence along the northern and eastern boundaries of New Spain. In an order dated 11 July 1722, the Council of the Indies instructed the viceroy, the Marqués de Casafuerte, to uphold the transfer of the Hopi territory to the Jesuits. A cédula, dated 7 December 1722, was issued to the bishop of Durango confirming his jurisdiction over New Mexico along with the explicit right to make a visita. Two months later, another royal order was dispatched to Viceroy Casafuerte, commanding him to support a Jesuit expedition to the Hopi region with military forces. As will be noted later, however, the Jesuit campaign never got underway.[17]

Tapiz's successor, Bishop Benito Crespo y Monroy (1723–1734) continued to place pressure on the Franciscans in New Mexico. In August 1725, he made a visita to El Paso, and while there, he pledged to return to inspect the Santa Fe district as well. At the same time, Crespo designated two friars, one each in El Paso and Santa Fe, as ecclesiastical judges. Crespo explicitly instructed them that their duties included the enforcement of the arancel, and that monies collected from services and the tithe were to be remitted to Durango. Bishop Crespo was the first non-Franciscan prelate to pursue so concretely the diocese's dominion over the territory.[18]

The Franciscans did not bow gracefully to these developments. They vociferously protested to the government both Crespo's visita to El Paso and the transfer of the Hopi region to the Society of Jesus. In another cédula issued in 1726, however, the Crown upheld the decision on the Hopi and the bishopric of Durango's total jurisdiction over New Mexico. The friars in the colony responded by ignoring Crespo's appointment of ecclesiastical judges and his orders to them. In 1728, Bishop Crespo complained bitterly to the Order's provincial in Mexico City, Fray Luís Martínez Clemente, about the Franciscans' insubordination.[19]

That same year Bishop Crespo raised the stakes by announcing his plans to soon undertake a visita to the entire Kingdom of New Mexico. This development set off a storm of protest by the Franciscan Order in which arguments were exchanged in a series of letters between Crespo and the Franciscan Commissary General of New Spain, Fray Fernando Alonso González. González maintained that the Custody of Saint Paul operated in accordance with all royal decrees and within the parameters set forth by the Council of Trent. He insisted that, except for El Paso, the colony was outside diocesan boundaries.

Furthermore, since Durango was so far from the territory, it could never be governed efficiently by the diocese. González also warned that because of hostile natives, any episcopal journey north of El Paso would be a hazardous endeavor. Crespo countered in his letters to González by restating the original 1621 boundary description of the diocese and by referring to the recent royal decrees confirming Durango's jurisdiction over New Mexico. The bishop also pointed out that other areas of his diocese were equally as distant as New Mexico, yet no questions had been raised concerning the prelate's authority over those. In each of his letters, Crespo avowed that the planned visita of New Mexico would take place as soon as arrangements could be completed.[20]

This dispute over Crespo's intentions dragged on into 1729. The matter was finally referred to Viceroy Casafuerte's office, which naturally turned the issue over to the government in Spain. In December 1729, a new royal decree again confirmed complete jurisdiction and rights over New Mexico to the See of Durango. Secure in the earlier governmental rulings, however, Bishop Crespo had not waited for this new communication from Spain. Before the 1729 cédula arrived, Crespo left Durango in April 1730 for New Mexico.[21]

*   *   *

As Bishop Crespo neared El Paso in June 1730, Fray Andrés Varo, the custos of the Custody of Saint Paul, rushed from Santa Fe to confront the prelate. Varo was a gachupín friar who had arrived in New Spain by 1717. He had only been posted to New Mexico in 1729, bearing his appointment as custos. Varo would remain in the colony for over thirty years and held the office of custos on at least three other occasions. He was approximately forty-seven years of age at the time of Crespo's visita, and Varo would quickly establish his reputation as a steadfast defender of his Order's traditional rights and privileges in New Mexico.[22]

Custos Varo clearly intended to limit Bishop Crespo's inspection to the El Paso area, therefore avoiding any new precedence in the jurisdictional dispute. In a letter dispatched to Crespo on 19 June, Varo wrote that he was submitting to a visita of El Paso "with much weariness." On 6 July, about five leagues west of El Paso, the custos and his companions met Crespo and his retinue. Their exchange of greetings left Varo feeling "mortified and annoyed." For about a week the two groups stayed in El Paso, where Varo pressed the bishop to offer authorization papers specifically stating that Crespo might proceed north of that villa. Bishop Crespo's response did not satisfy Varo, but Crespo refused to be turned away. Eight days after their arrival in El Paso, the party departed northward into the heart of the Custody of Saint Paul.[23]

The best sources for what transpired during this first-ever episcopal visit of New Mexico by a prelate of Durango are a diary/report submitted by Varo to the Franciscan Commissary General of New Spain, two lengthy reports drafted by Crespo near the conclusion of the inspection for Viceroy Casafuerte, and Crespo's logbook of the entire visita of the diocese (1729–1732). Both men's records are naturally very partisan, as revealed early in their writings. Shortly after greeting the bishop and his companions, Varo wrote, "[W]e appeared before him [Crespo], although we did not have to comply with this obligation to which we had been poisoned to attend and to revere to [one] of the Princes of the Church." For his part, perhaps with tongue-in-cheek, Bishop Crespo stated, "I found the Father Custos of the missions in this province, New Mexico, with the surprising attitude, which had never crossed my mind, of opposition to my exercising jurisdiction in the said province." One can imagine the tension in the air during their trek to the north.[24]

Failing to stop Crespo in El Paso, Varo's aim now was to limit the bishop's access to the Franciscan mission operation as much as possible by denying Crespo the opportunity to inspect the churches and records belonging to the Custody of Saint Paul. At Isleta, which they reached on 23 July, and next, Alburquerque, Crespo was not allowed to enter any Franciscan buildings, although the bishop performed the sacrament of confirmation at each place. In Alburquerque, Crespo stayed at the residence of the brother of Governor Don Juan Domingo de Bustamante. At Santo Domingo, between Alburquerque and Santa Fe, Crespo spent the night in the mission's convento because no other satisfactory lodging was available. A violent argument took place there, however, between Varo and Crespo over the type of reception that should be staged for the bishop's arrival in the colony's capital. Crespo, of course, desired a bishop's full ceremonial entry, an idea that Varo considered "scandalous" even to entertain. The two antagonists reached a compromise that the custos described vaguely as an entrance befitting "a Prince of the Church and no more."[25]

Varo next wrote of the tactics used by the Franciscans to keep Crespo out of the Franciscan church in Santa Fe. The custos had the altar moved to the front doors of the church, and he and several friars stood directly behind it, thus physically barring the bishop from entering. Crespo could conduct mass and perform other sacraments, but not from inside the Franciscan structure. Varo claimed that this method was "as they did it in El Paso." Whether the custos meant that was how other episcopal visitas to El Paso were managed or that was how Crespo had been treated earlier on this inspection is unclear. In addition to this frigid reception, Bishop Crespo received quarters in the governor's palace, not the Franciscan convento, during his stay in Santa Fe.[26]

Bishop Crespo remained in Santa Fe for about two weeks, and disputes between him and the custos occurred almost daily. Crespo did inspect some mission books and performed a few marriage ceremonies, all executed "with violence," according to Varo. Crespo ordered Varo to call in the friars from the missions to Santa Fe for a meeting, creating another conflict, although the

Franciscans eventually relented and the conclave took place. In an effort to derail the visita, Varo even appealed to Governor Bustamante, claiming that Crespo's inspection undermined Bustamante's rights as vice-patron. This occurred despite the fact that the Franciscans had never recognized the office of governor as invested with those rights! Governor Bustamante, however, supported Crespo and urged Varo to cooperate with the bishop. Bustamante's position incited a bitter quarrel between him and Varo.[27]

During the latter part of August, Varo, Crespo, Bustamante, and their escorts began an inspection of the Franciscan missions north of Santa Fe. According to Bishop Crespo, he personally examined every mission in New Mexico during this visita, except Laguna, Acoma, and Zuñi. Varo stated that north of Santa Fe, Crespo visited only Nambé, Picurís, San Ildefonso, Taos, and the Spanish settlement of Santa Cruz de la Cañada. Crespo's log noted confirmations of Puebloans from all missions but Santa Clara. He does not state that the confirmations took place at each group's mission, and it was not unusual for Puebloans to gather at others' missions for ceremonies. Furthermore, since Crespo was being denied complete access to the Franciscan facilities, perhaps the bishop included missions he only briefly viewed, and Varo listed only visits of more lengthy duration. Nonetheless, the inspection followed the pattern outlined previously, including the ongoing disputes.[28]

When the party returned to Santa Fe on 29 August, Bishop Crespo moved forcefully to extend his authority over the colony. He presented the Franciscans with an arancel to follow in determining charges for services to the region's Spanish citizens. Crespo noted that this was a well-known procedure to which the mendicant orders conformed in areas where they administered to nonnative peoples. More shocking to the Franciscans, though, was the bishop's appointment of Don Santiago Roybal, a secular priest residing in Santa Fe, as Crespo's new vicar and ecclesiastical judge for New Mexico. The nomination of a non-Franciscan to such a post constituted a totally unprecedented move and sent Varo into a rage. In fact, according to Varo, their argument became so heated that Crespo threatened to declare null and void all sacraments performed in the past or those to be made in the future by the friars.[29]

Both sides now realized that continued open acrimony benefited neither side, and, according to Varo, they agreed to suspend their hostilities. The bishop's visita continued (Varo mentions only Pecos and Galisteo), and by late September Varo and Crespo had returned to El Paso. After some minor unspecified problems there, Bishop Crespo concluded his inspection and during the first week in October departed New Mexico.[30]

*   *   *

Though a prelate of the See of Durango had finally made a visita, the struggle over jurisdiction now only intensified. Bishop Crespo's two reports to

Viceroy Casafuerte clearly threatened the Franciscans' position in New Mexico. By informing the government that he had made an inspection of the northern region, posting an arancel, and appointing Roybal as vicar and ecclesiastical judge, Crespo severely damaged Franciscan autonomy in the colony. Moreover, Crespo made a series of recommendations that, if enacted, would further weaken the Franciscans. The bishop suggested a reorganization of the Church's presence in New Mexico that included the placement of secular priests in the predominantly Spanish settlements of El Paso and Alburquerque. Crespo also opined that the government could reduce expenses for New Mexico by consolidating some missionary assignments, and, thus, shrink the number of friars billeted to the Custody of Saint Paul. Specifically, the bishop claimed that one missionary priest would be sufficient to take care of both Acoma and Laguna, and another could administer to Pecos and Galisteo.[31]

Perhaps even more harmful to the Franciscans was Crespo's condemnation of them as missionaries. The bishop claimed that "there has not been, and is not, any minister who understands the language of the Indians." Consequently, the Puebloans' conversion proceeded far too slowly. Since the friars had not mastered their neophytes' languages, the most fundamental of Catholic rites, confession, rarely took place. Since the missionaries were forced to rely on interpreters, penitent Puebloans avoided the humiliation inherent in a crowded confessional. This unhappy situation existed, noted Crespo, despite the fact that "the languages are not so difficult that they cannot be comprehended in a short period of friendly intercourse and communication; because in those I heard, I found ease in pronunciation, which is not the case with many others of this diocese."[32]

In addition to submitting Varo's diary/report to the government, the New Mexico friars attempted to discredit Crespo and his competency as a bishop. They produced affidavits purporting to show that the bishop gave a dispensation to the governor's brother, Don José Perea Bustamante, for a manslaughter incident he allegedly committed, simply because of his relationship to the governor. The Franciscans also claimed that Crespo performed a marriage between Joseph Maesa and Gertrudis de Maesa (a stepsister) even though the bishop knew that Joseph was engaged in an adulterous relationship with the stepmother.[33]

While the Maesa matter cannot be confirmed (Crespo's logbook notes only the dispensation), there might have been some truth to the Franciscans' charge concerning Governor Bustamante's brother. The bishop's logbook of the visita does not include any dispensation for any reason concerning Don José Perea Bustamante, but on 26 August 1730, just before Roybal was appointed vicar and ecclesiastical judge, Governor Bustamante made a gift of 6,000 pesos to Crespo to create a benefice. Perhaps it was not pure coincidence that Crespo funded Roybal's position at exactly 6,000 pesos.[34]

Naturally, Crespo's visita set off a wave of official reports, opinions, and investigations involving numerous offices in New Spain, including the See of Durango, the Custody of Saint Paul, the Province of Santo Evangelio, the Franciscan Commissary General, the Audiencia of Mexico, and the Viceroyalty. The arguments concerning the jurisdictional conflict, both pro and con, reiterated those previously developed and do not bear repeating here. As these documents piled up in Spain, however, the King requested an opinion from the Franciscan hierarchy in Madrid.

Fray Francisco Seco, Procurador General of the Indies, drafted the document solicited by the royal government. Because of its detail and fresh arguments, this report deserves some attention. Seco's *Memorial* began with a brief early history of New Mexico and its relationship with the diocese of Durango. He noted that since 1649 the Custody of Saint Paul and its mission operations had been financed only by the Real Hacienda, despite the fact that state and church rulings required episcopates to assist in funding missionary activities within their jurisdictions. Seco cited the government's decree in 1681, which confirmed the dominion of the Franciscans over New Mexico during the Puebloan rebellion, and he compared this arrangement with those the King had conceded to other regions, such as Baja California, where the missionary effort was directly beneficial to the maintenance of the empire's boundaries. The Procurador General quoted from the *Recopilación de las Indias* (Book 3, Law 3, Title 7), which stipulated that a diocesan boundary was not to exceed fifteen leagues in radius. New Mexico, Seco pointed out, was at least four hundred leagues from Durango. Seco advised that this great distance would result in very few visits by the Durango bishop, and that the prelate would have little firsthand understanding of New Mexico's special problems. Seco closed by requesting a complete renunciation of the Durango diocese's jurisdiction over the Custody of Saint Paul and a ban on further episcopal visitas.[35]

Seco's recommendations regarding New Mexico, however, went unheeded. While the government did temporarily suspend the appointment of Roybal as vicar and ecclesiastical judge, the Crown vigorously confirmed all other rights of the bishopric of Durango over New Mexico. Crespo's negative assessment of the Franciscans' evangelical performance, especially their failure to speed up the conversion of the Puebloans, stood as a primary factor in this decision. The government concluded that Santo Evangelio, the only Church body directly responsible for the Custody of Saint Paul, was too remote from the region and had proven unequal to the task. Consequently, it was believed that the diocese of Durango might act as a more effective overseer of the missionary effort in New Mexico.[36]

A lull in the controversy occurred over the next four years. Bishop Crespo fell seriously ill and resigned from his position in 1734. The diocese remained without a bishop until the installation of Don Martín de Elizacoechea in 1736.

Prior to his appointment, Bishop Elizacoechea was dean of the cathedral cabildo in Mexico City. His promotion from that prestigious post may have reflected the gravity of the jurisdictional conflict and the general concern with
the pace of conversion among the native people along the northern frontier. To
further attest to Elizacoechea's ability, he later became bishop of the diocese of
Michoacán.[37]

While less is known of Bishop Elizacoechea's administration in Durango,
he also made a visita to New Mexico during the summer of 1737. This second
inspection by a Durango prelate apparently lacked the pyrotechnics of Crespo's visita. In a rather subdued and conciliatory letter to Elizacoechea, Fray
Andrés Varo, again custos, offered his assistance to the bishop during the inspection. Bishop Elizacoechea later wrote that Varo had been very cooperative
"notwithstanding his opposition to the *entrada* (entrance), which he made
[known] to me."[38]

Bishop Elizacoechea's evaluation to the government of the Franciscan missionary operation among the Puebloans, while not as scathing as Crespo's, still
proffered a negative assessment. Elizacoechea stated that the missions around
El Paso functioned well, and he conceded that the region as a whole comprised a difficult, dangerous, and remote area in which to work. Nonetheless,
the bishop "recognized that [the missions provided] very little instruction, guid-
ance, and education" to the "poor, miserable Indians." According to Elizacoechea, the friars' lack of competency in the Puebloans' languages was the
fundamental problem. He found that only three of thirty missionary priests
were fluent in the natives' speech. (Two of these, Fray Pedro Díaz de Aguilar
and Fray Manuel Zambrano, were in New Mexico when Crespo made his
visita and claimed that none knew Puebloan languages.) Elizacoechea also
complained that some of the friars did not live in accordance with their Christian faith and their Order's vows, which set a bad example for the Puebloans and
other native people in the region. The bishop closed his report with a recommendation that missionaries assigned to New Mexico "be not too young nor
too old, but a mature age, sensible and prudent."[39]

The Franciscans objected to this second visita and petitioned, once again,
to have Durango's jurisdictional authority overturned. The surviving documents, however, show the Franciscans protested less vigorously this time. The
results, though, were the same. A ruling by the Council of the Indies in 1738
and a royal decree the following year absolutely maintained the bishopric of
Durango's jurisdiction over New Mexico and the Custody of Saint Paul.[40]

*   *   *

After the protests, reports, and government edicts from Elizacoechea's visita
had been filed, the conflict over jurisdiction seemed to fade as a matter of serious concern to the prelates in Durango and the Franciscans in New Mexico. As

for the bishops, once their jurisdiction was upheld, they appeared to lose interest in the colony. Bishop Elizacoechea did include the Franciscan missions at Junta de los Ríos in a visita he conducted in 1742. These missions had not been part of any earlier inspections. The See of Durango also began to approve any construction of new churches and chapels for the Spanish population of New Mexico, such as the building at Tomé in 1743. Another bishop's inspection of the El Paso and Santa Fe districts, however, did not occur until 1760. Hence, the Franciscans' claim that the diocese would significantly ignore New Mexico appears to have been valid.[41]

The Franciscans did not complain, though. The lack of attention by the bishops meant that very little changed in the day-to-day operations of the Custody of Saint Paul. They continued to make most of the decisions concerning the mission operation, the assignment of friars, and generally exercised autonomy over many religious affairs as they had done for over a hundred years. True, the government ultimately confirmed Roybal's titles and the clergyman did begin to perform some religious functions in the Santa Fe district, but Roybal and the Franciscans avoided any significant controversies. Furthermore, in order to strengthen their position, the Franciscans initiated a reform effort within the Custody of Saint Paul (see chapter 9). Instead of incessantly challenging episcopal authority, the Franciscans must have sensed that their interests would be better served by not pressing the issue.

The jurisdictional conflict, however, significantly weakened the Franciscans' power. The negative assessments levied by Crespo and Elizacoechea against their mission program placed the friars in a vulnerable position with His Majesty's government. Moreover, New Mexico governors supported their own criticisms of the missionaries by echoing the bishops' complaints. The establishment in principle of diocesan control meant that in any future conflict with the secular side of the Church, the Franciscans would be at a distinct disadvantage. As will be seen later, when the next episcopal visita occurred in 1760, the friars offered virtually no resistance or protest. Thus, the two-decade struggle with Durango was another important factor in the decline of the Franciscan position in New Mexico.

CHAPTER 8

Church and State Interlude

Fortunately for the Franciscans in New Mexico, the years of struggle over diocesan control did not coincide with an equally assertive local government. For seven years after Governor Flores's sudden resignation in 1715, no New Mexico executive held more than an ad interim title as governor and two officials claimed that title at the same time. The political infighting, along with a military debacle in 1720, severely disrupted local political authority. Although the governor's office was fully restored with Bustamante's appointment in 1722, his administrative record was one of the weakest during the eighteenth century, despite the fact that he held office until 1731. Governor Cruzat y Góngora (1731–1736), Bustamante's successor, left behind an unremarkable legacy as well. Thus, for over twenty years, the expansion of local political power in the Kingdom slowed noticeably.

The Custody of Saint Paul, however, was unable to take advantage of the weaker governor's office to recover any of its lost power. Certainly a significant portion of their energy and time was devoted to their struggle with the See of Durango. In addition, an increased interest in New Mexico's affairs by the government and Franciscan hierarchy in Spain filled some of the void created by the less-than-assertive governors. The Franciscans themselves did little to promote their position in the colony by energetically improving the missionization program until the 1730s. The result was that while very little changed in local church and state affairs for virtually two decades, the Franciscans' position continued to deteriorate.

* * *

When Governor Flores resigned abruptly in December 1715, Captain Don Félix Martínez bestowed on himself the title of ad interim governor. Martínez was the commanding officer of the Santa Fe presidio at that time and had been a thorn in Flores's side during the latter's administration. Indeed, Captain Martínez had been an unruly subordinate and had instigated several conflicts with Flores. Martínez, a native of Galicia, had soldiered in New Mexico since the reconquest. Before assuming command in Santa Fe, he had held several military postings, including commander of the El Paso presidio. Martínez aspired to be appointed governor in 1712, and it was this disappointment that likely influenced Martínez's disruptive relationship with Flores and his later blatant grab for power.[1]

Captain Martínez held the office of governor for about thirteen months, although the government in Mexico City never recognized his pretension. Martínez's stature in New Mexico was further complicated by Flores's continued presence in the region. The former governor claimed that Martínez owed him financial restitution for presidial supplies that Flores had procured earlier. The animosity between the two men grew so heated that Martínez even had Flores incarcerated for a brief time. Obviously, this entire affair unsettled and diminished the civil government in the colony.[2]

As had occurred previously during the Rodríguez-Vargas controversy, Martínez viewed the Franciscans as potentially important supporters in his claim to the governorship. Martínez went out of his way to foster good relations with the friars. He issued several bandos instructing the population of New Mexico to comply with the Franciscans in matters of faith. During the spring of 1716, Martínez ordered the alcaldes mayores to post the Edicts of Faith in their districts. When the Franciscans complained to Martínez that some Puebloan groups were shirking their assignments in the preparations for Corpus Cristi Day, Martínez issued stern and detailed orders to the Puebloans to comply in readying the colony for this religious celebration.[3]

One of the most important accomplishments Martínez could achieve, both to endear himself to the Franciscans and cement his position with the government, would have been to successfully bring the Hopi back into the Spanish fold. To that end, Martínez organized the most ambitious expedition to reduce the Hopi since the reconquest era. The Franciscans closely cooperated with Martínez in this effort. Fray Francisco de Irazábal, the resident friar at Zuñi, turned his mission into a virtual supply depot to support the campaign. In addition, Irazábal functioned as a quasi-intelligence officer by sending a steady stream of reports to Martínez detailing what the terrain would be like, where water sources were located, and any news the missionary had of the Hopis' condition. Custos Fray Antonio Camargo and Fray Domingo de Araoz accompanied the army during the entrada. Despite the Spaniards' impressive effort, the Hopi proved to be as recalcitrant as ever and rejected the Franciscans.[4]

Also during the Martínez period, the Franciscans recognized the potential dangers inherent in this charged political atmosphere. Regarding the problems between Martínez and Flores, Custos Camargo admonished the missionaries on several occasions to steer clear of that dispute. Camargo also directed the friars to stay away from Santa Fe unless they had permission to be there. If the Franciscans encountered any problems with the governor's office or the alcaldes mayores, they were to turn the matter over to the prelate.

A new element, however, was prominent in these many directives to the friars. Realizing that many of their difficulties with governors Chacón and Flores originated with the slow pace of converting the Puebloans, the missionaries were now exhorted to improve their efforts. Instructions from the provincial office of Santo Evangelio and the custos to the friars included orders to master the neophytes' languages and to teach the Puebloans "in the clearest possible terms" the articles of faith, the sacraments, and other tenets of Catholicism. The missionaries were to set a better example of the Christian ideal in their own daily lives, and in general always to work untiringly to fulfill their holy vows. Clearly, the Franciscan leaders believed that by improving the mission operation, they could better ward off attacks from the local government.[5]

In January 1717, shortly after news of the failure of the campaign against the Hopi reached Mexico City, the viceregal office moved to end Martínez's questionable authority. Captain Don Antonio Valverde y Cosío was appointed ad interim governor of New Mexico and was ordered to remove Martínez from all authority. Valverde was a veteran of New Mexican military and political affairs, having previously served as an alcalde mayor and commander of the El Paso presidio.[6]

Captain Valverde moved quickly to assume his office in Santa Fe and to carry out his instructions, but Martínez was not yet willing to bow to the inevitable. As Valverde approached the capital, Martínez issued orders for his arrest. Valverde, warned of his impending incarceration, sought asylum at the mission of San Ildefonso, Fray Juan de Tagle's bailiwick. Despite Martínez's obvious ambitions, the pretender to the governor's office now backed away. Churches, in Spanish custom, represented sanctuaries where an individual might escape harm or avoid pursuit by the law. This tradition of the right of asylum in church and state relations was still very strong. Indeed, as Elizabeth Howard West has established, the Church's immunity in this matter was not challenged in New Mexico through most of the eighteenth century. Thus, Martínez could not seize Valverde.[7]

At this point, Martínez, foiled in his attempt to get his hands on Valverde, seemed to acknowledge the hopelessness of his position, but he also knew that he was in a legal quandary. His actions, especially toward Valverde, were likely to have adverse consequences. After delaying into June, Martínez turned over his office, but not to Valverde. To buy himself time to get out of New Mexico, Martínez surrendered the governorship to an old comrade-in-arms, Captain Don Juan Páez Hurtado. Páez, who had been an officer with Vargas's reconquest army, kept the office for almost a month before finally turning the governor's palace over to Valverde. When he did, in July 1717, Valverde had Páez and the entire Santa Fe cabildo (who had supported Martínez) arrested and sent in chains to Mexico City. The civil authority in New Mexico had virtually disintegrated.[8]

Valverde served as ad interim governor until 1722, and, in the process, restored some political stability to the Kingdom. Not much is known of his relationship with the Custody of Saint Paul, although Valverde appears to have enjoyed at least benign relations with the friars. The Franciscans, at least tacitly, supported Valverde in the numerous lawsuits engendered by the Martínez-Páez episode. Conversely, in later documents, the missionaries were critical in their allegations that Valverde had enriched himself at the expense of the inhabitants of the territory.[9]

The primary concern for Valverde's administration, as ordered by viceregal officials in Mexico City, was to counter the growing French presence on New Spain's northern frontier. As discussed previously, the Spanish government had been increasingly alarmed by French incursions into Texas since the 1680s. More recently, French traders had appeared along the southern Río Grande, and New Mexico officials and missionaries were hearing accounts of French agents selling arms to native people on the Great Plains. Valverde was ordered to respond to these developments by establishing a mission and Spanish settlement in southeast Colorado.[10]

To that end, Valverde led a large reconnaissance party into that area in 1719, accompanied by Fray Juan Jorge del Pino as chaplain. The following year another expedition was launched under the command of the lieutenant governor, Don Pedro de Villasur. On the Platte River, a Pawnee party, perhaps accompanied by French traders, ambushed this force and over thirty Spanish soldiers were slain. Among the dead was Fray Juan Mingues, a missionary with fourteen years of service in New Mexico. This catastrophe reduced the Spanish military forces in the colony by at least a third. Therefore, much of Valverde's attention during the remainder of his tenure had to be directed toward the defense of the region.[11]

Even had they been so inclined, the Franciscans of the Custody of Saint Paul were in no position to exploit this disaster to strengthen their position. They had enough problems of their own. As noted in the previous chapter, the struggle with the bishopric of Durango was escalating during this period. In addition, the missions in the Junta de los Ríos district were temporarily abandoned in 1718, primarily because of damaging raids by hostile natives, probably Apaches. The Franciscans also received a harsh rebuke from their Vicar General in Spain, Fray José García. García was incensed that complaints about the Custody of Saint Paul (probably from the Chacón-Flores era) were a topic of concern at the Spanish court. García warned the friars to cease their bickering and to avoid future disputes with the local government officials. The Vicar General urged the missionaries to review their vows, especially that of poverty, in light of their everyday lives. To drive the point home, García forbade the friars to engage in any form of commerce or to accept any luxury gifts. Conventos were to be furnished only with the base necessities. All mission fathers were to master the language of their charges to ensure the Puebloans' total understanding of Catholicism. Finally, all Puebloan forms of idolatry or paganism were to be confronted sternly and eradicated.[12]

*   *   *

Don Juan Domingo de Bustamante, a nephew of Valverde, began his term as a regularly appointed governor in 1722. Thus, for the first time in seven years, a fully invested executive was in charge of New Mexico's affairs. Prior to his appointment as governor, Bustamante held the rank of lieutenant general in El Paso. Hence, as so many of his predecessors since the reconquest, Bustamante was a military man. Some of New Mexico's inhabitants later charged, however, that Bustamante's only qualification for the post as governor was his relationship to Valverde who, it was said, paid 20,000 pesos to secure his nephew's appointment. There appears to be merit to the complaint that Bustamante was not particularly qualified for the governorship. Though he served as New Mexico's chief civil and military authority for nine consecutive years, Bustamante accomplished, much less attempted, very little to benefit New Mexico.[13]

One reason that might explain Bustamante's lackluster administration is that he enjoyed less autonomy in office than any of his fellow governors since before the Pueblo revolt in 1680. Partially in response to Spain's worries concerning French activities along the northern frontier and to the turmoil that had plagued the governor's office in recent years, Viceroy Casafuerte dispatched a *visitador*, Don Antonio Cobían Busto, in 1722 to examine the conditions in New Mexico. Cobían was in the region for several weeks, shortly after Bustamante began his administration. The visitador recommended that new settlements be created, especially north of Taos and south of Isleta, to secure the flanks of the central area of New Mexico, and that the military capabilities of the Kingdom be strengthened. Obviously, the presence of a viceregal representative in New Mexico, immediately after his installation in office, must have restricted Bustamante's freedom of action.[14]

Four years later, Governor Bustamante had to contend with an even more important visitor to his jurisdiction. Brigadier Don Pedro de Rivera had been assigned by the government to undertake an inspection and review of the entire northern frontier. For four months, Brigadier Rivera thoroughly scrutinized all aspects of the Spanish establishments in New Mexico. Rivera's report and recommendations to Madrid concerning New Spain's northern frontier led to the *Reglamento de 1729*. These regulations issued by the monarchy spelled out in explicit terms how presidial garrisons were to be managed and how relations with peaceful and hostile natives were to be conducted. The overall thrust of the Reglamento de 1729 prescribed a more pacific policy toward native people; punitive measures were only to be used after all peaceful means failed. Although New Mexico was still remote from centers of Spanish government, and governors could enjoy some latitude in their activities, Cobían and Rivera's time in New Mexico and the 1729 Reglamento restricted some of Bustamante's freedom to govern.[15]

Governor Bustamante may have been further hampered in his efforts to freely administer his region by developments associated with the status of alcaldes mayores in New Mexico. After the Bourbons took over the Spanish Crown, the government altered the process of selection and tenure of these district officials. Previously, alcaldes mayores in New Mexico served virtually at the whim of the governors. Under the Bourbon policy, alcaldes mayores were still appointed by governors but were confirmed in office by the Council of the Indies. These district officers then served for life, unless they voluntarily retired or were found guilty of misconduct in their official duties. By the time Bustamante assumed his office, many alcaldes mayores had held their posts long enough to have carved out their own little fiefdoms, safe from a governor's capricious desires. Thus, a new bureaucracy was established in New Mexico that would force governors to be more circumspect in their relations with the alcaldes mayores.[16]

Whether restricted by royal inspectors or alcaldes mayores, the fact remains that Bustamante's nine-year term in office can only be described as somnolent when compared to his predecessors. Though attacks by Apaches and other natives declined somewhat during the 1720s, they still posed a threat to New Mexico's security and continued to disrupt the lives of the territory's inhabitants. Bustamante, however, launched no military campaigns against marauding natives. Granted, the presidial garrison was still undermanned after the Villasur debacle in 1720. Indeed, according to a 1723 report, the Santa Fe presidio was down to twenty-three soldiers. As a result of Cobían's and Rivera's visits, however, the military was at full strength by 1730. Of course, the Reglamento of 1729 stressed a more conciliatory native policy, but these regulations were issued seven years into Bustamante's administration. Bustamante was later charged in his residencia with only being interested in self-enrichment and with having amassed a fortune of 200,000 pesos while in office. Perhaps that is the best explanation for his rather torpid style of governing.[17]

Bustamante's do-nothing method of governance clearly contributed to the rather poor relationship between himself and the Custody of Saint Paul. The Franciscans were chagrined that the new governor failed to support them in their efforts to retain the Hopi region as part of the custody's jurisdiction. As noted in the previous chapter, the Spanish government in 1722 transferred the Hopi province to the Jesuits at the recommendation of Bishop Tapiz, the Durango prelate. The Franciscans in New Mexico continued to protest that decision throughout the 1720s, and they attempted to have it overturned by successfully reestablishing missions among the Hopi people.

To that end, the Franciscans launched two entradas to the Hopi mesas during Bustamante's tenure. The first occurred in 1724, when two veteran missionaries, Fray Antonio de Miranda and Irazábal, the priest at Zuñi, made the trek to implore the Hopi to return to the Catholic faith. Miranda and Irazábal were received politely by the Hopi, and the two friars remained among them for several days, during which time they even preached a sermon. The Hopi, however, only made vague promises to consider the Franciscan entreaties. In 1731, a newly arrived Franciscan, Fray José de Archundía, made the same journey, but with no better results for the Order. In neither of these entradas did the Franciscans receive any assistance (financially or militarily) from Governor Bustamante, and the missionaries charged that the Hopis' resistance to the friars stemmed significantly from this lack of support. Hence, when Brigadier Rivera made his inspection of New Mexico in 1726, the Franciscans complained of Bustamante's failure to support the mission program and the governor's overall corrupt policies toward Spanish citizens and native people.[18]

From that point, the relationship between the missionaries and Bustamante plummeted. In 1727, Bustamante charged that the Franciscans embarrassed him and created a "scandal" in the colony when they did not greet him at the door of the Franciscan church in Santa Fe on Corpus Cristi Day, as was the custom. This incident grew even more ugly the following day, when the governor and his entourage forced their way into the church and demanded to receive communion. Some of Bustamante's party were armed and the friars refused to perform the sacrament until they divested themselves of their weapons. When Bustamante refused to order his men to do so, the Franciscans withdrew without giving communion to Bustamante or his men.[19]

Later that same year, the custos, Fray Antonio Camargo, penned a cryptic directive to the missionaries. Without acknowledging specific incidents or names, Camargo informed the friars that the bitter invectives being hurled at them were a cross they would have to bear. He advised the Franciscans to avoid coming into contact with certain officials and to avoid any actions that might leave them open to condemnation by the local authorities. If any problems developed with civil officials, the missionaries were not to respond, but to turn the matter over to the custos.[20]

Governor Bustamante, it should be remembered, proved to be a further irritant to the Custody of Saint Paul during its disputes with Bishop Crespo and that prelate's visita in 1730. Indeed, even before Crespo's inspection, Bustamante sent the bishop a report on the state of affairs in New Mexico and encouraged Crespo to come and inspect the missions. Time after time during Crespo's visit, Bustamante sided with the prelate during disputes with the Franciscans and housed Crespo in the governor's palace in Santa Fe. Even when a desperate Custos Varo was willing to recognize Bustamante's rights as vice-patron over the Franciscans in New Mexico, the governor still supported the bishop of Durango. As noted previously, it was likely Bustamante's gift of 6,000 pesos that funded Santiago Roybal's appointment as Crespo's vicar and ecclesiastical judge for the colony. In 1731 after Crespo's visita, the governor adamantly rejected a request from Vice-custos Fray José Antonio Guerrero that Roybal's positions be overturned.[21]

The Franciscans did attempt to even the score with Bustamante during the governor's residencia in the summer of 1731. The formal investigation into Bustamante's administration was conducted inexplicably not by the incoming governor, but by one Don Francisco de Sierra. Perhaps the new governor was delayed, or the selection of Sierra to hold Bustamante's residencia was a manifestation of the government's concern about New Mexican affairs. Whatever the reason, the Franciscans took this opportunity to launch a scathing attack on Bustamante's activities as governor. The Franciscans reported to Sierra that Bustamante poorly maintained and equipped the presidial garrison, abused mission inhabitants, enriched himself through illegal slave trading, and failed to protect the colony from Apache raids. More specifically to the mission operation in New Mexico, the friars pointed out how Bustamante had failed to bolster the two entradas to the Hopi region. In addition, the governor encouraged the Puebloans to "abhor" their mission fathers, allowed the friars to be "humiliated" by Bishop Crespo, and generally treated the Franciscans "with great impudence." Though Bustamante was found guilty of some charges, especially illegal trading activities with non-mission natives, none of the Franciscans' complaints concerning the mission program were found by Sierra to be significant.[22]

Don Gervasio Cruzat y Góngora (1731–1736) followed Bustamante as the governor of New Mexico. Very little is known of Cruzat or his administration. The new governor seems to have enjoyed better relations with the Franciscans than did Bustamante, although that conclusion must be based on the dearth of documents for that five-year span. While the lack of materials is certainly not conclusive in passing judgment of Cruzat's interactions with the Custody of Saint Paul, the fact is that most archival sources on church and state relations are concerned with conflicts and controversies. Hence, the scarcity of documents dealing with matters between Governor Cruzat and the Franciscans at least strongly suggests that the period was rather quiet.

From what materials do exist, Governor Cruzat seems to have been supportive of the Franciscans. The best example of their relationship involved a complaint filed by Vice-custos José Antonio Guerrero against two Spaniards, Martín Hurtado and Pedro García, for disrupting a mass in Alburquerque during the spring of 1733. Hurtado and García entered the church during the sermon by Fray Pedro Montaño and in loud voices, mixed with profanities, called Montaño "a governor of Hell." What prompted their outburst is unknown. No background information exists for García, although Hurtado was a longtime resident of Alburquerque, who had at one point held the rank of captain in the military, and, in 1714, was the alcalde mayor of that Spanish villa. In 1723, he was involved in some minor political disputes with Governor Bustamante, but those seem to have had no bearing on his anger toward Montaño. Fray Pedro Montaño only arrived in New Mexico in 1728.[23]

Why the Franciscans asked for Governor Cruzat's participation in this matter was likely a legacy of the recent visita by Bishop Crespo. In the past, Hurtado and García would have been brought before either the ecclesiastical judge or the Inquisition. In 1733, of course, the ecclesiastical judge was Santiago Roybal, a secular clergyman and Bishop Crespo's appointee. The Franciscans had no desire to bring Roybal into the matter and legitimize his position in the colony. Why the Inquisition was not used is unknown, other than the Franciscans' increasing reluctance to employ the Holy Office in these affairs. Governor Cruzat accepted the vice-custos's complaint and ordered Don Juan González Blas, the alcalde mayor of Alburquerque, to conduct an investigation. Both Hurtado and García were found guilty, and García was incarcerated. Hurtado was probably not jailed because of his poor health and advanced age; he died in 1734.[24]

The only other concrete interaction between Governor Cruzat and the Franciscans occurred in June 1733. During Cruzat's inspection of the mission at Galisteo, the governor admonished the inhabitants to always obey and cooperate with their mission father. Perhaps Cruzat did this simply at the behest of the new missionary there, Fray Francisco Benito Cayetano de Otero.[25]

In general, Governor Cruzat's term in office was a reasonably calm and peaceful period for New Mexico. Apache attacks on the colony continued to decline, and the Navajos and Utes seem to have been at peace with the Spanish as well. Consequently, the colony experienced some economic growth during the early 1730s, especially in agricultural and livestock production. The

biggest headache for Cruzat concerned an investigation of three alcaldes mayores who were charged with abusing the Puebloans in their districts. All three
were found guilty, but only two were removed from office. Thus, Cruzat's
tenure as governor seems to have been one of the more peaceful and harmonious periods in eighteenth-century New Mexico.[26]

* * *

One of the most important changes in the missionary operation during this
period, from Governor Flores's resignation through the end of Governor
Cruzat's administration, was an increase in the number of friars serving in
New Mexico. When last considered, twelve to fourteen missionary priests
maintained the eighteen missions and three Spanish villas in the Santa Fe district. Between 1715 and 1736, at least twenty-eight new Franciscans arrived in
the Kingdom while, at most, ten friars left the region or died while in service.
Some of these recent arrivals were soon posted to El Paso or Junta de los Ríos,
but the gain in friars augmented their contingent in the Santa Fe district to almost thirty, a level close to that requested time after time since the reconquest
period.

While the growth in the number of missionary priests was noteworthy, the
rate of increase was very uneven. Between 1715 and 1719, only three new friars
appeared in the Santa Fe district: Fray Juan de la Cruz, Fray Juan Jorge del
Pino, and Fray Juan Antonio Sánchez. Sánchez was soon posted to the El Paso
missions, however, where he served during most of his tenure as a missionary
for the Custody of Saint Paul. Furthermore, another friar, Fray Jerónimo
Liñán, left during the same period. Thus, New Mexico gained, at best, two friars by 1719.[27]

Over the next decade, ten more Franciscans appeared in the colony, or
about one per year. These new friars were Fray Pedro Díaz de Aguilar, Fray
Diego Arias de Espinosa, Fray Andrés Ceballos (Zevallos), Fray Antonio Esquer, Fray Antonio Gabaldón, Fray José de Irigoyen, Fray Pedro Montaño, Fray
Juan José Pérez de Mirabal, Fray Andrés Varo, and Fray Manuel Zambrano.
Three missionaries were removed from the Franciscan rosters during these
years: Fray Juan Mingues, killed during the Villasur massacre; and Fray Juan
de Tagle and Fray José López Tello, who retired from the field with over forty
years of service in New Mexico between them. In 1727, Governor Bustamante's
letter to Bishop Crespo (noted earlier) included a short report on the Franciscan roster in New Mexico. In the Santa Fe district, all eighteen missions and
the three Spanish villas each had at least one resident friar. That represented a
first for the colony since 1680.[28]

If the missions were fully staffed in 1727, Bishop Crespo did not find them so
during his visita three years later. In his report to Viceroy Casafuerte, Crespo

claimed the mission operation was short by seven priests. It was no mere coincidence, probably, that seven new friars arrived in the Santa Fe region within a year of Crespo's inspection. This represented the single greatest increase in missionaries since the reconquest era. Among the new Franciscans were Fray Juan Aguilar, Fray José de Archundía, Fray Ignacio Díaz, Fray Francisco Larias, Fray Miguel Loreno, Fray Francisco Benito Cayetano de Otero, and Fray Manuel Sopecho. Only four of these replacements, however, remained for any length of time. Archundía, Díaz, and Larias were all absent from the Custody of Saint Paul roster within three years.[29]

Besides the seven sudden new arrivals in 1731, the buildup in missionary priests continued between 1729 and 1736, as eight more Franciscans entered the Santa Fe district. These friars included Fray Francisco Manuel Bravo Lerchundí, Fray Jacinto González, Fray Gabriel Hoyuela, Fray Juan Miguel Menchero (who was briefly in New Mexico previously in 1729), Fray Juan Carlos de Oronzoro, Fray Juan José de Padilla, Fray Juan Tejada, and Fray José de San Antonio Terrón. This entire contingent did not serve permanently as mission priests in the territory. Menchero held various posts over the next two decades (see chapter 9), but was rarely active as a missionary. Hoyuela and Oronzoro would mainly labor in the El Paso region.[30]

Therefore, while fifteen Franciscans were first posted to New Mexico within five years of Bishop Crespo's visita, only nine seem to have been permanently assigned as mission priests. Furthermore, three other friars departed during this period: Francisco de Irazábal left about 1732 with twenty-five years of service; Bravo Lerchundí remained only about five years; and Domingo de Araoz died in his mission at Santa Ana in 1731, after more than two decades in New Mexico. Nonetheless, by 1736, the Custody of Saint Paul's mission operation in New Mexico was at its greatest strength since the Pueblo revolt in 1680.[31]

It should be recalled that Bishop Crespo advised the government that the friars sent to New Mexico be "neither too young nor too old." The data on the thirteen Franciscans who arrived between 1715 and 1730 suggest that the missionaries posted to the Kingdom tended to be either youthful and inexperienced or advanced in years. At least five (Cruz, Gabaldón, Irigoyen, Pino, and Sánchez) were in their mid-twenties and/or recently ordained as priests. Gabaldón, as noted earlier, had not yet been ordained as a priest when he was sent north. Three of the replacements in the 1715–1730 era could be considered well along in years. Montaño and Varo were at least in their mid-forties when they entered New Mexico, and Ceballos was over fifty. Thus, over half of the Franciscans billeted to New Mexico in the fifteen years prior to Crespo's visita may have been too young or too old to suit the bishop.[32]

Did Crespo's criticism seem to have any influence on how the Franciscans selected New Mexico missionaries in the five years after the prelate's inspection? The answer is "somewhat." Of the fifteen posted to the colony between 1731 and 1736, substantial background information exists for ten. Of these, seven were between the ages of thirty and forty: Aguilar, Archundía, Díaz, Otero, Menchero, Oronzoro, and Terrón. Furthermore, all seven of these missionaries had been ordained priests for at least five years, although none were known to have frontier evangelical experience. While no extant documents make any reference to Crespo's criticism as a consideration in the selection of friars, the majority of new missionaries bound for New Mexico met the bishop of Durango's criteria.[33]

As the governors in New Mexico were under closer scrutiny by the Spanish government during these decades, so too were the Franciscans. The rather swift response by the monarchy to the transfer of the Hopi region to the Jesuits from the Franciscans and to other matters engendered by the dispute over diocesan control has been previously noted. In addition, Viceroy Casafuerte demanded in 1734 that Santo Evangelio submit a detailed report on the state of the mission programs in New Mexico and Tampico. The Viceroy noted that this had not been done in eighteen years. Later that same year, the court in Spain was the scene of a debate on the possibility of dispatching thirty-four gachupín Franciscans directly to the mission field of New Mexico. This number was later scaled back to twenty friars and was approved by the government, but this contingent of gachupines was never sent.[34]

The intention of the government to send such a large number of gachupín friars to New Mexico was probably based on two considerations. First, the Spanish government in Madrid under the Bourbons tended to hold criollos in low esteem throughout the eighteenth century. They would have reasoned that the slow pace of native conversions in New Mexico was surely a result of criollo ineptitude. Second, the Bourbons were generally suspicious of the loyalty and obedience of criollos in the New World. With New Mexico seen as a focal point for increasing French activity, the government likely was concerned about whether Spanish policy was being diligently carried out. Certainly there was a paltry number of gachupín friars in the Kingdom. Of the twenty-eight Franciscans who came to New Mexico in the 1715–1736 period, the nationalities of twenty-four are known. Only three (Cruz, Ceballos, and Varo) were gachupines, and six more were hijos de provincia. Fifteen, or well over half of the replacements, were criollos.[35]

Despite the ever-growing number of missionary priests in New Mexico, the conversion of native people seemed to be at a standstill. The criticisms from Bishop Crespo, the government, and the Franciscan hierarchy directed at the friars for their lack of success in converting the Puebloans already in the missions have been noted. Furthermore, no new missions were being successfully established. True, three attempts were made during these two decades to induce the Hopi back into the fold, but all of them failed. A new mission was created near Trampas for the Jicarilla Apaches in the early 1730s, but it was abandoned within a few years when these natives were forbidden to continue their trade with Comanches and other native people thought to be hostile to the Spanish. To the south, the Junta de los Ríos missions opened and closed with depressing regularity for the Franciscans. As previously noted, these missions were abandoned in 1718 but resumed operation within a few years. A rebellion among these natives and Apache raids caused their evacuation again in 1725. At least two of the Junta de los Ríos missions were reestablished in 1733, but these would be abandoned periodically over the next few decades. Hence, while the number of missionaries had grown remarkably, the Franciscans' goal of congregating more native people into missions was not being achieved in the Custody of Saint Paul.[36]

* * *

During the 1715–1736 period, Franciscan autonomy and position in New Mexico in relationship to the government continued to decline, though at a much slower pace than during the Chacón-Flores era. The chaos in the governor's office during the Martínez-Páez-Valverde controversies, Governor Bustamante's incompetence, and the presence of royal inspectors all contributed to slowing the growth of local government authority. On the other hand, the higher governmental offices in Mexico City and Madrid expanded their interest in the activities of the Custody of Saint Paul and intensified the pressure on the Franciscans to carry out their duties to the native population. In short, the monarchy wanted results, or it would intervene, as the government had when it transferred the Hopi region to the Jesuits. Upon factoring in the growth of influence by the See of Durango in New Mexican affairs, the Franciscans' position by 1736 was diminished compared to two decades earlier.

By the 1730s the Franciscans had come to realize that their main problem stemmed from not fulfilling their primary tasks: the converting to Christianity and instilling the trappings of civilization in the native people of New Mexico. Bishop Crespo had directly pointed this out, and so had several of the governors. Even to many friars, both in the Custody of Saint Paul and in the Franciscan hierarchy, it had become obvious that greater effort and commitment would be required in the evangelical process. Only through more baptized natives and Spanish-acting Puebloans could the Franciscans hope to silence their critics and solidify their position in the Kingdom. With that recognition and the largest number of missionary priests available than at any time since the reconquest, the Franciscans now attempted to reform the mission operation and expand their field of labor.

CHAPTER 9

An Era of Reform

MORE THAN three decades after their return to New Mexico, the Franciscans had not achieved their evangelical goals nor had they made much progress to that end. Lack of success in converting and civilizing the native people of the region had significantly contributed to the deterioration of the Franciscan position within the Kingdom. The friars' inability to extirpate Puebloan social and cultural customs had provided a springboard for assertive governors, such as Chacón and Flores, to expand civil authority at the expense of the Order in New Mexico. The Custody of Saint Paul's failure to restore the Hopi mission field was the primary reason why that territory was transferred to the Jesuits. Bishop Crespo's harsh denunciation of the Franciscans' performance as missionaries clearly figured in the government's decision to uphold the See of Durango's jurisdiction over New Mexico. While the Franciscans labored under many difficulties, especially severe personnel shortages, the fact of the matter was that the Custody of Saint Paul had not fulfilled its purpose in New Mexico. Thus, the friars had to shoulder most of the blame for their ever-diminishing power and influence.

Certainly the Franciscans had known for some time that there were problems with the mission operation in New Mexico. Various custos of the Custody of Saint Paul and officials in the upper echelons of the Order in Mexico City and Spain had on numerous occasions since the 1690s pointed out the friars' shortcomings. A stream of directives urging the missionaries on to greater efforts in their work among the Puebloan people has been noted. Most of these admonitions, however, were not vigorously or effectively pursued.

Beginning in the late 1720s and continuing over the following two decades, the Franciscans strove to right their ship and improve their status in the Kingdom. Efforts were initiated to produce more zealous and industrious mission priests, and to spur them on to greater achievements. More emphasis was placed on mastering the Puebloan languages and providing a regimen conducive to that goal. A determined attempt was begun to expand the mission field, especially among the apostate Hopi and the long-hostile Navajo people. In short, for the first and only time during the eighteenth century, the Franciscans energetically tried to attain their goals as missionaries and, by extension, to restore their position in New Mexico.

*   *   *

The first evidence of a reform in the mission operation came in a directive sent by Custos Fray Antonio Camargo to the Franciscan missionaries in December 1727. Camargo had been in New Mexico since 1699, serving in various missions in the Santa Fe district and holding higher offices for the Custody of Saint Paul, including a previous term as custos. Camargo, as noted earlier, had been one of the missionaries who took part in the 1716 expedition to the Hopi, and he was very aware of the mission operation's strengths and weaknesses. Indeed, he had just completed a thorough inspection of the missions prior to his issuing his 1727 *patente*. It included what had now become routine instructions for the friars to diligently attend to their duties, to avoid luxuries, and to set a good example for their neophytes. Camargo, however, went further. He decreed that the missionaries devote their free time to learning the Puebloan languages, and, to ensure the friars' compliance, Camargo announced that he would begin examining them in their proficiency in native languages. Never, since the reconquest of New Mexico, had the Franciscan missionaries been so compelled to master Puebloan languages.[1]

Camargo's decision to increase the pressure on the friars to learn the local languages was likely influenced by the jurisdictional dispute with the See of Durango. Since the early seventeenth century, governmental and ecclesiastical policies required clergymen to be fluent in their parishioners' language. Bishops were responsible for ensuring that this regulation was met, and, indeed, these prelates had sometimes used the excuse that regular clergy were deficient in speaking local languages to replace them with secular clergy. Perhaps Camargo was hedging his bets concerning the outcome of the conflict with Durango. Bishop Crespo had already made his visita of El Paso in 1725, and the Custody of Saint Paul had lost in every decision made over the past decade by the government since the controversy had erupted. If the bishopric of Durango's jurisdiction was upheld, the Franciscans would have to be more fluent in indigenous languages in order to maintain their hold on the missions.[2]

That the friars in New Mexico had failed to gain mastery in Puebloan tongues was no secret by the end of the 1720s. The Franciscans offered two reasons why this fundamental missionary skill eluded their grasp. The most frequently cited excuse was the difficulty and diversity of Puebloan languages. Within the missions of the Santa Fe district, there were three completely unrelated language groups: Keresan, Tanoan, and Zuñian. The Tanoan language also had three distinct subgroups: Tiwa, Tewa, and Towa. These subgroups had similarities of structure; however, they were virtually mutually unintelligible. To complicate matters even more, significant dialectic differences often existed within each language group from village to village. When one further considers the additional languages spoken in the Kingdom by native peoples such as the Suma, Hopi, Apache, Navajo, and Ute, the missionaries worked in an environment that rivaled Babel.[3]

The Franciscans arrived in New Mexico without any pertinent language preparation. As noted previously, the missionary training facility at Santiago de Tlatelolco offered only Nahuatl, Otomí, and Tarascán. Some missionaries, retired or on leave from New Mexico, would occasionally be available to the friars-in-training to answer questions or to provide some idea of what the frontier mission environment was like. These opportunities likely offered no more than the chance to pick up a Puebloan phrase or two, assuming that the New Mexico veterans spoke native languages. Only one New Mexico missionary proficient in a Puebloan language, Fray Antonio de Miranda, is known to have been assigned to Santiago de Tlatelolco, and he was there only one year. Finally, there were no published grammars or vocabularies in existence for an inexperienced missionary to study before he arrived in New Mexico.[4]

A second explanation often given by the Franciscans concerning their language deficiencies was the friars' frequent transfers within the colony. Between 1694 and 1730, the typical missionary in New Mexico was assigned to five different missions during his tenure in the colony and averaged less than three years at any one post. Moreover, the decisions concerning assignments to missions did not seem to reflect the experience a friar might have garnered previously in regard to native languages. The career of Fray Antonio Esquer is a good example of this pattern of assigning priests. Esquer arrived in the Santa Fe district in 1724. Within the first eleven months, he worked at Galisteo (Tano) and San Ildefonso (Tewa). After a gap in his known service, spent perhaps at Cochití, Esquer was posted for two and a half years to San Felipe (Keres) and for fifteen months to Pecos (Towa). The much-traveled Esquer was then sent to Santa Clara (Tewa) for three months before going back to Pecos for about six months. Fray Antonio next seems to have split about eighteen months between Zía and Acoma (both Keres), before landing again at Santa Clara. Thus, within less than a dozen years, Esquer served at seven different mission sites and was confronted by four different languages.[5]

Had the missionaries been left at one site for longer periods, or at least been allowed to labor among Puebloans of the same language group, they might have achieved greater fluency. During the first half of the eighteenth century, six friars were cited for their mastery of a Puebloan tongue. Five of these priests were stationed at a single mission for a lengthy period of time or were placed in missions within a single language group. Fray Antonio de Miranda spent all but two of thirty-seven years among the Keres of Laguna, Acoma, and Zía. Fray Pedro Díaz de Aguilar worked eleven out of fourteen years with the Keres, at Laguna, Zía, Santa Ana, and San Felipe. Fray Francisco de Irazábal was initially at Zuñi for thirteen years. Fray Manuel Zambrano devoted all but two of his first thirteen years to work among the Keres at Zía, San Felipe, and Santo Domingo. Fray Juan José de Padilla was billeted thirteen out of seventeen years with the Keres of Zía and Laguna. Only Fray José de Irigoyen appears to have mastered the various Tanoan subgroups, despite being transferred often among these Puebloans.[6]

No official explanation or policy statement exists which might reveal why missionaries were moved about so often and haphazardly. Furthermore, the friars often complained about this situation. One factor must have been the personnel shortages during the first three decades after the reconquest. With the Custody of Saint Paul habitually understaffed, friars had to be juggled about to compensate for illnesses, deaths, and retirements from the field. Perhaps the most likely reason the missionaries were reassigned so frequently was that the local Franciscan leaders were looking for a suitable match between priest and Puebloan group. This would explain why some friars stayed in one place for extended periods: their missions functioned well. Whatever the reasons, the fact that more than thirty years after the reconquest most Franciscans did not speak their neophytes' languages spoke volumes about the general state of the mission operation in New Mexico.

* * *

In the summer of 1731, less than a year after Bishop Crespo's visita of New Mexico, Fray Juan Miguel Menchero returned to the Kingdom bearing specific instructions from the Franciscan Commissary General of New Spain, Fray Fernando Alonso González, to reform and intensify the mission field of the Custody of Saint Paul. In addition, Menchero held joint appointments as visitador and procurador for the custody. Over the next twenty years, Menchero would be one of the primary figures in the Franciscans' twin goals to improve and expand the mission program.[7]

The Franciscan leadership in New Spain appears to have had considerable faith in Menchero's abilities. He was an hijo de provincia who had professed his faith in 1714 in Puebla at age nineteen. Early Franciscan documents refer to him with the title of Don, one of the few friars so noted. His parents and grandparents were described as merchants, and the Menchero family also owned land near Mexico City. After Menchero's ordination, he held several offices in

Puebla, including chaplain at the convento of Santa Clara and censor for the Holy Office. In addition, Menchero had been entrusted with conducting a visita of the Custody of Saint Paul in 1729. During the nearly twenty years he worked in New Mexico, Menchero was at various times custos and procurador, and he was appointed to other special assignments, including visitador to the Custody of Tampico. Thus, Menchero seems to have been a highly esteemed friar when he arrived in New Mexico.[8]

The instructions Menchero brought from Commissary General González for the New Mexico missionaries were lengthy and unusually specific. Each mission priest was to keep detailed accurate records of expenses and the income generated by the mission's livestock and crops. Friars were no longer to accept payment of any kind from their neophytes for religious services rendered. The Franciscan vows of poverty were to be strictly maintained. In addition, missionaries were to see that native people were paid in advance for any labor services they performed outside the missions. To avoid any hint of scandal, Puebloan women were not to be employed within the conventos. The friars were to endeavor to keep their mission churches and other buildings clean and in good repair. The restrictions on friars becoming embroiled in civil disputes were reiterated, as were the instructions to refer all problems with local officials to the custos. Missionaries were to remain at their assigned posts at all times. Furthermore, should friars leave their missions without permission to come to Santa Fe, they would be disciplined, including a punishment of banishment to Zuñi for six months for a first offense. The Franciscans were to promote the Puebloans' mastery of the Spanish language to speed their understanding of Catholicism. To that end, friars were to distribute Spanish language primers, readers, and catechisms to the Puebloans and teach directly from those items. And finally, missionaries were to learn Puebloan languages, and to promote that goal, friars would not be moved about so often.[9]

In 1732, Commissary General González ordered Menchero to return to Mexico City to inspect the training school at Santiago de Tlatelolco and make recommendations to improve the friars' missionary preparation. Perhaps to gain a comparative perspective, Menchero stopped off in Querétaro to look at the Propaganda Fide facility located in that city. In his report to the Commissary General, Menchero focused primarily on the psychological aspects of missionary training. According to Menchero, friars needed better preparation to cope with adversity; individual initiative should be inculcated within prospective missionaries to help them address the unforeseen difficulties inherent in mission operations. Training should enhance future missionaries' religious zeal and evangelical commitment. Mission priests must be encouraged to face the dangers associated with frontier service with fortitude, although Menchero did not suggest encouraging martyrdom. While one must wonder how such mental and emotional traits were to be instilled in young men, Menchero's report clearly implied disappointment with the character of many of New Mexico's friars. He viewed their personal and training deficiencies as major stumbling blocks to reinvigorating the Custody of Saint Paul's missions. Menchero's inspection and assessment of Santiago de Tlatelolco, however, had little effect. The school's rector claimed that no changes were needed, and no records indicate that any reforms were ever instituted.[10]

The effort to reform the missionaries' performance in New Mexico stalled as well, although not from a lack of attention by the different custos. In 1734, Custos Fray José Ortiz de Velasco, based in El Paso, inspected the northern missions. Ortiz found many of the old problems still in place. The friars continued to absent themselves too frequently from their missions without permission. Furthermore, when Ortiz administered language examinations to the friars, very few passed them. Consequently, the indoctrination of the Puebloans in the foundations of Catholicism still fell far short of the Franciscans' goal. Fray José cajoled and threatened his friars by promising that those who attained language proficiency would not be transferred from their missions, and warning that those who were negligent in their duties would be punished. Ortiz closed with a passionate plea for the missionaries to live "according to the examples set by St. Francis and St. Paul."[11]

The same message was repeated shortly after Bishop Elizacoechea's visita. In 1738, Custos Fray Juan García, likewise billeted in El Paso, inspected the Santa Fe district. He found that many of the missions were dirty and in disrepair. Worse, García found Puebloan paganism common and indications that sacrilegious behavior was endemic. The custos noted dismally, "that nothing is progressing nor has progressed since past times; I saw waste, not hope." García rebuked the missionaries and reminded them yet again to adhere to the instructions brought by Menchero in 1731 from the Commissary General of New Spain.[12]

Concern over the reports coming out of New Mexico, including the negative assessments from the Crespo and Elizacoechea visitas, evoked a further response from the Franciscan hierarchy. The new Commissary General of New Spain, Fray Pedro Navarrete, ordered that an investigation of the New Mexico mission operation be conducted in Mexico City. While the aim of the investigation was likely to minimize the damage from the two reports by the Durango bishops, the candor of the questions and responses suggests that this inquiry was to be a critical assessment of the evangelical performance of the Custody of Saint Paul. Three former visitadores who had also served as missionaries in the Kingdom gathered at Santiago de Tlatelolco to be interrogated. The three

Franciscans were Fray Francisco de Lipianí (Lepiane), who had also served in
the El Paso and Junta de los Ríos districts; Fray Luís Martínez Clemente, who
had labored in the Junta de los Ríos area; and Menchero.

Lipianí, who testified first, noted that despite Crespo's allegations, some
friars did know Puebloan languages, though their level of fluency was often "insufficient." He blamed the problem on the region's diversity of languages, a
situation similar to what he had experienced previously in missions in
Coahuila. Lipianí further admitted that, in his opinion, some New Mexico
missionaries were incompetent and others too old for the rigors of frontier service. Martínez Clemente seconded much of Lipianí's testimony, but he added
that many friars were forced to rely on native interpreters to communicate with
their neophytes because the priests were unable to speak Puebloan languages.
When Menchero's turn came, he produced two affidavits from local alcaldes
mayores that attested to the fluency in Puebloan languages of two friars: Fray
Pedro Díaz de Aguilar and Fray José de Irigoyen. Menchero stated, however,
that many other mission priests were not as capable, and that created in New
Mexico a situation in which "there was nothing to admire." Despite the criticism brought into the open by these proceedings as to the depth of New Mexico's mission problems, nothing seems to have come from this inquiry.[13]

The inability to inform and reinvigorate the friars' evangelical effort spawned
frustration and desperation in some Franciscans, and it was perhaps this frustration that was at the root of an unprecedented incident occurring in July 1743.
Two friars, Fray Francisco de la Concepción González and Fray Antonio Esquer, were summoned before Custos Fray Gabriel Hoyuela and formally
charged with disobedience and creating scandals. The most significant allega-
tion was their supposed encouragement of a bizarre plot to foment a Puebloan
rebellion (see chapter 10). After the custos found them guilty, he sentenced
both friars to receive twelve lashes. On 28 July 1743, both men were brought
from their rooms, stripped, and whipped. Hoyuela stopped the beatings short of
the prescribed twelve blows when Concepción and Esquer pleaded for mercy
and promised to amend their behavior. The two friars were then confined to
cells in the convento of Santa Fe for a period of time, and each signed an oath
promising to uphold the tranquillity of the colony and swearing their future absolute obedience to their Franciscan superiors.[14]

This is the only recorded incident of such physical and psychologically hu-
miliating punishment being meted out to any New Mexico friar during the
time period of this study. As will be noted in the following chapter, Concepción
was later exonerated of all charges when it became apparent that he had been
framed by local civil officials and that the entire affair was actually an outgrowth of widespread church-state tensions in the 1740s. Nonetheless, this
harsh and unprecedented punishment was also likely a reflection of the Fran-

ciscans' inability to reform many friars' performances as missionaries and of the
need to set an example.

Indeed, by the mid-1740s it must have become apparent that the attempt to
reform the performances of the missionaries had borne little fruit. Much of the
blame for the failure, however, must be laid at the feet of the Order itself and its
inflexibility in the structure of the mission operation. In the 1730s Commissary
General González, Menchero, and Custos García all promised not to move friars as frequently in order to make it easier for missionaries to master the
Puebloan languages, but the friars continued to be frequently rotated from mission to mission. In fact, where friars averaged about 2.8 years per assignment
prior to 1730, the average actually and inexplicably dropped slightly to about 2.6
years over the next two decades. Furthermore, the excuse of personnel shortages was no longer valid. The rapid expansion in the number of friars in New
Mexico during the 1730s was noted previously, and their strength remained
high into the 1750s. There exists no Franciscan rationale why this seemingly
simple reform was not realized.[15]

One might further ask why no former New Mexico missionaries were teaching Puebloan languages at the training school of Santiago de Tlatelolco. As
noted earlier, Fray Antonio de Miranda, cited as fluent in the Keres tongue,
was posted to the school; however, he apparently did not actually teach Keresan
there. In a 1739 Santo Evangelio roster, Miranda is listed only as a notary at
Santiago de Tlatelolco. Miranda had previously served thirty-seven years in
New Mexico and would have been over sixty by then. Perhaps his long years of
labor on the frontier had sapped his strength, although later, during the 1740s,
he was listed at various times as Santo Evangelio's provincial secretary. Perhaps
Miranda simply lacked the aptitude to teach. Nevertheless, Miranda was the
only veteran New Mexico friar fluent in language to whom prospective missionaries might have turned prior to their assignment in New Mexico. The
shortsightedness of the Franciscan leadership in not offering the study of
Puebloan languages to potential missionaries remains a very perplexing issue.[16]

*   *   *

If reforming the evangelical capabilities of most of the friars failed, the Franciscans enjoyed more success, at least for a time, in expanding their mission
field. Through vigorous efforts, they opened more new missions in the Custody
of Saint Paul during the 1740s than at any time since the decade after the reconquest in 1694.

The first area of expansion occurred among the *genízaro* population in the
Kingdom. The Spanish in New Mexico defined genízaros as non-Puebloan native people who had been, at least nominally, converted to Christianity and
who now lived as Spanish. During the eighteenth century, most genízaros

entered New Mexico as slaves, traded to the Spanish by the more dominant, nomadic native groups such as the Apaches and Comanches. While this form of slave trading was supposedly outlawed earlier and was vehemently condemned by the Franciscans, it still continued, especially in the 1720s during Governor Bustamante's administration.[17]

In 1740, during the administration of Governor Gaspar Domingo de Mendoza (1739–1743), the Franciscans and the local government cooperated in opening two genízaro settlements near the mission at Isleta. The two communities, Valencia and Tomé, were inhabited by formerly enslaved native people who had been able to prove they had been poorly and unjustly treated by their masters. About forty families were moved into the region, and by 1744, they were building a church. The Franciscan missionary at Isleta ministered to these people. In 1747, another genízaro community was established at Abiquiu, southwest of Taos, and was administered to by the mission fathers of that pueblo. While these new genízaro settlements were obviously important to the defense of the Kingdom, their existence represented an enlargement of the religious sphere of the Custody of Saint Paul as well.[18]

A more difficult and ambitious undertaking by the Franciscans during this period was their renewed effort to return the intransigent Hopi to Catholicism. It will be recalled that in the 1720s the government transferred the Hopi territory to the Jesuit sphere of mission operations. Since the reconquest, the Franciscans had failed to induce the Hopi to return to mission life despite numerous attempts. The Spanish government was anxious to secure the Hopi region and to incorporate them into the defense of northern New Spain. Though the Franciscans had strongly objected to losing jurisdiction over the Hopi, His Majesty's government rebuffed every petition by the Franciscans to have the transfer overturned. However, by the end of the 1730s Philip V was becoming impatient with the efforts of the Society of Jesus to reduce the Hopi. Thus, the stage was set for the Franciscans to approach the Hopi once again.[19]

The Franciscan missionary most associated with the campaigns into the Hopi provinces in the 1740s was Fray Carlos José Delgado. Delgado was a gachupín friar who had originally come to New Spain in 1708 as a priest with the Propaganda Fide. For unknown reasons, Fray Carlos left that organization's facility at Querétaro in 1710, and transferred to New Mexico. By 1740, he had been part of the Custody of Saint Paul for three decades. Delgado had labored primarily at Jémez, Taos, and Isleta, though he had also served terms in the El Paso and Junta de los Ríos districts. His career seems to have been unremarkable up to 1740. He had been appointed Commissary of the Inquisition for New Mexico once, but he had never held other higher offices, nor had Fray Carlos been singled out for any distinction in his service. Now, at the age of sixty-five,

Delgado would lead the most determined efforts by the Franciscans to restore the Hopi people to the Spanish fold.[20]

Despite his advanced age, in the late summer of 1742, Delgado led an expedition to the Hopi territory. Another friar, Fray Pedro Ignacio Pino, assisted him. Pino, a criollo, had only recently arrived in New Mexico and was newly ordained as a mission priest. The entrada was accompanied by three Spanish soldiers and about a dozen Puebloan auxiliaries.[21]

At the time of Delgado's expedition, the Hopi were plagued by internal turmoil, so timing might have been partly responsible for the entrada's relative success. Delgado avowed that the Hopi people had favorably received him and Pino, and, consequently, the missionaries returned to New Mexico optimistic that a future expedition would bear fruit. In addition, the expedition returned with 441 Puebloans, mostly from Tiwa clans that had fled New Mexico in the 1690s. Delgado claimed that they might have brought more back, had the expedition been better supplied and escorted by more soldiers. Nonetheless, the relocation of so many Puebloans back to the colony was a notable accomplishment.[22]

Delgado had hoped to resettle the refugee Tiwas quickly and return to the Hopi mesas to take advantage of the momentum created by the first entrada. Governor Mendoza, however, would not approve establishing these Tiwas in their former mission villages of Alameda, Pajarito, and Sandía until he received clearance from Mexico City. Therefore, the Tiwas were held first at a location known as Viní (near the Acoma and Laguna missions) and were then dispersed among several missions, with the majority of them going to Isleta and Jémez. Delgado was the one to shepherd the Tiwas through these various moves. Fray Carlos petitioned Governor Mendoza to return to the Hopi in 1743, but Mendoza, who was soon to be relieved, refused to sanction the expedition.[23]

It was not until 1745 that Delgado got his wish to again venture westward. This entrada to the Hopi was larger, as eighty Puebloan auxiliaries accompanied Delgado and two other friars: Fray José de Irigoyen and Fray Juan José Toledo. Irigoyen had been in the colony for over two decades and, as noted previously, was fluent in several Puebloan languages. Toledo, a criollo, was new to the region, having only arrived in 1743, and was relatively young (twenty-eight). Delgado did not succeed in getting the Hopi to embrace the Spanish religion anew, but he still believed that progress was being made. A few more Tiwas returned with the Spanish, and Delgado's report on the entrada was enthusiastic. Indeed, the indefatigable Franciscan wrote excitably about the potential of opening a mission at a place he called "El Gran Teguayo" (twenty to thirty leagues northwest of the Hopi settlements) for native people whom, Delgado had heard, lived there.[24]

Delgado's two expeditions to the Hopi had one concrete result for the Franciscans. Shortly after the second entrada, the Jesuits submitted a lengthy report to the viceregal office in Mexico City, noting the problems the Society of Jesus were experiencing in reducing the Hopi people. The Jesuits claimed that they did not have enough priests, that the distances from southern Arizona were too great, and that hostile Apache bands between the Jesuit missions of Pimería Alta and the Hopi province made the whole operation too risky. Indeed, the Jesuits stated that as many as six Spanish soldiers would be required for each priest during the first four years after opening the Hopi mission operation, which would make the endeavor very expensive for the government. The Jesuits did not specifically ask to be relieved of the Hopi region; however, one could easily interpret that the Society of Jesus was suggesting that if the Franciscans were making progress, why not let the Custody of Saint Paul continue its efforts? His Majesty's government did come to that conclusion. In 1746 jurisdiction over the Hopi province was returned to the Custody of Saint Paul.[25]

Meanwhile, the Franciscans were having difficulties in getting the Tiwas who were brought out earlier from the Hopi region assigned to their own mission. Delgado had baptized over one hundred of them at Isleta, but the wheels of Spanish government turned slowly. It was not until the summer of 1748 that the necessary official sanctions were gained, the land surveyed, and a fortification constructed (the government feared that the Tiwas might flee again). The new mission at Sandía (northeast of Alburquerque) was thus opened, and 350 Tiwas, apparently all that remained of the original group of over four hundred, occupied one of their former pueblo sites. Fray Juan José Hernández, a criollo who had previously worked mostly in the El Paso district, was given charge of the Sandía mission.[26]

Besides their efforts with the Hopi and the runaway Tiwas, the Franciscans also achieved some successes in the 1740s with a group of native people the friars had heretofore not dared approach: the Navajos. The primary difficulty in bringing Christianity to the Navajo people had been the fact that these natives were semi-nomadic, without a tradition of living in permanent villages as the Puebloans did. To get the Navajos into congregations, the antithesis of their way of life, was an imposing problem. Indeed, the Spanish mission system throughout the New World was never very successful in converting native people who were nomadic or semi-nomadic. Of course, that the Navajos had long been implacable foes to the Spanish further complicated Franciscan efforts to induce them into the mission operation.[27]

In 1744, between his two treks to the Hopi region, Delgado (accompanied again by Irigoyen) made an entrada to the Navajo territory. Using gifts of cloth, beads, and tobacco, Delgado claimed that he was well received by the Navajos. The seemingly tireless Fray Carlos reported that he and Irigoyen converted five thousand (no doubt an exaggeration) of these people within a short time. The following year, Delgado journeyed briefly again among the Navajos with more positive results, although the friar made no mention whether beads and tobacco were once more distributed. In his reports to Santo Evangelio and the government, Delgado noted that these entradas had not cost His Majesty's royal treasury any additional monies, and he urged that missions be established quickly among the Navajos to take advantage of the promising start created from his and Irigoyen's efforts.[28]

The news of Delgado's work among these longtime enemies of the Spanish was, of course, well received in Mexico City and Spain. The King seemed especially pleased that Delgado's accomplishments were carried out "without any assistance and without any expense to my royal treasury." The monarchy ordered that a full report and assessment be made by the viceroy, the Conde de Fuenclara, and further directed that all possible aid should be made available for the Franciscans' effort to missionize the Navajo people.[29]

The viceroy moved relatively quickly to carry out His Majesty's wishes. In June 1746, Viceroy Fuenclara ordered that four missions be installed among the Navajos under Delgado's direct leadership. Fray Carlos was to select the mission sites personally, and three other missionary priests would assist Delgado. In addition, thirty presidial soldiers were to be assigned to guard the missions and the friars and to help the Franciscans as needed. Finally, all financial costs of this campaign were to be borne by the royal treasury in Mexico City. Delgado's efforts among the Navajo, therefore, had further enhanced the Franciscan position in New Mexico.[30]

Before this seemingly well-planned and coordinated mission program was launched, however, other developments involving the Navajos altered the course charted by the viceregal government. Before Viceroy Fuenclara's instructions arrived in New Mexico, Menchero, who had been serving in various capacities in the custody, undertook his own entrada to the Navajo people. During the summer of 1746, without the assistance of any other friars (or, at least, none were mentioned), Menchero went among the Navajo with stunning results. Using gifts of tobacco and cloth, and promising good treatment, he persuaded about five hundred Navajos to congregate in a mission Menchero called La Cebolleta, a few leagues north of the mission at Laguna. In the mission history of New Mexico, this was an unprecedented success, and convincing semi-nomadics such as the Navajo to enter the mission system must have caused considerable Franciscan self-satisfaction.[31]

Over the next three years, despite the fact that the viceroy's strategy was scrapped, the Franciscans' work among the Navajos proceeded well. By 1749, another mission was in operation nearby at a site called Encinal, and six friars were working among the Navajos. Curiously, the two missionaries in charge of these new sites were relatively new, inexperienced friars. Fray Manuel Bermejo, a gachupín, had come to New Spain in 1743 and had only just arrived in New Mexico when he was given La Cebolleta. Fray Juan Sáenz (Sanz, Saanz) de Lezáun, who administered Encinal, was an hijo de provincia. Fray Juan was in his mid-forties and had been an ordained priest for over a decade, but he had only arrived in New Mexico in 1748. Three of the other four missionaries—Fray Andrés José García de la Concepción, Fray Manuel Gómez Cayuela, and Fray José López Trigo—had been in the region less than five years, although each man was in his forties. It seems that the Franciscans were employing mature friars for this delicate new mission field, but priests who had not become jaded or complacent with the evangelical process.[32]

Thus, by 1749, the Franciscan reform effort to expand the mission operation had achieved some noteworthy results. Several entradas to the Hopi mesas had created optimism that these apostates might return to the Catholic fold. Moreover, jurisdiction over the Hopi once again resided with the Custody of Saint Paul. Over four hundred Tiwas had returned to New Mexico through Delgado's efforts, and to the new mission opened for them at Sandía. Delgado and Menchero's unprecedented success with the Navajo people and the two missions at La Cebolleta and Encinal appeared to bode well for the Navajos' further conversion to Catholicism. While the Franciscans' attempts to reform the attributes and attitudes of many of New Mexico's friars had been less than fruitful, the expansion of the mission field gave reason for hope that the Custody of Saint Paul might succeed in its responsibilities to convert and to civilize the indigenous population, and, by extension, to restore itself to a prominent position in the Kingdom.

*   *   *

A primary factor concerning the mission operation that stands out during this reform period was the relatively large number of friars in the Custody of Saint Paul. The rapid increase in their numbers between 1730 and 1736, which brought their personnel levels to the highest point since the reconquest, has been noted. These levels were maintained over the following thirteen years (through 1749), as at least fourteen new friars entered the colony, while thirteen were removed from the custody's rosters. According to a 1744 report written by Menchero, an ordained missionary staffed every mission in New Mexico, and Taos, Zuñi, Pecos, and Santa Fe each had two friars.[33]

An examination of the background of the new arrivals suggests that the Franciscans were continuing to try to assign mature, more experienced friars to New Mexico. The ages of twelve of the fourteen new friars are known, and at least eight were between thirty and forty-nine years of age. Fray José Blanco was thirty-one; Fray Angel García, thirty-nine; Fray Manuel Gómez Cayuela, forty-six; Fray Agustín de Iniesta and Fray Francisco de la Concepción González, thirty-three; Fray Juan Sáenz de Lezáun and Fray Antonio Zamora, forty-five; and Fray José López Trigo, forty-three. Three others were in their twenties, and Fray Manuel José de Sopeña was over fifty.[34]

Criollos still made up the majority of new missionaries being posted to New Mexico. Of the fourteen who arrived between 1736 and 1749, only two were gachupines: Fray Manuel Bermejo and Fray Manuel Gómez Cayuela. Likewise, only two were classified as hijos de provincia: Fray Francisco de la Concepción González and Fray Juan Sáenz de Lezáun. The remaining ten were all identified as criollos.[35]

Some very experienced friars left the colony during this same period. Of the thirteen who departed, at least eight had over two decades of service in the New Mexico mission field. Fray Andrés Ceballos had twenty-three years when he exited in 1749. Fray Juan de la Cruz had labored twenty-nine years when he left in 1746. Fray Antonio Esquer departed in 1749 with twenty-five years of service. Fray José Antonio Guerrero had toiled twenty-nine years when he exited in 1743. Fray Juan Antonio Sánchez left the same year as Guerrero, but with twenty-five years experience. Fray Antonio de Miranda, with thirty-seven years in the field, was reassigned to Santiago de Tlatelolco in 1737. Fray Antonio Camargo had thirty-eight years of tenure when he, too, departed in 1737. Fray Carlos José Delgado finally retired from mission work with thirty-nine years of service in 1749. Despite the lengthy terms in the field that some Franciscans were amassing, no friars are known to have died in New Mexico during the 1736–1749 period.[36]

Perhaps the long years of service in the Kingdom helps to explain the Franciscans' failure to improve the zeal and evangelical qualities of the friars. If 1736 is taken as an approximate mid-point of Menchero and others' reform efforts, there were twenty-five friars toiling in the Santa Fe district. Their average time in the colony was about twelve years, and well over half of the missionaries had more years of service. It seems safe to assume that by the time a friar had worked in the mission field for a dozen years, he would have become fairly set in his routines, having reached his own unique modus operandi that allowed him to at least peacefully coexist with his neophytes. By then, these veteran friars probably lacked the flexibility and fervor (if they ever possessed those qualities) to respond favorably to the reform initiatives of this era.

Of course, there are usually exceptions to any rule, and certainly, Fray Carlos José Delgado was one. It was this most elderly of missionaries who expended so much effort with the Hopi and Navajo people in the 1740s. What motivated a friar of such age and length of service to suddenly undertake such extraordinary efforts is unclear. Delgado did not record much in the way of rationale. In his reports and other correspondence, Delgado alluded to his wish to see the Hopi province returned to Franciscan jurisdiction, a desire that was fulfilled. Otherwise, Delgado noted simply that the apostate Hopi and the Navajo should have the spiritual benefits of Catholicism. Never did Delgado mention the reforms launched by Menchero or others. Nor did Fray José write zealously of perhaps receiving a martyr's crown. One is left simply with the impression that Delgado was a missionary who strove to fully realize his evangelical calling in the twilight of his career.[37]

Two unique developments concerning the office of custos also occurred during this period. The first anomaly concerned the number of different friars who held the office. In addition to the three Franciscans noted earlier in this chapter, Menchero, Fray Andrés Varo, Fray Juan José Pérez de Mirabal, and Fray Juan Carlos de Oronzoro also wore the mantle of custos. Prior to the 1730s, the prelate post seemed to pass back and forth among a smaller number of individuals. While there exists no official Franciscan explanation for this trend, perhaps it was a natural outgrowth of the reform era. As the Franciscans grappled with the problems manifested among many missionaries, the Order searched for a prelate who might prove equal to the task of reinvigorating the Custody of Saint Paul.

A second surprising and baffling development was that several of the New Mexico prelates were based in the El Paso district. This seems difficult to reconcile with the apparent focus of the Franciscans during the 1730s–1740s era. Why not ensure that the custos was close to the greatest concentration of friars and missions? The extant documents are mute in offering any rationale for locating the custos in El Paso. Perhaps it was to narrow the distance in Franciscan communications between Mexico City and New Mexico. With the difficulties previously noted regarding the Junta de los Ríos missions, placing the custos closer to that region might have been thought beneficial. It should also be recalled that Bishop Crespo's appointee, Santiago Roybal, was in El Paso during much of the 1730s. Maybe the Franciscans wanted the custos there to keep watch over that secular clergyman. More likely, the custos was in El Paso as a shield against further inroads from the See of Durango. The result, however, was that most missions and friars were remote from the custos's management and authority. A vice-custos was in the northern district, usually in Santa Fe, but he had to attend to his own religious responsibilities. Despite the fact that reform policies were developed and ordered, the typical friar remained immune from corrective measures and coercion. With many mission priests avoiding onerous or difficult duties, such as learning their neophytes' language, the rate of conversion of the Puebloan people proceeded at a snail's pace.

Indeed, one might inquire as to how committed the Franciscan hierarchy in Mexico City was to ameliorating the problems in New Mexico. While Commissary General González's intentions seem clear, as did Menchero's and those of the different prelates of the Custody of Saint Paul, the same degree of interest by Santo Evangelio appears lacking. The provincial documents between 1737 (the date of Bishop Elizacoechea's visita) and 1749 hardly mention New Mexico. Many of the perplexing problems of the Kingdom never rippled the waters of the issues with which the Franciscan province was concerned. Why was more care not taken to see that missionaries were not transferred so often? Why was appropriate language instruction not offered to prospective missionaries? Why was the custos in El Paso when perhaps that official might have been more effective in Santa Fe? All of these issues were properly the domain of Santo Evangelio, but the answers are not to be found among that province's documents. Santo Evangelio was a large and territorially vast Franciscan province. The New Mexico mission field was but one distant responsibility among many.

*   *   *

Although it was not obvious at the time, when the elderly Delgado left New Mexico in 1749 for the comparably less arduous duties of the Order's *hospicio* (alms house/orphanage) of Santa Barbara del Pueblo de Tlatelolco, the reform era in New Mexico had essentially run its course. The results of this period clearly were mixed. On the one hand, the many attempts to improve the qualities and skills of the mission priests had fallen well short of the ideal. Thus, the Franciscans remained vulnerable to criticism and censure from the government. That would prove to be their Achilles heel. On the other hand, their success in opening missions for the Navajo people and the renewed optimism that the Hopi might return to the fold represented considerable achievements. Unfortunately for the Custody of Saint Paul, the Franciscans' work with the Navajo people (discussed later) was soon undone, and the friars were not to return to the Hopi mesas for another quarter century. The last effort by the Franciscans in New Mexico to carry out their assignments and to solidify their position in the Kingdom had come to naught. Their shortcomings were soon to provide a springboard for the local civil authority to further weaken the power and position of the Franciscans in New Mexico.

CHAPTER 10

The Franciscans Overwhelmed

T HROUGHOUT most of the 1730s, while the friars were caught up in their controversies with the bishopric of Durango and trying to reform the custody's mission operation, the Franciscans had experienced a time of relative calm in their relations with New Mexico's government officials. As noted previously, the Franciscans and Governor Cruzat enjoyed a rather peaceful relationship, far removed from the bitterness characteristic of Bustamante's administration in the 1720s. Cruzat's term ended in 1736 but, as no regular appointee was available, Mexico City dispatched to Santa Fe another ad interim executive, Don Enrique de Olavide y Michelena. Olavide served barely two years with no significant eruptions between church and state. Thus, for almost eight years, longer than any other period since the reconquest, the missionaries and the governors avoided any notable confrontations.

This time of peace proved to be only a calm before the tempest. Beginning with the administration of Don Gaspar Domingo de Mendoza (1739–1743), the tranquillity between church and state rapidly broke down. Conflict followed conflict between Franciscans and local officials throughout the next decade, and, by 1750, the Kingdom was locked in the most severe period of internal strife since before "the year eighty." The Franciscans were angered by what they perceived to be a lack of support from civil officials during the friars' efforts to expand the mission operation to the Hopi and Navajo people. On the other hand, the governors who served in this period were under growing pressures from external forces, namely Comanche raiders and French traders. Consequently, these officials resented any interference and criticism from the missionaries that might weaken their executive authority over the colony. The struggle between the Franciscans and the governors climaxed in the early 1750s, and by 1760 civil authority in New Mexico clearly reigned supreme.

* * *

Don Gaspar Domingo de Mendoza arrived in Santa Fe to receive the governor's baton in January 1739. Within a very short period, Mendoza was forced to contend with the threats posed by Comanche attackers and adventurous French traders. While Apache pressure ebbed in the 1730s as noted previously, by the end of 1739 the Comanche people began to assert their power on New Mexico's eastern and northern boundaries.

Though these early raids paled in comparison to those with which Mendoza's successors had to contend, Comanche pressure steadily increased throughout his term in office. By 1740, the Comanche people realized the fortuitous position they enjoyed over trade routes on the southern Great Plains. Strategically placed now between the Spanish and French, the Comanches moved to protect their hard-won gains. In addition, the Comanches' predisposition to engage in vendettas was fanned by several episodes in which they believed they had been cheated in trade exchanges with Puebloans and Spaniards. Supplied by the French and sometimes in concert with the Ute people, the Comanches effectively began to harass the peripheral areas of the colony.[1]

That French interests were becoming a factor in the area and a boost to Comanche strength was made abundantly clear during Mendoza's first year in office. Before 1739 was over, the Mallet brothers (Pierre and Paul) led a group of other traders from the northeast into New Mexico. Governor Mendoza had them detained for nearly a year but eventually allowed them to leave, save for two who elected to remain in the Kingdom. Many New Mexicans, including Santa Fe's vicar and ecclesiastical judge, Don Santiago Roybal, appreciated French trade goods. Roybal sent along an order for more goods with the Mallets when they departed. French traders would be back.[2]

One scholar of this period has suggested that Mendoza was a relatively inactive executive for New Mexico, which certainly was the crux of the Franciscans' controversies with Don Gaspar. As noted in the previous chapter, Delgado made his encouraging entrada to the Hopi in 1742. Fray Carlos complained that he might have returned with more Puebloan exiles had the governor better supported the expedition. In addition, Delgado wanted to resettle these Tiwas in their former pueblos quickly and return to the Hopi mesas to take advantage of the momentum created by his initial visit. Mendoza, it will be recalled, refused to allow the Tiwas to be resettled in their former lands (now occupied by Spanish settlers), pending a decision from Mexico City or Spain. As it happened, the Tiwa refugees would not receive a permanent home (Sandía) for more than five years. Furthermore, the governor would not sanction another entrada to the Hopi during his administration. Toward the end of Mendoza's administration, Franciscans were complaining strongly to Mexico City officials that the governor "does not assist us with anything."[3]

In fairness to Governor Mendoza, several points should be considered concerning the Franciscans' charges. With New Mexico coming under ever-growing pressure from the Comanche people, to have denuded the Santa Fe presidio to support Franciscan entradas on the far western frontier would have invited disaster. With Comanche traders frequently showing up at missions and Spanish settlements, news of a reduction in the garrison at Santa Fe would be disseminated quickly among hostile native bands. As to placing the returned Tiwas on their former lands, that decision necessitated viceregal authority (if not Madrid's), especially since those lands now belonged to others. Surely the Franciscans knew that. Finally, while a reduction of the Hopi would have been a significant achievement for his administration, Mendoza was to be relieved soon, probably before any definitive success with the Hopi could be realized. Thus, Franciscan interests and goals in this instance diverged from those of the governor's and gave rise to the friars' complaints.[4]

One other event in church and state relations during the Mendoza term in office merits consideration. During the winter of 1742–1743, Luís María Mora (Moreau), one of the French traders who had remained behind when the Mallet group departed, was accused of sorcery and fomenting rebellion among the Puebloans of Tesuque. Mora was found guilty of these charges and condemned to death. The entire matter was handled by the civil government, but prior to Mora's execution the Franciscans requested a stay to allow for an Inquisition investigation into the affair. Mendoza agreed to postpone Mora's death sentence. It was the subsequent Holy Office inquiry, however, which eventually led to the punishment meted out to the missionaries Concepción and Esquer (see chapter 9). Concepción specifically was implicated for being too lenient while serving as the mission father at Tesuque in suppressing Mora's activities. Though Mora was put to death shortly thereafter, the matter with Concepción was not finished, as we shall see.[5]

In 1743, Don Joaquín Codallos y Rabal replaced Mendoza as governor of New Mexico. Codallos was a veteran of the Spanish army, and he held the rank of sergeant major at the time of his appointment. The Codallos administration, like that of Mendoza, was forced to concentrate on defensive issues. Comanche and Ute attacks on the colony's settlements reached a crescendo during his term. Major assaults were made on Pecos and Galisteo in 1746 and 1748. Indeed, Codallos was obliged to garrison a detachment of the presidial forces at Pecos. In the north, a series of raids were launched against Pueblo, Spanish, and some of the newer genízaro settlements. A 1746 Comanche assault on Abiquiu resulted in four deaths and the kidnapping of twenty-three women and children. The threat to their lives became so oppressive and continuous that in March 1748 the citizens of Abiquiu, Ojo Caliente, and Quemada petitioned Codallos to allow them to temporarily evacuate their communities. Codallos reluctantly agreed, though it must have seemed as if Spanish control in New

Mexico was being rolled back. A smallpox epidemic in 1748 further added to the misery in the Kingdom.[6]

Behind the escalating Comanche pressure, a French presence seemed to lurk. A lone French deserter was found in the area and brought before Codallos in 1744. More ominously, in the last year of Codallos's term in office (1748), the governor was informed that a large party of Frenchmen was among the Comanches trading weapons.[7]

As to his relationship with the Franciscans, Codallos seemed to have begun on a fairly good note. Delgado wrote that Codallos had been supportive of the Franciscan entradas to the Hopi and Navajo in 1744. Indeed, when Navajo leaders asked Delgado about meeting the Spanish leader, Codallos readily agreed with Delgado's request to do so. Delgado later reported that Codallos fully cooperated in the matter, treated the Navajos graciously, and promised to protect them, as they were now vassals of His Majesty.[8]

The interactions between Governor Codallos and the missionaries, however, quickly soured. By June 1744, Codallos had written to the Franciscan Commissary General of New Spain, Fray Pedro Navarrete, complaining about the missionary program and the behavior of missionaries. He claimed that three missions—Zuñi, Pecos, and Galisteo—were currently without resident friars. Santa Clara had gone six months without the services of a missionary before the recent installation of one. The governor asserted that friars generally were absent too frequently from their posts. Codallos further believed Santa Fe did not have enough priests (at that time there were two), and should be assigned one more. He specifically condemned the attributes of two friars to Navarrete. Puebloans had cited numerous abuses by Fray Juan José Hernández in each of the four different missions in which he had served. The other friar, Fray Francisco Benito Cayetano de Otero, Codallos derisively dismissed as "useless for he does not like the Indians of any Pueblo."[9]

The enmity between the Franciscans and Codallos was further evidenced in yet another controversy involving the unfortunate Fray Francisco de la Concepción González. Concepción, an hijo de provincia, had come to New Spain from his birthplace of Burgos. In 1727, he entered the Order at age twenty-one at San Francisco de México. Nothing is known of his career until 1739 when he arrived in New Mexico. As already noted, he was seen as having a connection to the Mora incident at his mission of Tesuque, and, along with Father Antonio Esquer, was whipped under orders of the custos. Shortly after receiving this punishment, Concepción was ordered to Mexico City to be questioned by Santo Evangelio leaders. Fray Francisco was deemed by them fit to serve in the mission field, and he made the long journey back to New Mexico.[10]

Upon Concepción's return, however, the hapless friar soon was embroiled in another controversy, now with Governor Codallos. The governor charged the friar with incompetence and banished Concepción, under military escort, to the El Paso district. The Franciscans assigned him to the even more remote Junta de los Ríos district, pending an investigation. That Franciscan inquiry revealed a tangled web of issues that had been festering since shortly after Fray Francisco first appeared in New Mexico. The main problem was that Concepción had made some powerful enemies among local civil authorities. The missionary had first made a foe of Don Antonio Guerrero, then alcalde mayor for Taos. Don Antonio blamed Concepción for unstated reasons in the death of a good friend who had perished of dropsy. Guerrero was also a close friend of Mendoza's lieutenant governor, Don Bernardo de Bustamante. Don Bernardo was no friend of the Franciscans, as seen in the context of Bishop Crespo's visita. Guerrero, Bustamante, and Mendoza, according to the Franciscan investigation, conspired to "ruin" Concepción by falsely implicating him in the Mora incident.

The matter became more complex with Codallos's involvement. When he arrived in New Mexico to replace Mendoza, Codallos became betrothed to Mendoza's daughter. Such a relationship was likely to influence Mendoza's residencia, and Concepción injudiciously attempted to intervene in the upcoming wedding. According to Franciscan documents, Concepción earned Codallos's hatred for that. Fray Francisco still did not know when to leave well enough alone. He next complained loudly that Codallos used the native people of Tesuque as unpaid labor for his own purposes, and Concepción attempted to send a letter to the viceroy stating as much. To extract revenge and unburden himself of a troublesome priest, Codallos solicited false testimony regarding Concepción in order to have him removed. The Order's investigation exonerated Concepción of all charges, but for the duration of Codallos's term in office, the friar remained at Junta de los Ríos, out of the governor's sight.[11]

The Franciscans also made their share of complaints to Mexico City concerning Codallos. In 1748, Menchero was organizing an entrada to the Gila Apaches, hoping to maintain the momentum in the western region that the Franciscans had built with their overtures to the Hopi and Navajo peoples. Menchero reported to the Franciscan Vice-Commissary General of New Spain that he was forced to delay the expedition indefinitely because Codallos refused to release any horses or supplies for the entrada. That Comanche raids must have harried Codallos and the presidial force especially at that time did not seem to register with Menchero. The friar also reported that Codallos was less than helpful in opening the mission for the Tiwa at Sandía, as noted previously. Indeed, even after the King's cédula arrived in Santa Fe ordering that the new mission be erected, Menchero had to press Codallos several more times to get the governor to initiate the process of surveying boundaries and preparing the mission grounds.[12]

As to Codallos's abilities as governor of New Mexico, one rather peculiar event stands out early in his administration. In February 1745, Codallos wrote to Viceroy Conde de Fuenclara that he had uncovered documents in the local archives that placed New Mexico's boundary with Nueva Vizcaya much further south than was currently agreed. In fact, according to Codallos, the real boundary was the Río Nombre de Dios (a.k.a. Río Sacramento), just a few leagues north of the villa of Chihuahua (about forty-five leagues south of the accepted boundary). Codallos asked that this boundary change be officially recognized by the viceroy, claiming it would improve the defenses of New Mexico and enhance livestock production for those Spaniards living between El Paso and Chihuahua (without stating how). No governor, at least since the reconquest, had made a similar petition, and no reply from the viceregal offices has been uncovered. There is no further evidence that Codallos even pursued the matter.[13]

The Franciscans also received a reminder during this period of their reduced autonomy regarding the bishopric of Durango. In 1747, a new bishop, Don Pedro Anselmo Sánchez de Tagle, appointed a church notary for Santa Fe. Bishop Sánchez selected Felipe de Tafoya, a layman with extensive civil service experience in New Mexico. In addition to his notarial duties, Tafoya was instructed to see that the friars strictly adhered to the diocese's arancel. There is no record of any Franciscan protests regarding this development, which ten years earlier would have generated a blizzard of protestations.[14]

Governor Codallos was to have ended his tenure in office in 1748, but the man chosen by the royal government to replace him, Don Francisco de la Rocha, relinquished his appointment at the last moment, citing poor health and advancing age. Codallos remained as governor for almost another year before the commander of the cavalry at the Santa Fe presidio, Captain Don Tomás Vélez Cachupín, took over the reins of civil authority as ad interim governor. Though not a regular appointee, a status that often fostered benign interactions between governors and missionaries, church and state in New Mexico became locked in a decisive conflict during Vélez Cachupín's administration.[15]

*   *   *

In early January 1749 the veteran missionary and yet again custos, Fray Andrés Varo, was finishing an *informe* (report) on the state of the mission operation in the Custody of Saint Paul for Viceroy Conde de Revillagigedo (the elder, 1746–1755). The report, ordered in 1747, was the first in-depth Franciscan account of the New Mexico missions in almost thirty years. While the Franciscans were not completely satisfied with mission affairs, recent years had brought some successes—the Delgado entradas to the Hopi, relocation of Tiwa refugees at Sandía, and the two new missions among the Navajo. Thus, Varo must have worked on his report with a certain degree of pleasure. As previously established, Fray Andrés had been a stalwart and assertive spokesman for the New Mexico missionaries for two decades.[16]

The initial portion of the informe related briefly the number of missions and their grouping into the three districts of Santa Fe, El Paso, and Junta de los Ríos. Varo then described the physical environment of the region and its agricultural and livestock capacities. The local economy, he noted, suffered from a shortage of currency, and exchange was usually based on barter. Around Santa Fe, though, the custos claimed that the piñon nut was sometimes employed as a medium of exchange. The most onerous aspect of life in New Mexico, Varo pointed out, was the constant threat posed by hostile native raiders.

The royal treasury financially supported the missions, Varo thankfully acknowledged, with 330 pesos allotted per year for each ordained friar and 230 pesos per lay brother. At that time in the Custody of Saint Paul, the government supported thirty-six missionaries and one lay brother. Four additional friars were in the custody at the expense of the viceroy, explicitly assigned to the new Navajo missions. The Franciscans also received some compensation, usually in goods, from the Spanish population for religious services; Pueblans and Navajos in missions were exempt from these fees. Varo admitted, though, that the Pueblans usually provided "a little corn, wheat and beans" to help sustain their respective resident priest. The custos further admitted that some friars did, on occasion, trade with non-mission natives, but most often barter was used for slaves held by the Comanches, Utes, or Apaches. Extra produce from the missions was stored and used in exchange for these captives or was distributed among the Kingdom's poor, of which, Varo regretted, the colony had too many.

Custos Varo then moved on to a more detailed description of each mission and a census of the population at each. The census figures offered by Varo were clearly based only on estimates and are thought to be generally too high. According to Varo, every mission had at least one priest except for Pecos and Galisteo, which were served by the same friar; two Franciscans were assigned to Santa Fe. Missionaries posted to Alburquerque, Isleta, and Jémez were at the moment detailed to assist with the new Navajo missions, as were Menchero and four other friars. In all, eight Franciscans were serving with the Navajo. Five friars were assigned to El Paso and four to the Junta de los Ríos, although only one was in the latter district at this time, as flooding had forced the other missions to be temporarily abandoned. Another friar was ill and was recuperating away from New Mexico.

As to needs of the custody, Varo noted that additional friars would be helpful, especially to stabilize the missions at Junta de los Ríos. He also reported that a presidio located closer to the Junta de los Ríos missions would provide much-needed security. Hostile native people frequently raided that region, and the presidio at El Paso was simply too far away to deter those assaults. Otherwise, the custos was content with the state of the mission program.

Any self-satisfaction enjoyed by Varo and the other Franciscans in New Mexico soon evaporated during the Vélez Cachupín administration, which began in the early spring of 1749. Described by one historian as "young, full of ambition and not a little impetuous," Vélez Cachupín had only recently arrived in New Mexico to command the cavalry at Santa Fe. Previously, he had served as a cadet in a regular army battalion in Havaña. He apparently came to the attention of the Conde de Revillagigedo and was for a time part of the viceroy's household. The rapid leap to holding a governor's baton must have been a heady experience for the young officer.[17]

The governor inherited a territory under considerable duress, primarily from Comanche raiders. During the first two years of his administration, these assaults reached terrifying levels for the Spanish and Puebloans, especially at Pecos and Galisteo. Vélez Cachupín, to his credit, brought peace to the region to a significant extent by the end of his first administration (1754). First, he took a strong stance against French traders in the region. Those who appeared in 1750 and 1752 were arrested, had their goods confiscated, and were dispatched to Mexico City to be dealt with by officials there. To compensate the Comanches for any lost French trade and to foster their dependency, the governor increased Spanish trade contacts with them. Vélez Cachupín saw that the Comanches were treated fairly, and he bestowed courtesies and honors on those who kept the peace. On the other hand, the governor pursued unrelenting war against native people who assaulted the Kingdom. In November 1751, he achieved a significant victory over the Comanches that led shortly thereafter to a period of relative harmony between the two sides. Vélez Cachupín also negotiated a peace treaty with the Ute people during his term in office.[18]

Governor Vélez Cachupín could be uncompromising and domineering in his relationship with the region's Spanish population. In November 1749, at the high point of the Comanche threat to New Mexico, the citizens of Chama (in the northern area of New Mexico) petitioned Vélez Cachupín to be allowed to temporarily abandon their settlement. It will be recalled that Governor Codallos had allowed similarly threatened citizens to flee their communities. Vélez Cachupín did not. He sternly denied their requests and promised that anyone who disobeyed the order would forfeit all property and be sentenced to a four-year enlistment in a presidial force.[19]

In a like manner, the new governor set the pattern early on for his relationship with the Franciscans. No sooner was he installed in office in April than Vélez Cachupín wrote Custos Varo, in an overbearing tone, demanding that the custos prepare a full report on the mission program. Moreover, until the report was delivered, Vélez Cachupín declared he would be unable to certify the release of the annual Franciscan alms from the treasury. Vélez Cachupín had probably been ordered to get the report in his instructions from the viceroy, or had discovered the order among the documents Codallos turned over to him. The matter was quickly resolved, as noted above, since Varo had already finished the report, but the affair foreshadowed the type of administration Governor Vélez Cachupín was to follow in his relationship with the Franciscans.[20]

The next serious blow to the Franciscans, however, came not from the new governor but from an official somewhat shrouded in mystery: Don Antonio de Ornedal y Maza. Ornedal arrived in New Mexico in April 1749, bearing Vélez Cachupín's ad interim appointment. Ornedal was in New Mexico officially for two reasons: to serve as the residencia judge for Governor Codallos and as visitador for presidios in Nueva Vizcaya and New Mexico. Like Vélez Cachupín, Ornedal was part of the Viceroy Conde de Revillagigedo's extended household, and the two men probably knew each other. He remained in New Mexico into late July carrying out his duties. Nowhere in his written official duties was he asked to examine the operations of the Custody of Saint Paul, but from his own initiative, at the behest of Vélez Cachupín, or on secret instructions from the Conde, Ornedal composed a stinging report on the condition of New Mexico's missionary effort.[21]

Much of what Ornedal wrote to the Conde was not new. He repeated the earlier criticism that the friars were absent from their missions too often, and, therefore, neglected their spiritual duties to the Puebloans. Ornedal reiterated the complaint that the Franciscans were neither learning native languages nor teaching their neophytes Spanish. Throughout the entire Kingdom, Ornedal claimed, only three missionaries were fluent in the Puebloans' languages. Consequently, no progress had been made since the reconquest in civilizing or Christianizing the Kingdom's native population. If the friars were not moved so frequently they might master these languages, but Ornedal claimed the Franciscans ignored the governor's just rights under the Patronato Real to determine friar assignments that might promote longevity!

Ornedal also charged that the Franciscans regularly exploited their mission charges. Priests extorted grain and livestock from the Puebloans and forced them to labor for their resident friars without any compensation. Even worse, Ornedal reported, the missionaries often engaged in prohibited trade, especially with enemies such as the Comanches, for the friars' own profit.

Ornedal found much to condemn even with the Franciscans' most recent achievement, the two Navajo missions. He claimed that the Franciscans were not providing enough attention to this effort, and, specifically, that not enough friars were toiling with these recent converts. Indeed, the four friars recently billeted to New Mexico solely to work with the Navajos, he alleged, had not yet been placed in these new mission sites, which directly contradicted Varo's report.

But at the heart of the missions' shortcomings were the friars' defects as evangelicals. These were not zealous, self-sacrificing priests. Most of them, Ornedal wrote, were too timid for the rigors and dangers of a frontier environment. Furthermore, it was not the best friars who were sent to New Mexico, but the dregs of the Order. Or, as he bluntly put it, "the major portion of the Religious that are found in this custody are those that have not been able to adhere to the Rules of the Province [Santo Evangelio] and they are given this [assignment] as punishment." Ornedal claimed that those friars who amended their behavior were reassigned, but those who did not remained as missionaries in New Mexico.[22]

Ornedal offered the viceroy some proposals to improve the situation in the Kingdom, most of which had been brought up previously by others. He noted that many missions in the Santa Fe and El Paso districts were in close proximity to one another and could be consolidated under a single missionary. He believed the same could be done to those in the Junta de los Ríos, although Ornedal admitted he had not seen those missions. In the predominantly Spanish communities of Santa Fe and El Paso, he argued, secular clergy should replace the Franciscans. These alterations, of course, would save His Majesty's government money.[23]

In the juxtaposition of Ornedal's report with Varo's just completed informe, two wildly different descriptions of the New Mexico mission operation were presented. One is left to consider their relative veracity. It seems unlikely that Ornedal visited each mission, although he infers that he did (save for those at Junta de los Ríos). His report lacks the specificity and the mission-by-mission minutiae so often seen in previous written assessments by Franciscans, bishops, governors, and other Spanish officials. The Franciscans later charged that Ornedal visited no missions, though that, too, seems farfetched considering the modes of travel in the region and the proximity of missions to Santa Fe, Alburquerque, El Paso, and other Spanish communities and presidios. The reliability of each report might be better judged from what each author omitted. Varo overlooked the language problem, yet numerous instances have been noted that the Franciscans themselves were acutely aware of their deficiencies. On the other hand, Ornedal failed to give the Franciscans any credit for their recent successes in expanding the mission field by opening Sandía for Tiwa people brought from the Hopi region and the two Navajo missions.[24]

The authors of the two reports obviously had their own agendas. Varo's motives are easy to ascertain. Fray Andrés wanted the Franciscan operation to be seen in the best possible light, especially in view of their recent evangelical achievements, the return of the Hopi territory from the Jesuits' jurisdiction, and their feeble but ongoing dispute over diocesan control. In addition, this was the Franciscans' first major self-evaluation of New Mexico's missions in thirty years. Varo would want to accentuate the positive.

Ornedal's aims are not so clear. In his report, he avowed his friendship to the Franciscans and swore that he bore them no ill will. That he acted outside of his official duties, however, is obvious. Was this going over and above the call of duty simply to help the Franciscans fulfill their evangelical duties? Was Ornedal hoping to impress the Conde and win another post for himself? Was he acting in league with Vélez Cachupín, perhaps based on their previous friendship from their time spent together within the viceroy's family? Had he been verbally or otherwise instructed by Revillagigedo to take a more expansive look at a region long known for contentious church and state relations? Any and all of these are real possibilities, but all lack documentation.[25]

Whatever the motivations and relative merits surrounding each report, that both would arrive in Mexico City at about the same time, if not in the same official pouch, was potentially embarrassing and damaging to the Franciscan position in New Mexico. After three decades without the Franciscans providing such an assessment of their mission operation, that Ornedal's informe so contradicted Varo's weakened the custody's report. Furthermore, Ornedal's report reinforced all of the negative charges that the Franciscans had been trying to disprove, especially through the custody's renewed effort to expand the mission field. The Franciscans were outraged and embittered by the Ornedal report, but their reaction placed them on a collision course with New Mexico's civil authority.

* * *

From the Franciscan perspective, the year 1750 proved to be the darkest of times since the Pueblo uprising in 1696. The hard-won effort to expand the missions to the Navajo people abruptly and irreversibly collapsed. Further west, the Jesuits appeared among the Hopi and for a brief moment, rekindled Franciscan fears that their jurisdiction over that area would be once again taken from them. The controversies ignited by the Ornedal report led to divisions and conflicts within the ranks of the friars. Finally, Governor Vélez Cachupín subdued the Franciscans to a degree greater than any previous New Mexico official could ever have hoped.

In April 1750, the Navajos residing in the new missions at Encinal and La Cebolleta suddenly expelled the resident friars and began to leave the area. Trouble had been brewing at these missions for at least a year. Vélez Cachupín had been forced to curtail supplies and reduce the number of Spanish soldiers for these missions to respond to Comanche pressures on the eastern borders. In addition, the governor had accidentally wounded a Navajo with an arrow during a visit the previous October, frightening many of these neophytes. Navajo relations with their Puebloan neighbors at Acoma and Laguna were strained by disputes over water. While there are no written complaints or re-criminations, that the Franciscans had assigned inexperienced missionaries (as noted previously) to be in charge of each Navajo mission perhaps contributed to the failure.[26]

The main problem, however, was the Navajo people's traditional mobile lifestyle. The previous year they came close to bolting from the missions and were only persuaded to remain with difficulty. From that time onward, Navajo leaders repeatedly told friars and civil officials that adult Navajos would never be domiciled in a permanent settlement, nor would they be Christians. They did not mind their children being sprinkled with water as it might make them somewhat more powerful, but mature Navajos had little use for the Christian way. Indeed, the Navajos admitted that the primary reason they had tried mission life was Menchero's original promise of gifts.[27]

Despite their pleas, the Franciscans were unable to convince the Navajos to return to the missions. They simply refused to countenance Spanish-style living arrangements and Christianity. The Navajos said that friars might stay with them in their wanderings, but they would only tolerate the priests' presence, nothing more. Thus, the reduction of the Navajo people, begun with such optimism by Delgado six years earlier, was over, and with it one of the few Franciscan achievements since the reconquest.[28]

During the same year, the Franciscans learned that the Jesuit missionary Jacobo Sedelmayr had recently made two entradas into the region of the Gila-Colorado rivers. Sedelmayr's goal was to promote the expansion of Jesuit missions toward California, but his travels brought him into territory considered to be part of the Hopi province. Even though the Jesuit priest did not make contact with the Hopi people, the Franciscans were alarmed by Sedelmayr's travels. The following year a major rebellion by the Pima permanently halted all Jesuit expansionist intentions in the area, though the Franciscans would not realize that result until much later. For the moment, the custody worried that Sedelmayr's entradas would open anew the jurisdictional question concerning the Hopi people.[29]

Despite these seemingly ominous developments, it was the Ornedal informe that consumed Franciscan attention throughout the year. Friars in the Santa Fe district authored several lengthy Franciscan rebuttals. Typically, these refuted categorically all of Ornedal's negative criticism while at the same time offering counterallegations of abuse and misuse of power by Vélez Cachupín and the alcaldes mayores. According to the Franciscans, Puebloans were being forced by those officials to work without pay for the Spaniards' private interests. What the Puebloans produced in the way of woven goods or agricultural and live-stock commodities was taken without fair compensation. The Kingdom was not being defended adequately, and His Majesty's soldiers were ill-equipped and harshly treated. The governor and alcaldes mayores were profiteering from their own illegal trade with the colony's enemies. A rebuttal drafted by Varo was judged by Santo Evangelio officials to be so incendiary that it was suppressed and was only given to another viceroy in an abridged form ten years later. Among other things, Varo described Vélez Cachupín as "childish . . . without maturity, knowledge, or experience." Varo also claimed that governors often amassed 50,000 to 60,000 pesos during a term in office from the illegal slave trade and by cheating Spanish soldiers. Even the venerable and ancient Fray Carlos José Delgado wrote from his retirement at the Franciscan hospicio in Tlatelolco. He avowed that the colony's officials "hated and persecuted the fri-ars." He added that these same officials, including the various governors, rou-tinely sexually assaulted Puebloan women sent to work in the Spaniards' houses. When the Franciscans interceded on behalf of native people, the friars were charged with disturbing the region's peace and were often expelled from the territory. Delgado cited the punishments meted out to Concepción as an example of wha might befall a missionary who ran afoul of a governor or an al-calde mayor.[30]

The most detailed and influential response to Ornedal's charges came from the provincial of Santo Evangelio, Fray José Ximeno, and was directed to the Viceroy Conde de Revillagigedo. The provincial began by questioning whether Ornedal even had the right to comment on the New Mexico missions in light of his stipulated official duties as residencia judge and inspector of presidios. Xi-meno gave little credence to Ornedal's claim that he had been moved to report by "the loud and constant complaints" made by Puebloans. Which Puebloan groups? What were the aggrieved natives' names? Usually an informe such as Ornedal's would give specific evidence.[31]

Ximeno then made a point-by-point rebuttal of Ornedal's charges. Yes, mis-sionaries were sometimes away from their posts, but other responsibilities, such as serving as a chaplain on an army campaign, necessitated their absences. As to Ornedal finding no written grammars of Puebloan languages, that did not prove friars were not fluent. In fact, how could Ornedal have understood the al-leged Puebloan complaints if native people had not been taught to speak Span-ish? In the matter of ignoring the governor's rights as vice-patron to determine Franciscan assignments, the head of Santo Evangelio denied that a New Mex-ico governor had such prerogatives.

Fray José next considered the accusations concerning friars exploiting Puebloan workers and engaging in trade for their own benefit. To the first, Ximeno answered yes, missionaries did have their neophytes working at various tasks. Labor skills, however, were part and parcel of becoming a civilized Spanish citizen. Likewise, it was true that mission priests sometimes involved themselves in trade. The provincial thought that the major reason for their commercial activity was that the custody's yearly royal allowance was often in arrears, thus leaving missions destitute.

As to the reorganization of New Mexico's missions, Ximeno flatly rejected those suggestions. He did not believe that the citizens of El Paso and Santa Fe were of such number and wealth that they could support secular clergy. Ornedal's redrawing of mission assignments showed, Ximeno wrote, that the visitador must not have visited these missions. Otherwise, Ornedal would have known how difficult the terrain was and that routes between missions were not safe. The provincial reminded Conde de Revillagigedo that mission priests did not work regular hours. A friar might be needed at any time, often with little notice, day or night. If a missionary had to travel three, four, or more leagues to provide a sacrament, some Christian rites might never be administered or be offered too late.

Ximeno closed with some speculations as to what could have motivated Ornedal to write such things against the Franciscan missionaries in New Mexico. The provincial finally admitted he did not have the answers, but he wanted the viceroy to know "that this [Ornedal's] report is nothing more than a hypocritical manifestation of some hidden and blind passion which it served like a blind man's guide, bringing it, stumbling along, without warning of the stones over which it is falling."[32]

That Franciscans would dispute Ornedal's findings comes as no surprise, and the Order must have known their protests were expected. To add weight to their refutations, between July and November 1750, the Franciscans in New Mexico collected affidavits from local citizens attesting to the missionaries' exemplary behavior and attention to their responsibilities. In all, the current assistant governor and captain general of Nueva Vizcaya, former alcaldes mayores of New Mexico, and other influential citizens of the Kingdom made thirteen testimonials. According to these witnesses, the friars were diligent in carrying out their responsibilities to the Puebloans; the priests did not engage in trade for their personal advantage; and many of the Puebloans were fluent in Spanish because of the missionaries' teachings. None of these men addressed the issue of whether friars were fluent in Puebloan languages, although Don Antonio de Ulibarrí volunteered that Puebloan languages were diverse and difficult to master. Surprisingly, and perhaps giving credence to these statements, two of the witnesses—Don Ramón García Jurado and Captain Bernabé Baca (Vaca)—had clashed with the Franciscans during their time in local government.[33]

Support for the custody from individuals such as these was potentially the most effective response the friars could marshal to Ornedal's charges. While some of these men who testified might have viewed this episode as an opportunity to get back at their own political enemies, or, through some convoluted process, to again attain government posts, most were too advanced in years to hope for the latter. Three of the thirteen currently held positions: Don Francisco Guerrero and Gerónimo Jaramilla were part of the Santa Fe presidial garrison, and Don Alonso de Gastessi was the assistant governor and captain general for Nueva Vizcaya.[34]

At this point, Governor Vélez Cachupín did the unexpected and unprecedented: he effectively ended the controversy. First, Vélez Cachupín moved to unify the local government's posture in the affair. No current alcalde mayor or other civil officer was permitted to provide testimonials either for, or, more importantly, against Ornedal's informe. In addition, no New Mexico official was to attest to or certify any Franciscan reports. By implication, only Vélez Cachupín's name could legitimize Franciscan reports leaving the Kingdom. Any deviation from these instructions by an official could result in a 200-peso fine and loss of position. Furthermore, to put a stop to the custody's criticism of the local government, Vélez Cachupín directed that Franciscan mail could not leave the Kingdom, except for correspondence pertaining to the Inquisition, without the governor's approval. In this manner, Vélez Cachupín silenced the Franciscans, something no governor had ever been able to do, without challenging the Holy Office. Astonishingly, he made it work.[35]

What motivated Vélez Cachupín's stance against the Franciscans is unclear. There are no written statements that are clearly anti-religious, or, for that matter, anti-Franciscan, except in his assessments of the friars' evangelical performance. While he seems to have been less generous than many governors, Vélez Cachupín bought new vestments, linens, and an altar screen for the mission church at San Juan. Certainly, New Mexico was under dire threat from Comanche raids in 1750. The governor must have viewed the Ornedal matter as relatively unimportant and distracting. Any competent leader would have wanted a united administration in such times. Vélez Cachupín's propensity to be personally domineering in his dealings with the Franciscans was noted previously. The friars later charged that, beginning at this time, their mail was often tampered with and sometimes stolen. Vélez Cachupín even threatened on one occasion, according to Varo, to have two friars clapped in irons, thrown over mules, and driven from New Mexico. Whatever the reasons or the methods, Franciscan correspondence from New Mexico soon slowed to a trickle.[36]

Matters worsened when an internal Franciscan struggle also erupted in 1750. For some time in the custody, two friars held appointments as commissaries of the Inquisition, one in El Paso and one in Santa Fe. In 1750, Varo held that position for El Paso. In Santa Fe, Fray Pedro Montaño, a criollo, was the representative of the Holy Office. Fray Pedro had been in the custody since 1728, just before Varo arrived, but most of his service had been in the El Paso district. Like Varo, Montaño was over sixty years of age. Indeed, they seemed to have much in common, except that Varo was a gachupín. Nevertheless, a most acrimonious controversy now broke out between these two friars and soon involved other missionaries as well.[37]

The dispute was ignited by Vélez Cachupín's actions toward the Franciscans. Since Vélez Cachupín had exempted Inquisition documents from government control, Varo (still custos) from El Paso asked Montaño to initiate an Inquisition investigation against the governor. This would have created a vast opening allowing testimonies, interrogations, and related reports to leave New Mexico unimpeded. Furthermore, starting Inquisition proceedings might intimidate Vélez Cachupín and force him into a defensive position. There was even a slim chance that the Holy Office could get Vélez Cachupín out of New Mexico. That tactic had worked in the seventeenth century, and Varo probably reasoned it was at least worth the effort.

The problem, however, was that Montaño refused to open Inquisition proceedings against the governor. When Varo turned to the vice-custos for the Santa Fe district, Fray José Manuel Trigo, to pressure Montaño to act, Montaño used his Holy Office powers to have Trigo placed in seclusion. Next, Varo wrote to the Holy Office in Mexico City asking to have Montaño recalled, and had Fray Agustín de Iniesta and Fray Juan Sáenz de Lezáun submit supporting testimonials. At this point, Montaño went on the offensive by attacking Varo's supporters. Trigo was accused of violating "the seal of the confessional" (soliciting women), and Iniesta was charged with having sexual relations with several women and fathering their children. A close friend of Varo's, Fray José de Irigoyen, was likewise accused and removed from his post at Alburquerque. By the time Montaño was removed by the Inquisition in April 1752, the custody had been riven by internal turmoil for two years. Hence, at a time the custody most needed to present a united front, the missionaries turned on one another, and, just as important, must have made a sorry spectacle of themselves in the eyes of both friend and foe.[38]

It is important to note that Vélez Cachupín did give something to the friars they had not enjoyed for a while: succor from Comanche raids. As noted earlier, by the end of his first administration, the governor had forged a peace with the Comanche people. Thus, Vélez Cachupín had supporters, even among the Franciscans. In 1751, four friars wrote glowing letters commending the governor for a victory over the Comanche. Fray Antonio Zamora's was typical: "Thanks to God for everything and Your Lordship, who, in defense of both majesties, desired, as a good vassal and Catholic Christian, to risk his life in such evident danger, the heroic action of an excellent and spirited chief." One of the testimonials was penned by Fray Agustín de Iniesta who, as just noted above, was mired at that moment in the Varo-Montaño conflict. In light of Vélez Cachupín's accomplishment, it is not surprising that some Franciscans applauded. At the same time, however, these letters are further proof of the absence of unity among the missionaries in their attitudes toward the governor.[39]

In 1753, Vélez Cachupín composed a long, comprehensive report to Mexico City concerning the state of the colony. While concerned in detail with such matters as trade, relations with native peoples, population figures, and other pertinent material, the document was highly critical of the Franciscans' missionary operation. One of their crucial failings, again, was language: "If they [friars] would also apply themselves to learning the languages of the barbarians, it would be very useful to the service of God, because their [natives] ignorance largely prevents their conversion since they are not able to understand the Catholic religion." As to the missionaries' evangelical fervor, Vélez Cachupín wrote, "The missionaries, overseers of that Holy Custody by orders of the King, should be more disposed to that endeavor because experience has shown that when these individuals have dedication and diligence, they can obtain the fruit of converting to the Knowledge of God many souls whose Holy spiritual devotions are His greatest pleasure."[40]

Such a withering condemnation of the Franciscans by a governor in the past would have quickly engendered a vociferous response. None was forthcoming, for now. Vélez Cachupín had muted the Franciscans; local government had clearly gained hegemony over the missionaries in New Mexico for the first time since its settlement.

* * *

Don Francisco Marín del Valle replaced Vélez Cachupín in August 1754. The Conde de Revillagigedo would have preferred to leave Vélez Cachupín in charge for a longer period, but His Majesty's government tapped Marín as New Mexico's new executive. It proved to be a poor choice. While Marín endeavored to maintain peace with the Comanches by adhering to his predecessor's policies, the new governor was less effective. Their attacks were not constant during Marín's administration, but by 1760 (Marín's last year in office), Comanche assaults were regaining their previous levels of destructiveness and frequency.[41]

Governor Marín continued Vélez Cachupín's policies toward the Franciscans. No one but the governor could certify Franciscan reports, lesser officials were still held to the same penalties if they provided testimonials for the Franciscans, and the proscriptions on the Order's mail remained in effect. As to the effectiveness of these policies, Franciscan documents from the 1750s were a fraction of what had gone before (based on what remains in the archives). Only toward the end of Marín's term did the friars seem to have become more efficient at smuggling reports through Inquisition pouches, as the quantity of the Order's correspondence increased somewhat after 1758. The friars also later claimed that Marín was cruel and disrespectful to them. On the other hand, Marín paid to set up the Confraternity of Our Lady of Light and to have a chapel constructed in Santa Fe for that *cofradía* out of his own pocket.[42]

Another significant development was that the number of personnel for the Custody of Saint Paul began to decline during the Vélez Cachupín-Marín era. It will be recalled that in 1749, Varo's report listed forty priests in the Kingdom: thirty-six regular appointees and four who had been sent to assist with the now-defunct Navajo missions. Three apparently valid rosters of New Mexico friars exist for the 1750s: a report in 1752 drafted and signed by Vélez Cachupín (as consistent with his policy), a 1755 visita by Custos Fray Jacobo de Castro (of which more will be said later), and a 1757 roster submitted for release of the Franciscans' yearly government stipends. The latter roster included additional notations through October of 1759. These documents reveal a marked decline in Franciscan numbers.[43]

The 1752 Vélez Cachupín roster listed thirty-three ordained friars in the Kingdom, down seven from Varo's 1749 total. Twenty-three missionaries were posted to the Santa Fe district, and ten were in El Paso. The large number in El Paso was partly because the Junta de los Ríos district had been abandoned temporarily for unstated reasons, and two other friars were there awaiting transport from the custody. Hence, the number of active Franciscans was only thirty-one. The twenty-three in the Santa Fe district were dispersed into twenty-two positions. The mission at Tesuque was listed as a visita for Santa Fe, and Pojoaque as a visita for the missionary at Nambé. Every mission site in this region had one friar, except Santa Fe, which had two.[44]

Castro's visita of the Santa Fe district in 1755 found only twenty-one friars present. At this time, there were twenty-three positions, since a mission had been opened at Abiquiu during the Vélez Cachupín administration. Tesuque and Pojoaque were still visitas. No missionary was at Zuñi at this time, and when Castro began his inspection, Alburquerque was also vacant. During the course of his visita, however, one of the Santa Fe-based friars transferred to Alburquerque. Thus, every site but Zuñi had one Franciscan priest (including Santa Fe).[45]

The 1757/1759 report first shows thirty-two Franciscans in the Kingdom; twenty-five were in the Santa Fe region, six in El Paso, and one laboring in the Junta de los Ríos. For the Santa Fe district, the same twenty-three positions were all staffed, and two missionaries were at both Santa Fe and Zuñi. The extra notations that cover the period to October 1759 reveal a Franciscan decline. Three left the Santa Fe district and two departed El Paso. Another

friar's name, Fray Antonio Gabaldón at Santa Cruz de la Cañada, bears a notation that he had just died. At the same time, four friars had arrived in the
Kingdom, though their mission assignments are not stated. Thus, at best, in
1759 thirty missionaries were in the Kingdom, where forty had served only ten
years earlier.[46]

These rosters reveal other factors concerning the mission program. For one
thing, they provide some insight as to whether friars were still being frequently
moved about. From the 1752 and 1755 rosters (in the Santa Fe district), only
nine of twenty-two sites still had the same Franciscan priest. Comparing 1755
with the 1757/1759 list, seven out of twenty-three positions were held by the
same friars. Taking into account all three rosters, five sites had the same missionaries over at least a seven-year period. Of those five, however, only three
were at Puebloan missions: San Ildefonso with Fray Juan Antonio Ezeiza, San
Juan with Fray Juan José Pérez de Mirabal, and Acoma with Fray Pedro Ignacio
Pino. Obviously, missionaries were continuing to be frequently moved.

Castro's report of his 1755 visita tells us more. Fray Jacobo was an hijo de
provincia from Galicia. He had professed at San Francisco de México in 1736
at age sixteen. Before arriving in New Mexico, he served in the Tampico custody where he was custos at least once. He came to the Custody of Saint Paul
by 1752 and remained until about 1762, serving primarily in El Paso and holding the title of custos three times. He appears to have been a competent and
committed friar.[47]

His inspection report of the Santa Fe district missions was unique in format.
First, he asked witnesses to respond to a battery of questions concerning each
friar's performance, including the following: Was the missionary usually at his
assigned post? How was Christian doctrine taught? Were feast days, masses, and
holy sacraments observed/administered as they should be? Was the arancel
posted and followed? The witnesses were Spaniards where possible, though at
fourteen missions those questioned were Puebloans. The answers were all sus-
piciously very similar, and, as one might expect in an official Franciscan report,
not one friar was found to be failing in his duties.

Castro's report reveals two important items. The first concerns the nature of
church and state interactions during the Marín administration. The local alcalde mayor or his lieutenant accompanied Castro to each mission and ob-
served the inquiry. Each of these officials refused to sign testimonials certifying
the proceedings, citing his instructions from Governor Marín not to do so. Indeed, Don Santiago Roybal, the representative of the diocese of Durango, certified the entire report. The document is also an indictment of the Franciscans'
failure to instruct their neophytes in the Spanish language. Of the fourteen missions where Puebloans were the only witnesses, in only two—Zía and Acoma—
were interpreters not required. Obviously, those who had condemned the

missionaries for not instructing their neophytes effectively in the Spanish language needed no better evidence than Castro's report that the Franciscans had fallen short in that duty.[48]

* * *

The ability of Governor Vélez Cachupín to silence the friars in New Mexico was a significant and symbolic achievement in the local government's interactions with the Custody of Saint Paul. If the Franciscans could neither present their views nor defend themselves in the higher councils of Spanish government, they were virtually impotent to influence affairs within the Kingdom. While the Order had seen a steady erosion in their position since the reconquest, Vélez Cachupín and Marín relegated the Franciscans to near powerless nonentities in New Mexico, except in spiritual matters.

It was not just the policies of these governors that were pivotal in the breakdown of the Franciscans' remaining power and prestige. The propagation of the Catholic faith was the major rationale for their existence in the Kingdom, but the friars' efforts among the Puebloans had been shown to be less than effective. Worse, the failure of the Navajo mission field foretold the end of Franciscan mission expansion. One last, half-hearted effort would be made in the late 1770s, but the mission program now stagnated. In addition, the Varo-Montaño dispute was a harbinger of further internecine conflicts to come. These fraternal arguments had occurred previously, as noted above, but the Varo-Montaño controversy had been especially intense. Within the next quarter century, some friars would arm themselves against their brethren. Unable to fulfill their evangelical duties, reduced in influence and prestige within the Kingdom, and lacking unity, the Franciscan position in New Mexico withered to insignificance.

CHAPTER 11

The Franciscan Collapse

IN THE 1760s two momentous events occurred that had tremendous significance for New Spain, and, perhaps more immediately, its northern frontier.
As a result of the Seven Years' War (French-Indian War), France gave up the
territory of Louisiana to Spain in 1763. While the two countries had been allies
during the war, for over eighty years French aspirations along New Mexico and
Texas's eastern boundaries posed a threat to Spanish security and shaped its
frontier policies. The Spanish monarchy's emphasis on defensive matters, as
seen repeatedly in previous chapters, meant that local government grew in importance in New Mexico at the expense of the Franciscans' position. Now, the
French threat had vanished.

The second major development occurred in 1767, when Charles III ordered
the expulsion of the Jesuits from the New World. Important to New Spain for
their superior education institutions, economic development, and mission operations, the removal of the Society of Jesus would have a profound influence
on growing Mexican nationalistic sentiment, and, ultimately, would be a factor in the Mexican independence movement. For New Mexico's Franciscans,
though, the expulsion meant three things. First, it reminded the missionaries,
yet again, that the direction in church and state relations inaugurated with the
Bourbon reign continued to reduce the influence of the regular orders. More
immediately, the removal of the Jesuits meant that a longtime rival and threat
for prestige and power in the mission field was suddenly gone. Finally, the Jesuit missions in northern New Spain were turned over to the Franciscans
(though not the Province of Santo Evangelio), which naturally stretched the
Order's resources to an even greater extent.

Both of these occurrences might have boded well for the Franciscans in New
Mexico. Spain's acquisition of Louisiana meant that French trade and intrigue
with native people would end. Thus, Spanish influence should increase with
the Kingdom's native enemies, especially the Comanche people. A reduction
in French, and by extension, native threats, could initiate a new era of mission
expansion. The royal government might again rely on the Franciscans to solid-

ify Spanish frontier holdings. New missions would bring more friars, and more friars equaled greater influence. That their Jesuit rivals were now gone should only enhance His Majesty's reliance on the Franciscans to spread Christianity and Spanish civilization during this era of peace. Perhaps a Franciscan restoration was on the horizon. It was not, however, to be a period of Franciscan renaissance in New Mexico. Instead, the next sixteen years (1760 to 1776) were characterized by a dramatic and irrevocable deterioration of the Custody of Saint Paul's missionary effort.

*   *   *

In 1760, a third episcopal visit of New Mexico took place. This bishop of Durango was not only a new prince of the Church but also a recent arrival to Mexico. Don Pedro Tamarón y Romeral was born near Toledo about 1695. He came to the New World with the bishop of Caracas, Don Juan José Escalona y Calatayud. In the New World, Tamarón received advanced education at the new University of Caracas and eventually obtained a doctorate in canon law. Over the next three decades, Tamarón served in several capacities for the Caracas bishopric, including vicar of the diocese and commissary of the Holy Office. He was appointed bishop of Durango in 1758 and installed in that city in March 1759. While his many duties in Caracas surely prepared Tamarón well for episcopal responsibilities, he seems an odd choice for Durango. Though he appeared energetic enough, he was by now well over sixty years of age. More importantly, Tamarón had not served within Mexico nor in such a rugged and remote environment as his episcopate encompassed.[1]

Bishop Tamarón arrived in El Paso in late April 1760. He had been traveling since the previous October, conducting the visita that was to take him through his entire diocese. One wonders about the impressions he had formed as he journeyed. Surely the vast expanses, the stark landscape, and the isolation of many of the settlements and missions he witnessed contrasted sharply with the more urban and comfortable existence of his life in Caracas.[2]

What he saw in the El Paso district did not elicit much response. At the time of Tamarón's arrival, six friars including the custos, Fray Jacobo de Castro, were serving in five mission sites in and around that villa. In addition, two secular clergymen were present, both appointees of Bishop Sánchez, Tamarón's predecessor. One served as vicar and ecclesiastical judge of El Paso; the other was the priest for Carrizal, a Spanish community established by Governor Marín in 1758. To foster good relations with the Franciscans, Bishop Tamarón turned over the office of vicar to Castro. Having inspected the missions and churches and performed confirmations, Tamarón, Castro, and about sixty others started north on 7 May. They arrived at Tomé, the first Spanish settlement in the Santa Fe district, eleven days later.[3]

This episcopal visita was carried out in a markedly different atmosphere than the previous two. This time Castro and the other friars were much more accommodating to the bishop of Durango. While Tamarón noted that the Franciscans maintained a legal challenge to Durango's jurisdiction, there were no protests or obstructions to his inspection. Indeed, Tamarón wrote, "I entered New Mexico with some misgivings. But when I found that I was not gainsaid in anything and that I was made free of everything, as if they were secular priests, I tried not to waste the opportunity."[4]

The Franciscans welcomed the bishop of Durango this time primarily because of the pressures they had experienced under Governors Vélez Cachupín and Marín. Indeed, acrimony had only become more acute the longer Marín was in office. In 1758, Custos Castro reported: "Nothing has sufficed to soothe his [Marín's] restless spirit, the passion, or hatred, with which he has looked upon all of us religious from the time he entered this kingdom, for he has always sought means to lower us in the estimation of the Indians and the settlers and to make us hated by them." According to Fray Juan Sáenz de Lezáun, the Franciscans made Tamarón aware of the abuses the missionaries had suffered under the last four governors (Mendoza and Codallos being the other two) and the alcaldes mayores. The bishop of Durango had thus come to be seen as a potential ally for New Mexico's friars.[5]

Bishop Tamarón remained in New Mexico conducting his inspection and performing confirmations through the first week in July. The first stages of his inspection went smoothly enough. Tamarón wanted Castro to assign a friar permanently to Tomé since that settlement had about four hundred citizens. Castro seems not to have objected, although no Franciscan would be assigned there during the next two decades. At Alburquerque, the bishop appointed Fray Manuel José Rojo (Roxo) to one of the vicar and ecclesiastical judge posts. (Later in the visita, the Franciscan priest based at Santa Cruz de la Cañada was appointed to identical titles as Rojo.). Governor Marín had an escort meet them at Sandía, and a chaise was provided for Tamarón's use at Santo Domingo. At each of these sites, Tamarón inspected the buildings and ledgers and performed confirmations. One friar was stationed at each place, but, except for Rojo, Tamarón did not deign to name them in his reports. On 24 May, local government officials, Don Santiago Roybal, and the Franciscans provided the bishop of Durango a full ceremonial entrance into Santa Fe. Tamarón remained there for about a week, inspecting church facilities, performing confirmations, preaching, and resting after the difficult trek from El Paso.[6]

From this point in his visita, however, the more missions Tamarón saw, the less he found to approve. At Pecos, which he visited first from Santa Fe, he complained that the natives did not know their catechism, nor, since a language barrier existed with the missionary, did they make confessions except when near death. Clearly angered by this situation, Tamarón ordered Castro to see that the friars improved their language skills. Tamarón noted the same deficiencies in Puebloan Christian religious knowledge and practices, and Franciscan language shortcomings with Puebloans at Picurís, Taos, Cochití, Jémez, Laguna, and Zuñi. There could easily have been more; the bishop did not see the neophytes at Santa Clara or the genízaros at Abiquiu, and for other missions his written report was ominously brief. Positive assessments were few. The native people at Tesuque were "somewhat more civilized." Tamarón described the mission priest at San Felipe as "very able." Puebloans at Acoma were more knowledgeable of the catechism than the others. He credited that to Acoma's missionary who understood their language, worked with them diligently, but "has had to whip them."[7]

During his travels in the Kingdom, Bishop Tamarón also received a thorough indoctrination in the conditions with which the missionaries contended. Going to and from Galisteo, a frequent target of Comanche raids, the bishop and his party were frightened of being attacked. Indeed, approaching that mission, Tamarón "had a good fright" when those Puebloans who came out on horseback to meet the bishop's party were first identified as Comanches. He could not inspect two missions, Santa Clara and Cochití, because the Río Grande was too swollen from the winter's melting snow. On the journey from Jémez to Laguna, he suffered from a lack of water. Concerning the heat, Tamarón wrote, "the sun burned as if it was shooting fire." The primary reason why his party decided to skip visiting Zuñi was the intense heat and drought conditions that prevailed west of the Río Grande.[8]

Tamarón departed the Santa Fe district from Isleta during the first week in July, and was back in El Paso by 18 July. He remained there for ten days, went next to Carrizal, and then exited the Kingdom on 30 July 1760. As far as it is known, that was the last time any bishop visited New Mexico during the Spanish period.[9]

More so than after the previous two episcopal visitas, Tamarón tried to implement diocesan control from Durango over the Franciscans in their day-to-day religious duties in New Mexico. He was clearly vexed by the Puebloans' noticeable lack of religious understanding and practices. Though he had not witnessed any idolatries, he was worried about the presence of kivas in some missions and ordered the friars to observe them closely. The native people's state of religious preparation "saddened and upset me more in that Kingdom [New Mexico] than in any other."[10]

The major failure was in language, though Tamarón noted Spaniards and Puebloans communicated well enough when it came to trade and commercial matters. The bishop strove to strengthen the Franciscans' language competency. As noted previously, he ordered Custos Castro to see that the friars improved. Before the bishop departed the Kingdom, he reiterated that order to Castro and instructed the custos to report to him on the missionaries' progress. In addition, Tamarón had noted that one missionary, Fray Tomás Murciano de la Cruz (apparently the one Tamarón praised at San Felipe), seemed to have special language skills. The bishop asked him to compose a guide to catechism and confession in the Keres tongue. Tamarón realized little success, though, in this matter. Castro did submit reports to Tamarón at least twice concerning language. In the first report (1761), he claimed that more Puebloans were confessing, but that Murciano was not having much success on the Keres catechism "because the interpreters confused him so greatly by the variety of terms" that they used. Castro again wrote in 1763 that some progress was evident, but that the "rebelliousness of the people" (friars? natives?) hindered grander achievements.[11]

In addition, Tamarón made a greater effort to have the Franciscans conform to policies set for the entire Spanish Catholic Church, and especially his diocese. From his return to Durango after his visita (1761) until his death in December 1768, Tamarón sent more communications to New Mexico than any previous bishop. One of the first was a papal bull and royal cédula establishing 8 December as a day to celebrate the Sacred Mystery of the Immaculate Conception. Regular clergy serving in missions or as parish priests were instructed in how to organize that special day. Friars were to hear confessions, offer communion, and spend the remainder of the day in devotional prayers. For that year's observance (1762), Tamarón relayed instructions that the King ordered prayers to be said for peace and an end to war among Christian princes, in reference to the Seven Years' War that Spain was losing. Tamarón sent other directives establishing feast days, explaining how to keep financial accounts, and clarifying what constituted fasting during the Lenten season. This latter missive accompanied the royal cédula that decreed the expulsion of the Jesuits. In 1765, Tamarón reissued an earlier edict (from 1759), stating that he felt compelled to do so in light of what he had seen during his visita. It included the usual admonitions for priests to remain in their parishes/missions and to keep parish books and registers current. In addition, this edict included such detailed instructions as to the length of sermons (no longer than thirty minutes, no less than fifteen), the manner in which priests were to question children regarding their understanding of Christian doctrine, and instructions that his clergymen were to frequently visit the gravely ill "lest the infernal wolf prey on his lambs in so terrible a crisis as death." From an immense distance, Tamarón tried to make the Franciscans in New Mexico an integrated part of his diocese.[12]

Even more importantly, Bishop Tamarón also attempted to place Spanish communities under the administration of secular priests. In 1765, he asked the royal government to secularize four predominantly Spanish towns in New Mexico: El Paso, Santa Fe, Alburquerque, and Santa Cruz de la Cañada. Tamarón offered three reasons why it was time to secularize these missions. First, he noted the long, and yet ongoing, conflict the Franciscans had waged over diocesan control, and their refusal to cooperate or acknowledge Don Santiago Roybal's offices of vicar and ecclesiastical judge in Santa Fe. Second, he pointed out the missionaries' many failures with the native peoples in New Mexico, citing specifically the friars' deficiencies with native languages. He had ordered changes during his visita, Tamarón wrote, but nothing had been done by the Franciscans to improve their evangelical performance. Finally, Tamarón claimed that the governor of New Mexico (Vélez Cachupín, again) and Roybal had recently informed him of evidence that witchcraft and other idolatries were occurring among the inhabitants of New Mexico.[13]

The bishop of Durango's desire to secularize these missions, as seen previously, was not an anomaly. Several governors, Durango prelates, and other officials had already suggested that at least El Paso and Santa Fe should be turned over to secular clergy. Tamarón's request mirrored a similar move at that time by the archbishop of Mexico to secularize ten other Santo Evangelio mission sites in central Mexico, including missions at Toluca, Texcoco, and the Franciscan facilities at Santiago de Tlatelolco. Of these, Toluca and Texcoco were secularized, but the viceroy left the others under Franciscan control. There is no evidence that Tamarón worked in concert with the archbishop, though Tamarón must have been at least encouraged by that prelate's actions.[14]

The viceroy, Marqués de Cruillas, was near the end of his administration (1760–1766) when the bishop of Durango's petition to secularize these missions was made, but he requested a Franciscan response to Tamarón's claims and intentions. It was a new viceroy, however, the Marqués de Croix (1766–1771), who received the Order's report, drafted by unnamed Santo Evangelio officials.

The Franciscans offered numerous specific reasons why these communities, especially El Paso and Santa Fe, should remain under Franciscan tutelage. El Paso was the residence of the custos, and as such was ideally suited as a central location for Franciscan mission operations throughout the custody. El Paso and Santa Fe were important as places for friars who became ill to receive treatment. As the most cultured communities, these villas also provided stimulation and restored vigor to long-isolated missionaries. Santa Fe and El Paso were the centers of government, and having Franciscans there improved communications between these two most important institutions. As to secular priests, the Franciscans claimed that the bishop of Durango was too far away to supervise them effectively. In addition, friars and secular clergy did not mix well, since completely different training and religious fraternal relationships shaped Franciscans. In all of these Spanish communities, parishioners would miss long spiritual associations that had been built between individual friars and citizens. Furthermore, the missionaries often had medical training, which seculars lacked, to succor the ill, and the Order was able to provide food from its stores for the needy in the colony. The report disputed that a secular priest could be supported financially by these communities. Indeed, recent Comanche raids had driven many destitute refugees into these communities; these displaced people might not be in these communities permanently, nor were they likely to be able to provide tithes to maintain a secular clergyman. Finally, the report noted that relations between the Franciscans and the bishopric of Durango had improved, especially as a result of Tamarón's visita.[15]

The Marqués de Croix turned these documents over to his *fiscal* (royal attorney) for a legal opinion, which was submitted to the viceroy in June 1768. The report was rather succinct in its recommendation that Tamarón's request be denied. Legally, the fiscal noted, the bishop of Durango had not followed proper procedure to place secular clergy in these four sites. His Majesty's law required that at least two secular priests be offered to the viceroy to select from to fill parish positions. In this instance, Tamarón had offered no names except one: Don Miguel de Larrañaga for El Paso. Unfortunately, Tamarón had not even presented any credentials for this candidate. Moreover, while the law allowed a parish position to be filled without competition if the post had been vacant for four consecutive months, Tamarón offered no claim that such a situation existed. In fact, the fiscal noted, the bishop's primary reason to secularize these missions was his dissatisfaction with the Franciscans' performance among the Puebloan population in New Mexico, but, he noted, that was no basis to secularize Spanish villas. The viceroy agreed and by 9 July 1768 the Franciscan Commissary General of New Spain was able to dispatch the government's favorable decision to Santo Evangelio and the Custody of Saint Paul.[16]

Two important developments, though, are discernible from this secularization matter. First, the Franciscans in New Mexico seemed to play a very small part in the controversy. Some of the points raised in the Santo Evangelio report to the viceroy must have been suggested by the custody. However, the reports, testimonials, opinions, and the like, which in the past would have flowed like a torrent from New Mexico's friars, were missing. Vélez Cachupín was the colony's governor into 1767, and it is entirely possible that Franciscan correspondence was again being restricted. Whatever the reasons, the custody played only a secondary role, at best, in its defense.

Second, it is important to note that the viceregal fiscal did not opine that these New Mexico mission sites could not be secularized. In fact, the fiscal seems to have ignored every point of rebuttal offered by Santo Evangelio. If there were secular clergy available from whom to choose and they were properly presented, the fiscal's recommendation to the viceroy might have been just the opposite. That possibility was surely noted by the Franciscans. Tamarón died, however, before 1768 ended. His immediate successor does not seem to have continued Tamarón's policies and methods of overseeing New Mexico. The secularization of these missions eventually did occur, though not until near the end of the century. Despite this momentary victory, throughout the 1760s the Franciscans' relations with New Mexico's governors continued to weaken.[17]

*   *   *

Governor Marín was still in power during Bishop Tamarón's visita. He did not play a significant part in that event, besides participating in the ceremonial welcome in Santa Fe and seeing to it that military escorts were available as needed. Unlike Bishops Crespo and Elizacoechea during their visitas, Tamarón did not stay in the governor's palace; rather, he resided at Don Santiago Roybal's quarters. Hostilities with the Comanche people had broken out again by 1760, and Marín likely had his hands full with that crisis. In addition, Marín should have already been relieved, and perhaps an episcopal visita did not merit much concern to an outgoing governor.[18]

One reason why Marín was still holding office in 1760 was that no regular appointee had arrived to replace him. For unknown reasons, the government was forced into a stopgap measure when it appointed Don Mateo de Mendoza as ad interim governor. He relieved Marín in the fall of 1760. Mendoza did not last long in office, however, as he was replaced by another ad interim appointee, Don Manuel Portilla y Urrisola, who assumed office in January 1761. Little is known of either man's administration. The Comanche threat was growing more perilous and is likely to have consumed much of their attention. Mendoza seems to have had a stormy relationship with the Franciscans during his brief tenure, though. At one point, he threatened to replace the Franciscan missionaries with Jesuit priests, though that was obviously mere bluster. It seems most likely, though, that from the autumn of 1760 to February 1762, when a regular gubernatorial appointee took the wand of office, the Franciscans enjoyed some respite from the ever-increasing power of the New Mexico governor.[19]

That Don Tomás Vélez Cachupín returned to New Mexico in 1762 as governor attested well to his abilities. Spain was doing poorly against the British in the Seven Years' War, and once again, Comanche, Apache, Pima, Ute, and other native people were running roughshod over much of New Spain's northern region. Certainly the government's selection of Vélez Cachupín was an indication of the gravity of the situation on the northern frontier. For the next five years, Vélez Cachupín was as relentless and successful as he previously had been. Once more, he relied on a combination of diplomacy, mutual respect, and military force to restore peace with most hostile native bands. By 1767, the Comanche people in particular were pacified along New Mexico's boundaries.[20]

Vélez Cachupín followed his previous path in regards to the Franciscans as well. He had not been in office six months when he submitted a damaging report to Viceroy Marqués de Cruillas (1760–1766). First, he charged that the Real Hacienda had overpaid the Franciscans for the past year. Indeed, the custody was short four missionaries, according to Vélez Cachupín. Two friars were supposed to be at Zuñi, but no missionary had been there for some time. Two other friars were to have been at Junta de los Ríos, but the governor claimed that those missions were unattended. Vélez Cachupín also thought the government was not getting its money's worth from six other missionaries who, because "of their advanced age and habitual indisposition," were unfit as mission priests. The six friars Vélez Cachupín complained of were aged—Manuel Zambrano, sixty-nine; Antonio Zamora, sixty-seven; Juan José Pérez de Mirabal, sixty-four; Juan Carlos de Oronzoro and José de Irigoyen, both sixty-three; and Juan Ezeiza, sixty—though others before them had served in the custody even later in life. The governor wanted Santo Evangelio to provide the four missing friars to New Mexico and replace the six invalids. Furthermore, if the custody was not going to maintain the Junta de los Ríos missions, those government stipends should be withdrawn permanently from the annual disbursements to the Franciscans.[21]

The Franciscan response to Vélez Cachupín's report once again came directly from Santo Evangelio, while the friars in New Mexico remained silent. The provincial first pointed out that sometimes friars were not at their missions when stipends were allotted. They might be in Mexico City taking care of the custody's affairs, or perhaps had been called to El Paso to meet with the custos. On the other hand, five friars were being dispatched immediately to fill shortages and to relieve certain missionaries. Of these five, only four actually made it to the Kingdom, and two of these friars (Fray Juan Tejada and Fray Francisco Xavier Dávila Saavedra) were already over fifty years of age, too old by Vélez Cachupín's standards.[22]

As to why the Junta de los Ríos missions were inactive, the provincial began by recapitulating the on and off nature of that effort. The missions there, the report noted, had performed up to expectations until 1725, "more or less." Since that time, hostile native raiders had constantly threatened those missions. Nevertheless, friars in twos, threes, and fours at various times were there (most recently, in 1759–1760), but the district was not safe for evangelical labor. The Franciscans, the provincial reminded the viceroy, had frequently asked that a presidio be built nearby to protect the friars and their neophytes. It had taken until 1760 for that request to be fulfilled. Now that a presidio had been established at La Junta, the work with those native people would resume. During the periods when these missions were vacant, though, the provincial claimed the friars assigned to them usually were assisting at missions in El Paso.[23]

While this was another incident putting the Franciscans on the defensive and calling into question their capabilities, the matter seems not to have gone any further. At least two of the Junta de los Ríos missions operated throughout the 1770s, though apparently not continuously. Moreover, there was no immediate reduction in the number of Franciscans supported by the Real Hacienda. In 1763, the government still supported thirty-four ordained friars and a lay brother. Significantly, as John L. Kessell noted, the custody was paid 11,450 pesos for 1763, while the presidio garrison at Santa Fe received over 32,000 pesos. From an accounting perspective alone, clearly the importance of the evangelical effort in New Mexico had been eclipsed by defensive concerns.[24]

From looking at the behaviors of New Mexico's residents, Governor Vélez Cachupín also did not think much of the friars' evangelical work in New Mexico. In January 1764, the governor called the Franciscans and Santiago Roybal to a conclave. There he presented them with materials and testimonials that had been collected by alcaldes mayores and soldiers from numerous settlements and missions throughout the Kingdom. According to Vélez Cachupín, it was obvious that "a pattern of nativism and paganism in the missions" had created "an aura" of sorcery and superstition among the Spanish and genízaro population. That Puebloans still met secretly in their kivas, worshipped idols, performed kachina dances, ingested hallucinogens, and indulged in other pagan practices was scandalous. Evidence suggested that these behaviors were common in at least thirteen missions out of twenty-one. Each one of these missions, the governor noted, had a friar currently in residence who apparently tolerated these scandals. Among the Spanish settlements, Vélez Cachupín's report mentioned Santa Fe, Alburquerque, Santa Cruz de la Cañada, Abiquiu, Tomé, Truchas, Chimayó, Belén, and Quemada. In short, virtually every Spanish community had residents who mimicked these idolatrous Puebloan behaviors. And what was the cause of this continued evidence of pagan activities? To Vélez Cachupín, the missionaries' lack of effort and incompetence in Puebloan languages had led directly to this sorry state of affairs. Vélez Cachupín's report on these matters went to the viceroy, Santo Evangelio, and to the bishop of Durango. It was this evidence of witchcraft and paganism to which Tamarón alluded in 1765 when he petitioned to secularize El Paso, Alburquerque, Santa Cruz de la Cañada, and Santa Fe.[25]

That witchcraft might be flourishing in the Kingdom gained further credence in 1772 when Fray Félix Ordóñez y Machado died under mysterious circumstances at Abiquiu. Not much is known of Fray Félix's life. He had arrived in New Mexico by 1754, and Abiquiu seems to have been his main place of service, though he was briefly at Santa Fe and Laguna. At his death, a young native female indicated that a local husband and wife played a role in the friar's demise. The government arrested many people in the area and found several guilty in contributing to Ordóñez's death, though no one was executed. Presidial patrols also found some witchcraft items and writings hidden in areas west of Abiquiu; these were destroyed. The local authorities obviously took this matter seriously, which further attests to the government's assumption of jurisdiction in an affair that once would have been the sole domain of the Franciscans.[26]

Although Spain had assumed control over Louisiana in 1763, and Vélez Cachupín had significantly secured New Mexico's borders with the Comanche people, defensive concerns for New Spain's northern frontier still dominated the attention of His Majesty's government. To that end, in 1766 the Marqués de Rubí, who had been dispatched by the government to assess frontier defenses and make recommendations, inspected New Mexico. The marqués was in New Mexico for almost two months and was escorted on his tour most of the time by Governor Vélez Cachupín. Missions seem to have been of little concern to Rubí, though native people were. Rubí's report concluded that for most of the northern frontier, Spain's control was a sham. He suggested a reorganization of the northern presidios and a general policy of pursuing peaceful relations with native people. Many of Rubí's recommendations would later become part of the *Reglamento de 1772* (of which more will be said later); however, this matter was another indication of the Franciscans' shrinking importance to His Majesty's government.[27]

Vélez Cachupín's administration came to an end in 1767, without further recorded incidence with the Franciscans. He had restored some measure of peace and security to the Kingdom, and many friars were undoubtedly grateful for that alone. His second term in office also coincided with a further erosion in the custody's position in New Mexico. Indeed, the friars seem to have gone into a shell when it came to contesting issues with Governor Vélez Cachupín.

* * *

Don Pedro Fermín de Mendinueta became the new governor in 1767. About forty-two years of age at the time, Mendinueta was an experienced military man with political administrative experience. He had seen action as a member of the Navy Guard against the British in Europe during the wars of the 1740s. He arrived in New Spain during the next decade at the rank of lieutenant colonel and served as *corregidor* (magistrate) for Mexico City. In 1763, he was promoted to colonel. His appointment as governor of New Mexico, therefore, was consistent with the pattern the Bourbon monarchy preferred for the frontier of New Spain: an experienced military officer with a background in political administration. Mendinueta would be the governor of New Mexico until 1778, longer than any other Spanish official's tenure there.[28]

Governor Mendinueta might have thought his administration would be a rather peaceful period. After all, France was no longer a threat to New Mexico's boundaries, now that the Spanish held Louisiana. French traders would not be bringing arms to the Comanche and other native people who had contested Spanish control over the area. Indeed, Vélez Cachupín had convinced the Comanche people that peace with Spain was preferable to war. Thus, Mendinueta and New Mexico's residents were justified in being somewhat optimistic that peace might become the norm in the Kingdom.

It was not to be. Whether as a result of mistakes on Mendinueta's part or just the fundamental nature of the differences between the Comanches and the Spanish, conflict resumed in 1768. Again, Comanche attacks were launched against Pecos, Galisteo, Taos, and the Spanish settlement of Ojo Caliente. In 1769, Comanche raiders sacked the Franciscan convento at Picurís. Mendinueta had that convento torn down and another built adjacent to the church in order to improve the mission's defenses.[29]

The situation in New Mexico was made more pernicious by a severe drought that began by the early 1770s. For over ten years, precious little rain fell in the region. Spanish and Puebloan crops failed and livestock losses were equally terrible. Wild plants and game grew scarce for the Comanche, Apache, Navajo, Ute, and other native people dependent on these foods. Since Puebloans and Spaniards had no surplus foodstuffs to trade with these traditional foes, there was little motivation for peace. In their desperation, Apaches, Navajos, and Utes also began to raid Puebloan and Spanish settlements. Among the missions assaulted in the 1770s were Laguna, Jémez, Cochití, Santa Clara, San Ildefonso, Zía, Sandía, Nambé, and San Juan, while traditional targets such as Pecos, Picurís, and Galisteo were raided again and again. Spanish settlements were also struck. Alburquerque, Abiquiu, Santa Cruz de la Cañada (now referred to as La Cañada or Cañada), and in May 1775, the capital itself, Santa Fe, experienced the terror of a Comanche attack. Livestock losses grew so great that the government in Mexico City was obliged to send 1,500 horses to New Mexico because the Kingdom's herds were virtually all stolen or dead. Food production declined even more since it was unsafe to be out in the fields. Many Spaniards crowded into Santa Fe for safety, while others headed south to El Paso. Mendinueta won a major victory over the Comanches in 1774, but the threat to the region's Spanish and Puebloan inhabitants remained great throughout the decade.[30]

Amid such unrelenting crises, Mendinueta obviously devoted most of his attention to military matters. When not campaigning directly, he had to make sure the presidial forces were always prepared. In addition, as a result of the Rubí inspection of the northern frontier of New Spain, His Majesty's government ordered the imposition of the Reglamento de 1772. Broadly concerned with two issues—promoting peace with native people and reorganizing the presidios—this new policy directive forced Governor Mendinueta to plan on closing the presidio at El Paso and relocating it southward to the isolated Spanish settlement of Carrizal. Another new presidio was to be added north of El Paso at Robledo (though this addition was never carried out), and Spanish settlements were planned between El Paso and Tomé. As yet another indication of the shrinking importance of missionaries in the eyes of the government, the Reglamento set higher presidial salaries, so that an army chaplain earned 480 pesos a year and a sergeant was paid 350 pesos. A mission priest's alms remained at 330 pesos.[31]

Governor Mendinueta's beginnings with the Franciscans in New Mexico were not positive. In January 1768, he wrote Viceroy Marqués de Croix, acknowledging Croix's decision not to secularize the four main Spanish settlements in New Mexico. Don Pedro wanted the viceroy to know that he and his predecessors had been treated rudely by the friars and were often berated from the pulpits. He had to endure these indignities, despite having provided some of the religious materials used in the churches. Furthermore, religious services and ceremonies were not always provided for the Spanish population, and many of the friars were incompetent as priests. Indeed, some Franciscans belonging to the Custody of Saint Paul were "known to be so repugnant" that even other friars had nothing to do with them. Governor Mendinueta begged the marqués to see that these problems were corrected if Franciscans were to continue serving as parish priests.[32]

The ongoing pressures brought to bear by the Comanches, Apaches, and others, coupled with these other defensive commitments, are likely to have added to Mendinueta's early dim view of the Franciscans. Asked by the new viceroy, Don Antonio Bucareli y Ursua (1771–1779), to report on native people and the missions in New Mexico, Mendinueta had little positive to say about the friars' evangelical capabilities. Neophytes were called together once a day "to say prayers, the Commandments, the Articles, and to partake of the Sacraments." Since the missionaries did not know the Puebloans' languages, and they, in turn, knew little Spanish, the Puebloans only memorized what to say; they really did not understand Catholic doctrine. At present, too, the Franciscans were shorthanded, Mendinueta reported. There were only sixteen ordained priests serving twenty-four locations. Zuñi had not had a resident priest for a long time. According to Mendinueta, a Franciscan would only go there once each year to administer to the inhabitants' sacramental needs. Mendinueta had urged the custos to station a friar there permanently, but so far, that had not happened. As to the Franciscans' potential for establishing missions among Comanches, Apaches, and other hostile people, Mendinueta saw that as extremely unlikely, based on current levels of evangelical zeal and ability.[33]

For most of Mendinueta's term, the Franciscans were very quiet. The unrelenting terror generated by Comanche and other raiders, coupled with the severe drought, must have made day-to-day existence depressing enough. Their numbers were waning as well. While Mendinueta reported a mere sixteen friars, a 1769 roster for the entire custody lists only twenty-seven. In El Paso, there were five friars, twenty-two in Santa Fe (Pecos, Galisteo, and Zuñi being vacant), and none in the Junta de los Ríos district. Later notations on that roster listed nine priests who died between 1769 and 1774. These included such once-vigorous and stalwart friars as Andrés Varo, Agustín Iniesta, Juan José Toledo, and Miguel Gómez Cayuela. No replacements for them were listed, which further validates the number of Franciscans reported above by Mendinueta.[34]

The Franciscans' evangelical performance and religious behavior were also concerns within the Order. In 1768–1769, Santo Evangelio sent Fray Pablo Antonio Pérez to New Mexico with the missions' supplies and to assess the friars' abilities and behaviors while there. Fray Pablo, however, reported that New Mexico's missionaries served God, fulfilled their duties, and were learned in the proper religious subjects. Pérez's assertions must be taken with some reservation, as his written report was noticeably vague and omitted any specific reference to individual Franciscans or missions.[35]

Custos Fray Juan José de Hinojosa was more candid and more disappointed in his visita report of 1772. He found some friars serving valiantly and running their missions "without a blemish." Other Franciscans, however, caused Hinojosa dismay. He was especially concerned that some friars were exceeding the bishop of Durango's arancel, at times charging Spanish residents double, and he admonished them to adhere to the established schedule of fees. Without naming individuals, the custos reported that some missionaries in the Santa Fe district did not obey the vice-custos, Fray Mariano Rodríguez de la Torre (the custos still being based in El Paso); others were not residing in their assigned missions; and a few were "disturbing the peace and causing a riot." Those friars breaking the Order's rule of obedience, Hinojosa decreed, were to desist in such behavior.[36]

That same year, the Franciscans were further embarrassed when Fray José Antonio de la Cruz Pollanco (Polanco), serving in the El Paso district, was accused of soliciting sex in the confessional from both genders. Not much is known of Pollanco's background other than that he was a criollo, born about 1727, and he first appeared in the custody in 1762. He had served briefly in Santa Fe, but most of his work seems to have been carried out around El Paso. As a result of these scandalous charges, Pollanco was quickly transferred out of New Mexico. It later came to light that among items he had left behind were things he had stolen; the friar was also a thief.[37]

Signs that the Franciscans in New Mexico had been significantly reduced in power were becoming commonplace. In 1772, the bishop of Durango ordered that in matters involving the responsibilities of ecclesiastical judges, especially those pertaining to marriage, Santiago Roybal would have jurisdiction in the Río Abajo area of the Santa Fe district. The Franciscan appointees (Fray Manuel José Rojo and Fray Andrés García de la Concepción) would assume these duties for Río Arriba. The next year, Viceroy Bucareli directed that church prelates were to submit the qualifications of their clergy to the appropriate bishop or archbishop. The rationale for this order was to ensure that the sacraments were only being performed by those clergy sanctioned to do so as established through the Patronato Real. Also in 1773, a royal cédula arrived that limited the right of asylum to one location for each Spanish community (two sites were allowed for large cities). These could be churches, chapels, missions, or conventos of the regular clergy, but the decisions as to which sites were designated as places of asylum were to be made by agreements reached between civil authorities and episcopates. Governor Mendinueta and the bishop of Durango left things as they had been in New Mexico, since the Kingdom was already in compliance with the cédula. In each of these issues, as far as is known, there were no Franciscan protests or claims of immunity from civil or episcopal jurisdiction.[38]

* * *

In the mid-1770s, the Franciscan hierarchy in New Spain made one last attempt to improve the mission operation in New Mexico and to rekindle the dying evangelical flame among those friars. Two Franciscans sent to the region were primarily responsible for this effort to rally the Custody of Saint Paul: Fray Francisco Silvestre Vélez de Escalante and Fray Francisco Atanasio Domínguez.

Vélez de Escalante arrived in New Mexico first. An hijo de provincia, Fray Silvestre professed in 1767 at San Francisco de México at about age seventeen. He was at that convento until he was ordained, probably early in 1774. By December of that year, Vélez de Escalante was serving in New Mexico at Laguna. The following month, he joined another recent arrival, Fray José Damián Martínez (Martín), as missionary at Zuñi. For a time, that remote Pueblo would have two missionaries in residence, compared to none or one since the 1750s. Fray Silvestre's career as a missionary in New Mexico was to be relatively brief. He became ill in New Mexico and died in 1780 at Parral, where he was being treated.[39]

The other reformer, Fray Francisco Atanasio Domínguez, was a criollo about ten years older than Vélez de Escalante. Born in Mexico City, he also professed at about age seventeen. He certainly was a more experienced friar than Fray Silvestre; his previous assignments included a stint as Franciscan commissary in Veracruz. The title given him by Santo Evangelio in 1775 for his upcoming inspection of the Custody of Saint Paul was that of "canonical visitor," a prestigious and potentially powerful designation within the Order. He was to visit each mission and report on its location, resources, the population it served, and the languages spoken by the inhabitants. All Franciscan buildings, books, and materials were to be inventoried. If any repairs were necessary, Domínguez was to see that those were carried out. Each Franciscan was to be evaluated as to his missionary performance, adherence to the rules of the Order, and Puebloan language skills. Domínguez was authorized to discipline and/or transfer friars as needed, but, in such matters, he was to be "prudent . . . pacific." If Fray Francisco had to chastise a friar, the canonical visitor "must not be too vociferous lest the defects of his brethren became known to the public." Finally, Domínguez was to find a route to connect New Mexico with the recently established Franciscan missions in California. Domínguez expected to carry out his instructions and return to Mexico City for another assignment. He was to remain away from Mexico City, however, until his death almost thirty years later.[40]

Vélez de Escalante took the first step to recharge Franciscan mission programs by leading an entrada to the Hopi provinces. He had been at Zuñi barely six months when he led a group of nineteen others west in late June 1775. They reached Walpi after a three-day march, but made no progress with the Hopi. On 3 July, Vélez de Escalante gave up and headed back to Zuñi. In October, he tried to convince Governor Mendinueta to support another entrada to the Hopi. If a large enough military force was used to pry the Hopi off their mesas and a presidio built to watch them, Fray Silvestre argued, the Hopi could be returned to the Catholic fold. Mendinueta was too hard-pressed by other, more aggressive hostile native people to launch an expedition against the Hopi, so Vélez de Escalante turned next to Mexico City for assistance. In May 1776, he wrote Fray Isidro Murillo (provincial of Santo Evangelio) that the Hopi could be converted, but it would require violence. The Hopi *caciques* (leaders), Vélez de Escalante wrote, barred their people who desired to practice Catholicism from abandoning their apostasy, and the caciques would never loosen their grip without Spanish might being applied. Vélez de Escalante justified the use of coercion through several supporting points: gifts and inducements had previously failed; if the Hopi were subdued by force it would serve as an example for Apaches, Comanches, and other natives; and Hopi reduction would open the door to the Cosninas (Havasupai) territory, a people who desired conversion. Thus, Fray Silvestre's major concerns and efforts were directed westward to the Hopi up to the time Domínguez appeared in the Kingdom.[41]

Domínguez arrived in El Paso in September 1775, though he was unable to go north for almost six more months. El Paso had been raided just a few days prior to Fray Francisco's arrival, and, to the north, Comanche attacks were widespread. Thus, the presidial forces were engaged in chasing these raiders, and none could be spared to escort Domínguez north. He apparently considered going without soldiers, but Hinojosa (still the custos) advised him he was "foolhardy" even to consider that. Domínguez filled this time by returning the goods stolen by Pollanco to their rightful owners and corresponding with the bishop of Durango (Don Antonio Macarulla, 1774–1781) over whether some of the custody's missionaries were properly certified to preach and to handle confession. He also decided to wait in El Paso in hopes that the royal alms, which were already a year in arrears, might arrive and he could carry them to the friars.[42]

With two new Franciscans in tow (Fray José Mariano Rosete y Peralta and Fray José Palacio), Domínguez was escorted north during the first three weeks of March 1776. The journey was relatively uneventful, and the group arrived in Santa Fe on 22 March. He stayed in the governor's palace for over two weeks, and Domínguez seemed to have interacted well with Governor Mendinueta. He agreed to Mendinueta's request to station one of the new friars at Pecos, since that mission was without a priest. However, Fray Damián Martínez apparently had become ill at Zuñi, and Rosete was posted there instead. (Palacio was to be the visita's secretary.) Domínguez was dismayed at the condition of the Franciscan archive and library in Santa Fe. Of the latter, he wrote Murillo that it would "make your Very Reverend Paternity laugh to see the books it contains and the state that it is in." Domínguez inspected the Río Arriba mission group between 10 April and 5 May. The Río Abajo missions took longer. Most of those were inspected between mid-May and early June, except for Isleta, Zuñi, Acoma, and Laguna. The last three were seen in December as Domínguez and Escalante returned from their failed effort to blaze a route to connect New Mexico to California (of which more will be said later). Because of other special circumstances noted below, Isleta was visited in early July 1776.[43]

Domínguez found the Franciscans' missions, conventos, and religious articles in appalling conditions, though he tried to find positive aspects in all he saw. At San Ildefonso, the cloister was "very pretty and cheerful." The pulpit that had been built for the mission at San Juan, Domínguez reported, was "exquisite," similar to what one might see in a cathedral. Pecos had a "pretty wooden confessional." Among the vestments, linens, candlesticks, paintings, and other religious items, he found some that were "pretty," "well made," and "in good condition."[44]

The decay, dirt, and desolation of the Franciscan facilities, however, soon overwhelmed Domínguez. That all the churches had earthen floors surprised him and caused him to describe most of them as "gloomy." At Santa Clara,

Fray Francisco described the adornments of the church as "so soulless that I consider it unnecessary to describe anything so dead." Half of the church's roof at Galisteo was "on the ground and the rest is ready to lie on the floor." He was shocked to find that although the mission at Sandía had opened almost thirty years before, no church had yet been constructed. The Puebloans made do there in the ruins of a pre-1680 church. Most often vestments, linens, and religious articles were "worn," "very worn," "ugly," "poor," "old," "very old," or "mismatched." At San Juan, the figure of Our Lady of the Rosary was decorated with "gewgaws," her dress and mantle were "tattered," and upon her head was "a moth-eaten wig." Even at Spanish churches, such as that at La Cañada, the pulpit was judged "a horror," and the confessional was "badly made." Over half of the mission bells, one of the most enduring symbols of Spanish mission churches (to this day), did not function. They were broken, cracked, or missing their clappers. At Santa Ana, ironically, the Puebloans were summoned to services at the church with a "war drum."[45]

The Christian and civilized behavior of the mission inhabitants lagged far behind what Domínguez thought he would find. For one thing, instruction in matters of the faith followed a sterile formula from mission to mission. Children were brought to the church each morning and evening to recite the catechism. Adults participated on Saturdays and feast days. Rosary was also said then. Mass was celebrated on Sundays and holy days, but confessions were usually carried out only when a Puebloan was gravely ill or near death; the necessity of using interpreters remained a problem. Only at Acoma and Jémez were more energetic and innovative methods being employed, according to Domínguez. Furthermore, the Franciscans told Domínguez that any sort of "explanatory discourse" was beyond the Puebloans' ability to comprehend. They cited a recent sermon against concubinage, given at Sandía by the custos (Hinojosa), which caused the husbands to go home immediately and beat their wives. Of course, a central problem was that the Puebloans were not fluent in Spanish. Domínguez most often wrote that the native people's Spanish language ability was "broken." Only at Tesuque, Nambé, Taos, San Juan, and Isleta did Puebloans speak Spanish somewhat better. As to the native people themselves, they were likely to be described as "timid," "quiet," or "peaceful." Some lagged behind in civilized behaviors, such as those at Picurís who Domínguez found to "abound in filth." On the other hand, Fray Francisco was pleased to note that the inhabitants at Isleta used mattresses on their beds like the Spanish.[46]

Generally speaking, Domínguez found that the Puebloans and their mission priests only peacefully coexisted, at best. At every mission the Puebloans, usually coordinated by their Spanish-appointed leaders, cleaned the church and convento, cooked meals for the friar, brought him firewood, managed the livestock, and provided other labor as might be required on a rotating basis. All Puebloan mission sites had plots of land set aside for growing corn, wheat, and beans for the resident friar; the vast majority of missionaries also had vegetable gardens. The size of the land area allocated for the friar, however, varied widely, based on the resources available and the nature of the neophytes' relationship with their missionary. Some friars were not supported well because of the drought conditions or local locust infestations. But at others, such as Taos and Picurís, Domínguez reported, the Puebloans did as little as possible for the mission priest.[47]

Christian and civilized characteristics, however, were not much better among the Spanish population, according to Domínguez. La Cañada was not a villa at all, but a ramshackle collection of ranchos. The inhabitants were niggardly in their obventions (payments for services such as baptism and marriage ceremonies) and first fruits (a symbolic contribution from what is produced) to the Church, and a local merchant who loaned the friar a measure of chocolate wanted to be repaid at what amounted to six hundred percent interest. As to La Cañada's residents, Domínguez wrote that they "are people of different classes which I refrain from describing in order to avoid prolixity and save confusion. Suffice it to say that most of them pass for Spaniards." Many so-called Spaniards in the Kingdom did not even know when they were born, Fray Francisco noted. The genízaros at Abiquiu were "examples of what happens when idleness becomes the den of evil." In Alburquerque, where a Third Order of St. Francis existed, Domínguez found that the lay body was in such disarray that meetings rarely occurred. He ordered the Third Order's members "to abandon the lethargy and laziness in which they lived." Even the capital of Santa Fe was but a collection of houses and ranchos without streets or order. Indeed, it "lacked everything," and the overall effect was "mournful." Here, too, the inhabitants resisted paying obventions and first fruits. Domínguez freely admitted that the local friar did not adhere to bishop of Durango's arancel; the citizens of the capital refused to pay that much! The people of Santa Fe, he further wrote, were selfish, greedy, and displayed "malice" toward the Franciscans.[48]

It was his brother friars and their behaviors that disappointed and worried Domínguez the most. There were twenty-two ordained missionaries in New Mexico at the time of his visita. Of the missions and Spanish settlements for which the Franciscans were responsible, all but Pecos and Galisteo had at least one priest. Zuñi had two, but Santa Fe, which normally had two friars, had only one in residence in 1776. Of the twenty-two Franciscans, eighteen were criollos, a noticeably higher percentage of New World-born friars than previously described. Perhaps reflecting the wave of deaths that had occurred between 1769 and 1774, the current friars were split relatively evenly between newcomers and seasoned missionaries. Nine were less than forty years of age;

thirteen were over forty. Six (over twenty-five percent) were at least fifty years of age. As to length of service in the custody, eight had five years or less, but thirteen had more than ten years (only one friar was between these two categories).

Domínguez was circumspect in his comments about his fellow friars in his official report to Santo Evangelio. The strongest criticism he levied against missionaries was that books and registers of baptisms, deaths, marriages, and other certifications were not up to date, or that the friar's inventory of materials belonging to a mission or church was not consistent with what Domínguez actually found. Six friars were admonished to bring these documents into line: Fray Manuel José Rojo (La Cañada), Fray Ramón Salas (San Juan), Fray Andrés García de la Concepción (Alburquerque), Fray Manuel Abadiano (Santa Ana), Fray José de Burgos (Zía), and Fray Estanislai Mariano de Marulanda (Cochití). Veteran friars were much more likely to be remiss in their record keeping. Each of these friars chastised by Fray Francisco had more than ten years of service in New Mexico.[49]

If in his report Domínguez was reluctant to condemn missionaries, he had as much difficulty finding priests to praise. Rojo might have had problems with his books and registers, but Domínguez found many residents of La Cañada who esteemed their priest, since "if they had not been struck by lightning, the father [Rojo] was responsible." Fray Andrés de Claramonte at Picurís worked diligently and selflessly under trying circumstances. At Abiquiu, Fray Sebastián Angel Fernández, an hijo de provincia and new to the Kingdom, was "very attentive . . . very zealous" in his work. Furthermore, Fray Sebastián's "love is so great" for the genízaros of Abiquiu. Fray José Manuel Marino, a criollo with less than three years in the custody, followed a teaching regimen of the "most exquisite manner" at Acoma. Marino was following in the footsteps of Fray Pedro Ignacio Pino (died at Acoma in 1767), who had developed a teaching strategy that went beyond rote memorization. Domínguez's greatest praise was reserved for Fray Joaquín de Ruíz, a criollo with more than a decade in New Mexico, who was over fifty years of age. At Jémez, Ruíz incorporated singers into catechism sessions and did extra work on Christian doctrine with married couples. Domínguez avowed that Ruíz's methods were a model for all New Mexico missionaries to follow, and he ordered Ruíz to write out meticulous instructions on how he taught (which Ruíz did). Thus, out of twenty-two mission priests, Domínguez commended only five.[50]

Actually, Domínguez's assessment of the New Mexico missionaries was considerably more negative than his official report revealed. In several letters written to Provincial Murillo, Domínguez detailed a litany of disgraceful behavior. Fray Francisco found that the El Paso district missionaries were not teaching their neophytes anything. The Franciscans there wanted only to obtain "tem-

poral goods" for themselves and procure luxuries "at the cost of the poor Indians' sweat and labor." Several missionaries had gone into debt to support their
extravagant lifestyles. One was over 700 pesos in debt to the tithe, from which
he had "borrowed" before it was remitted to Durango. Such worldly activities
meant mission duties were ignored; Domínguez found some parish books in
which no entries had been made for over five years. Worse still for Franciscan
records, he found pages from mission registers and books used to seal holes in
some convento windows. And finally, according to Domínguez, it was common
knowledge that some of the El Paso friars were engaged in carnal relations with
women who worked in the conventos.[51]

Eventually, Domínguez named individual friars who were particularly scandalous. Domínguez had transferred to El Paso Fray Ramón Salas, who had
been chastised for sloppy record keeping at San Juan. Later, he found Salas in
El Paso openly having an affair with a married woman. At Sandía, Fray Juan
José Llanos, a criollo who had been in the custody five years, was in possession
of "1,020 silver pesos." Domínguez charged that Fray Juan had obtained these
pesos through illicit trade and, incredibly, had stolen from Fray Sebastián
Angel Fernández's fund for the construction of new mission churches at Sandía
and Picurís. Furthermore, when Domínguez tried to transfer Llanos to Laguna, Llanos resisted the move.[52]

The matter involving the mission priest at Isleta was more detailed. It has
been noted that the official visita of Isleta was not carried out until July 1776.
Domínguez said he had been there several times, but he suspected that Fray
José Junco y Junquera, Isleta's missionary, was engaged in illicit trade. Hence,
Domínguez kept delaying an official inspection in the hopes of catching Junco
with evidence of illegal activities. Junco was a criollo, about forty years of age,
who had been in the custody fourteen years. Earlier, Domínguez had praised
the pulpit at San Juan and noted it was built by Junco during the missionary's
stint there. At Cochití, however, where Junco once had been stationed,
Domínguez had the current friar "erase completely" a note written by Junco in
the inventory records that Domínguez described as "indecorous, unbefitting
our [religious] state, and extremely defamatory of our holy habit." Isleta, it
should be pointed out, was well suited for illegal trade being the first mission
encountered by trade wagons coming into New Mexico from El Paso. It was
surrounded by several Spanish communities (especially Tomé), and was easily
accessible to non-mission natives. The mission grew a bounty of crops, had a
wine-producing vineyard, and was supplied by some of the most plentiful obventions and first fruits from nearby Spanish residents, all of which seems to
have gone into Junco's illegal commerce. Indeed, after Junco was removed and
sent out of the custody, Domínguez found other friars squabbling over who
should get Isleta. Domínguez chose Ruíz, the Jémez friar he earlier had

praised, as Isleta's new missionary. He must have believed Ruíz was less likely to become another Franciscan embarrassment.[53]

In yet another letter to Murillo, Domínguez listed friars who should not be serving as missionaries. Andrés García, Manuel Rojo, Mariano Rodríguez de la Torre, and José de Olaeta were described as "old and ill." Francisco Xavier Dávila Saavedra was "sicker than all the others." Even Damián Martínez, in the Kingdom less than two years now, was "very ill and disconsolate." While Domínguez had chastised Marulanda at Cochití for poor record keeping, he now described Marulanda as blind. Two other friars were also described as ill. Hence, at least nine friars were physically incapable of managing their missions.[54]

Others did not have the character to be evangelicals, Domínguez wrote Murillo. Patricio Cuellar was "a notorious drunkard" and José de Burgos "the same." There was Ramón Salas still fornicating with a married woman, and Fray José Manuel Marino was an "incorrigible and with public scandal." Mariano Rosete, who had just arrived in New Mexico with Domínguez, was already "not at all obedient to rule and [an] agitator of Indians." Though Domínguez had praised Sebastián Angel Fernández for his selfless work at Abiquiu, Fray Sebastián, too, "was not obedient to rule." Fray José Gómez Terán (in El Paso) was exposed as the friar who had embezzled the tithe bound for Durango and who lived "an unruly life." Because of personal failings, Domínguez believed seven friars should not be serving in the custody. "They are depraved, disobedient, bold characters and brothers who carry knives and blunderbusses as if they were highwaymen." Therefore, including the physically infirm, Domínguez concluded that over half of the Franciscans serving as mission priests had no business doing so.[55]

✳ ✳ ✳

Domínguez and Vélez de Escalante failed to rejuvenate and expand the missionary operation of New Mexico. In the latter half of 1776, the expedition they directed to forge a trail to California also failed. A last attempt to reconcile the Hopi during the expedition's return leg, Vélez de Escalante's great goal, likewise proved unfruitful. Even when Santo Evangelio selected Domínguez to serve a term as custos (through 1778) in El Paso, and with Vélez de Escalante his vice-custos in Santa Fe, nothing fundamentally improved with the Franciscan mission effort.

In August 1777, Vélez de Escalante pleaded with the New Mexico friars to keep their vows of poverty and not participate in trade. They should not leave their missions without permission; they should say mass every Sunday and on feast days; they should devote as much time as possible in teaching the Puebloans. That some friars were with women was obvious, and, as vice-custos, he ordered "all the friars not to keep suspect company or the counsels of women." He reminded his brethren that St. Francis had a "special precept" to avoid "talking and visiting with women." And once again, Vélez de Escalante admonished the missionaries to avoid disputes and conflicts with the civil authority.[56]

All of these matters had been the concern of various prelates of the custody for at least the last half century. Yet, something was different by now. Perhaps the Franciscans could have hid this decay during the episcopal visitas. It is extremely unlikely, however, that officials such as Ornedal or the governors who served up to the 1760s would have failed to report such scandalous and criminal behavior among the Franciscans had they been as widespread as Domínguez described. One cannot imagine that governors such as Chacón, Bustamante, or Vélez Cachupín would have neglected to name explicitly the friars who were having sexual relations with women or stealing from each other.

So, can Domínguez's descriptions of corrupt Franciscans in New Mexico be believed? First, Domínguez had nothing to gain by exaggerations except, possibly, to be recalled. He asked Murillo to relieve him from the custos office several times because the other friars hated and threatened him. To be relieved in such a manner, however, would have been a blot on the career that Domínguez was building. In addition, the worst charges were reserved for the letters he wrote to Murillo, and were not included in Domínguez's official report. In fact, he was especially circumspect in the latter, praising a few friars for some actions though, later, he was more critical of some of the same Franciscans in his letters to Provincial Murillo. Furthermore, Custos Hinojosa's visita of 1772 (noted above) alluded to every charge Domínguez made to Murillo. Hinojosa just did not make specific allegations against particular friars.

The collapse of Franciscan religious work among the inhabitants of New Mexico appears to have accelerated beginning in the late 1760s. This coincided with the second term of Vélez Cachupín and Mendinueta's administration; both governors were strong and assertive executives. Incessant attacks on missions and settlements by Comanche, Apache, and other native people during these years must have sapped morale among all Spaniards, including the friars. The severe drought only made the conditions of their lives more desperate. In addition, though the Franciscans might have applauded the Jesuits' expulsion, in the long run, what did that say about the direction of church and state relations? If the Society of Jesus was expendable, when might the Order of St. Francis suffer the same fate? Moreover, as seen previously, the royal treasury was often tardy in providing the missionaries with their stipends. Once friars accepted that commercial activity was a necessity to keep their missions provisioned, perhaps their decision to gain personally involved only a short leap.

Maybe cultural and societal changes taking place in the Enlightenment era (to which New Spain was no stranger) had altered the inclinations of young men who became priests, to the point that evangelical self-sacrifice, obedience, and zeal were less crucial. Quite probably, the reasons for the rapid Franciscan demise in New Mexico during the last half of the eighteenth century are to be found in all of these factors.

CHAPTER 12

Conclusion

DOMÍNGUEZ and Vélez de Escalante did not fulfill their goal to reform the Custody of Saint Paul. Fray Silvestre did not live long enough to see the ramifications of their failure. He died in Parral in 1780, possibly a victim of the smallpox epidemic that raged in the region at that time. Domínguez, though, remained in New Mexico and witnessed further ruination of the mission operation. When his term as custos expired in 1778, Fray Francisco stayed in the El Paso district for a while serving as chaplain for the new presidio at Carrizal. During the 1780s, he appears to have been in the Santa Fe district laboring at Zía, Jémez, and Santa Ana. In 1791, Domínguez was taking care of the mission at Isleta. He had departed New Mexico by 1795, although his circumstances were little improved; he was assigned to serve as chaplain at the remote presidio of Janos (about two hundred miles southwest of El Paso). In a letter dated 1 May 1795, he pleaded with the provincial of Santo Evangelio to be given a better assignment, but his entreaty was ignored. Domínguez remained at Janos at least until 1800, and he was dead by 1805. As far as can be ascertained, Domínguez never returned to Mexico City. The deterioration of the Custody of Saint Paul described in his reports and letters was certainly not well received by the Franciscan hierarchy in Mexico City, nor was the messenger ever welcomed back.[1]

Probably in direct response to Domínguez's reports, Santo Evangelio officials dispatched to New Mexico seventeen or eighteen new friars who arrived from Spain in 1778. Between 1777 and 1779, at least seven missionaries examined by Domínguez during his inspection departed the Custody of Saint Paul. Dávila Saavedra, Marulanda, and Rojo, all described as infirm by Domínguez, left. Salas and Marino, friars whose behavior Domínguez reported as scandalous, also departed the colony. With these fresh priests from Spain, the Franciscans reported in 1778 that every post in the custody was filled by at least one ordained friar. Never again, however, would so many Franciscans be in the Kingdom.[2]

If Domínguez felt satisfaction at seeing the arrival of these new Franciscans and the departure of those he had criticized, he could only enjoy it briefly. In 1780–1781, the inhabitants of New Mexico were ravaged by the great smallpox epidemic mentioned above. About a quarter of the population died from the disease, with the greatest losses occurring among the Puebloan population in the Santa Fe district. In a move designed to save money and citing a decline in the number of neophytes, Governor Don Juan Bautista de Anza (1778–1787) requested that the number of Franciscans supported by government alms be reduced to twenty (from thirty-four). Thus, the first official reduction in the number of Franciscan personnel since the beginning of Spanish New Mexico was so ordered by the government.[3]

The Custody of Saint Paul was able to manage some of the lost royal stipends by transferring mission assignments from the now-defunct Junta de los Ríos mission district. The Franciscan presence continued to decline, however, even when the colony's population rebounded quickly in the late 1780s. By 1788, Governor Fernando de la Concha desperately requested that more friars be sent to New Mexico. Governor Concha claimed that even Santa Fe was without an ordained priest. Only sixteen friars were in the Santa Fe district in 1792, though the Spanish and Puebloan inhabitants had grown to 28,000 (6,000 more than Domínguez had counted in 1776). Though five mission sites were secularized by 1797 (Santa Fe, El Paso, Alburquerque, La Cañada, and Tomé), there were no secular priests to administer to those parishes. In fact, no more than two secular clergy were ever in the region at any one time through 1821. Thus, the Franciscans were stretched desperately thin. The government did restore four stipends to the custody in the 1790s, but these were not sufficient to meet the needs of the rapidly growing population. Custos José Benito Pereyro reported in 1808 that six Puebloan mission sites were without friars. In 1821, as Mexico gained independence from Spain, twenty-three friars in the custody administered to almost 40,000 people. Considering distances, terrain, and climate, that on average each missionary was responsible for over 1,700 individuals presented a monumental challenge to the Custody of Saint Paul.[4]

The Franciscans' influence was virtually invisible in the considerations of government after 1776. Indeed, they were barely mentioned, if at all, in some of the most important official documents of the last decades of the Spanish period. After the creation of the Provincias Internas in the Bourbon political reorganization of the late 1770s, Teodoro de Croix, the first commandant-general of this new jurisdiction, inspected his territory. His long report and subsequent recommendations made only passing reference to the Franciscan missions in New Mexico. Governor Fernando de Chacón's report of 1803 only referred to the fact that the Franciscans received royal stipends as did he, the lieutenant governor, and presidial soldiers. Governor Chacón's remaining concerns were directed to the region's economic development. The *Exposición* of Don Pedro Baptista Pino, New Mexico's only delegate in 1812 to the Spanish Cortes in Cádiz, was less concerned with Franciscans than the religious condition of region's inhabitants. Pino urged that New Mexico be elevated to a diocese since the population was large enough to support a bishop. Pino lamented that a bishop of Durango had not visited the region since Tamarón in 1760. Pino claimed that there were twenty-two Franciscans in the colony, a number woefully insufficient for New Mexico's needs. Other than that, Pino found little else that the delegates in Cádiz needed to know about the Custody of Saint Paul.[5]

After Domínguez's inspection in 1776, the Franciscans seemed to have steadily declined in significance. Where once the direction of New Mexico's affairs was charted by numerous capable and assertive missionaries, by 1800, the average New Mexican must have had to search hard simply to find a friar. And what the Franciscans did beyond the spiritual seemed to have had little relevance to local or viceregal Spanish government officials.

* * *

The Franciscans' reduced circumstances at the end of the eighteenth century were set into motion, as seen previously, during the reoccupation of New Mexico after the Puebloan revolt. "The year eighty" temporarily freed the Puebloan people from the missionaries' hold and taught the friars a hard lesson. Their frequently described "timid" neophytes were capable of violent retributions against the missionaries. Indeed, Puebloan resistance to Governor Vargas's forces in 1694, the uprising in 1696 that provided the Franciscans with more martyrs, and repeated signs of Puebloan enmity during the following decade were powerful reminders to the Franciscans of what Puebloan wrath could inflict.

Had these priests been the veteran missionaries of the pre-1680 era, and had their numbers been sufficient in the 1690s, perhaps the Franciscans would have been capable of returning the mission program to its previous state. The fact of the matter, though, was that the friars were ill-prepared to reopen the missions. As noted, there were few pre-1680 priests in the Kingdom; most of the friars in 1694 were young and inexperienced. In addition, there were not nearly enough ordained priests, as less than half the pre-1680 number accompanied Vargas's expedition. Moreover, Franciscan personnel levels did not reach full capacity until three decades after the reconquest.

Two important patterns regarding the Franciscans were established during the reconquest. Understandably, fearful friars working alone among antagonistic Puebloans developed a dependency on government officials for protection. Thus, the Franciscans began the post-1680 epoch less assertive in their interactions with New Mexico officials than they had been prior to "the year eighty." Second, the mission priests sought accommodation with their neophytes. No longer was every kiva to be destroyed or every Puebloan religious article burned. Friars came to argue, as seen previously, that some Puebloan customs, such as face painting, were essentially harmless. In the Franciscans' efforts to mollify the Puebloans, to be less than rigorous in extirpating what heretofore friars had labeled pagan activities, the Custody of Saint Paul opened itself to criticism and denunciation from the local government and the diocese of Durango.

Local government, especially the office of governor, grew stronger during the eighteenth century and further weakened the Franciscan position in New Mexico. Part of this process was a result of His Majesty's officials' concern with securing New Mexico and solidifying the defense of the northern boundaries of the empire. French intrusions into the region and destructive raids by hostile native people had to be countered. Therefore, presidial forces replaced the ad hoc militias of the pre-1680 era. The governor was made captain general of these forces. Puebloan auxiliary units were formed, also under the command of the governor, not the Franciscans. Hence, the governors had greater interest in the Puebloan adoption of Spanish behaviors, once the sole bailiwick of the friars. The governors' term in office was also lengthened, and these officials were given significant controls over the Kingdom's economy, especially in the first decades after the reconquest. Where friars once dominated weak governors in New Mexico, the holder of the governor's baton now was much stronger.

Of course, bolstering the power of local officials at the expense of the Church was a hallmark of Bourbon political policy. The Bourbon family's assumption of the Spanish throne in the early eighteenth century launched a new era in church and state relations. This policy was aimed at augmenting Bourbon political control and improving the empire's economic potential. Thus, events that occurred in what previously were seen as marginal peripheral areas, such as New Mexico, now drew more interest from the government. Institutions that had retained elements of autonomy in regards to political control came under Bourbon pressures to eliminate that autonomy. Entities seen as hindering, challenging, or competing with Bourbon economic goals likewise were brought to heel. The Church fit both descriptions, and, consequently, was steadily weakened by the Bourbons throughout most of the 1700s. The strengthening of the office of governor did not happen in one royal decree, and, as seen here, some governors were less assertive than others. The trend was cumulative; in disputes between the Franciscans and local officials, His Majesty's government most often ruled in favor of civil and military authority.[6]

The Franciscans in New Mexico usually found His Majesty's government to be more supportive of the secular side of the Church as well. A significant factor underlying the Franciscans' hegemony in seventeenth-century New Mexico was their independence from episcopal jurisdiction. The Custody of Saint Paul's friars, as noted previously, enjoyed most of the rights and privileges of secular priests without suffering a bishop's control. During the 1600s, this was a powerful weapon, especially their ability to excommunicate their opponents. In addition, the Franciscans had in their hands most of the reins of spiritual authority over the Kingdom's inhabitants. To the Bourbons, though, missions were economic and political anachronisms. Throughout the Bourbon century, the monarchy's policy was to steadily eliminate these outmoded religious havens, and one way to do that was to strengthen the secular clergy, often through secularizing missions. For New Mexico, the government first needed to affirm episcopal jurisdiction over the Custody of Saint Paul. Again, this did not happen overnight, but by Bishop Tamarón's 1760 visita, the Franciscans had been forced to accept at least the forms of diocesan control. Since bishops were so far away and secular clergymen were scarce, the friars still exhibited considerable autonomy in day-to-day affairs. Symbolically and legally, though, Franciscan prestige and influence were weakened through the establishment of episcopal jurisdiction. In addition, the Holy Office's eighteenth-century policy of limiting the Franciscans' access to the Inquisition further sapped the friars' religious might over New Mexico's officials and other inhabitants.

* * *

The Franciscans had no shortage of human scapegoats to offer as excuses as to why the mission program was failing to fulfill its goals. The friars blamed government officials, bishops, secular clergymen, Comanches, Apaches, and even their Puebloan neophytes for the deficiencies in the mission operation. And to be certain, by 1730 at least, the Franciscans were acutely aware that all was not well in the New Mexico mission field. The friars also acknowledged that they were themselves partly at fault. The reform effort of the mid-eighteenth century was born out of the Franciscans' realization that the Puebloans were not being adequately indoctrinated into the faith nor acculturated as Spaniards. Furthermore, the Hopi missions had yet to reopen and Catholicism was not being propagated among other native people in the region, such as the Navajo. That surge in Franciscan reform measures peaked by 1750, but then quickly died out.

The question that remains is what role did the Franciscans play in their own breakdown? Some historians have concluded that the eighteenth-century missionaries were simply inferior as evangelicals when compared to their pre-1680 brethren. To one scholar, the seventeenth-century friars were "inflamed by millennial dreams and aglow with the spirit of apostolic renewal." These priests were "the most radical members of the Order" laboring to create "a theocracy, a utopia." In short, the New Mexico friars of the 1600s were "a legion of highly disciplined ascetic virtuosi." In comparison, those who served in the Kingdom after the reconquest were "not the zealous ascetics of the previous century"; they had "no desire to suffer martyrdom" in order to propagate their faith. If losing one's life for one's faith is the key measurement of evangelical fervor, then certainly the pre-1680 missionaries easily won that laurel. As many as forty-nine of these friars were killed by native people, four times more than the number slain after 1694.[7]

Not all New Mexico missionaries of the seventeenth century, however, were paragons of missionary devotion and virtue. Almost all of the friars abandoned the region with the colonists in 1601. Friars squabbled with the custos, especially over choice billets, and ten new missionaries exhibited so little commitment that they deserted the supply caravan in El Paso in 1659 rather than go on to serve in the Santa Fe district mission field. There are good reasons to suspect that the Franciscans were involved to some degree in the murder of Governor Luís de Rosas. Fray Miguel Sacristán committed suicide because of his participation in hiding an extramarital affair of Governor Juan Manso (1656–1659). There are individual cases of friars engaging in sexual relations with Puebloan women, and Fray Diego de Parraga admitted (in 1661) that he had fathered a child by a native woman. This is not meant to exonerate any deficiencies of the eighteenth-century friars, but simply to put their behaviors and characteristics into better perspective with those of their predecessors.[8]

There do not seem to be major differences in how Franciscans were deployed as missionaries in New Mexico between the seventeenth and eighteenth centuries. While no empirical study has been offered on the pre-1680 friars, archival records suggest that, on average, these missionaries were kept in the field about the same amount of time as those who came later. If the mission at Pecos is typical, the average tenure of a friar there in the 1600s was 2.5 years, almost identical to that of the eighteenth century. This seems to point to frequent transfers among missions, a problem cited by the friars in the 1700s. Two major differences do exist. First, more gachupín friars served in New Mexico during the 1600s, at least through 1640. After that date, however, criollos were the majority, as they were in the 1700s. Second, friars more often served in pairs at a mission site before 1680, a luxury few enjoyed after "the year eighty." Otherwise, the differences in the deployment of mission priests in the pre- and post-1680 periods seem almost inconsequential.[9]

Of course, this does not answer the perplexing question as to why obvious problems in the mission operations within the Order and the custody were not resolved. Why were friars kept in the mission field for such long periods, even when advancing age and physical infirmities clearly rendered them ineffective as evangelicals? Why were missionaries transferred with such frequency from mission to mission, often without consideration of their previous experience,

when the Franciscans admitted by 1730 that frequent transfer was not a beneficial policy? Inadequate personnel levels both in New Mexico and New Spain
might be an explanation, though the Franciscans never offered that as a defense. The custody claimed on one occasion, as noted earlier, that friars were
often transferred in an effort to establish good matches between Puebloans and
missionaries. That this policy continued, however, suggests that it was rare to
have a priest and Puebloan group establish a positive bond.

The most frequently cited Franciscan failure as missionaries, as repeatedly
noted, was in mastering Puebloan dialects and teaching Spanish to the neophytes. The critics of the Franciscans charged that the Puebloans did not really
understand Catholic doctrine, but merely memorized words to recite and
mimicked religious gestures. Puebloans avoided the confessional because interpreters had to be present for the friar to communicate with the penitent. Indeed, many instances of what some referred to as "pagan" activities could have
been a result of the Puebloans' imperfect understanding of Catholicism, or so
some officials accused the Franciscans.

The problem of language is another manifestation of a failure within the
Franciscans' mission policy. As noted previously, friars arrived in the Kingdom
without relevant language training, a glaring oversight in their preparation.
Once in the custody, the missionaries were exposed to a multitude of strange
languages. It seems incomprehensible that friars were then moved frequently
from mission to mission without regard to the language or dialect that the priest
would need to speak. That only a dozen or so Franciscans did become fluent
in a Puebloan tongue, usually because of long associations with one language
group, speaks volumes on the bankruptcy of the Franciscan mission program
regarding priests' language proficiency. How could Puebloans be grounded in
Catholic doctrine if the missionary could not communicate with them in their
native tongue?

Yet, the absence of language proficiency does not seem to have been a Franciscan failing specific to eighteenth-century New Mexico. There is no evidence
that a larger proportion of pre-1680 friars was expert in Puebloan languages;
neither did that group produce or publish Puebloan grammars or dictionaries,
or at least none that survived 1680. In addition, Franciscan language deficiencies were used as leverage by bishops, beginning in the mid-1600s, to secularize missions in other areas of New Spain. Nonetheless, the Franciscan
missionary school at Santiago de Tlatelolco continued to drill future missionaries only in Nahuatl, Otomí, and Tarascán. Thus, it seems that the failures in
native language proficiency by the Franciscans were more systemic and less an
aberrant shortcoming of New Mexico's friars.[10]

As to teaching the Puebloans Spanish, the Franciscans probably deserved
more credit than they officially received, though their efforts were uneven and

probably depended on the relationships between particular mission priests and their charges. That Puebloan interpreters were used in many of their people's interactions demonstrates that some neophytes were capable Spanish speakers. Many of the official reports noted previously as critical of the Franciscans, often included allegations elicited from Puebloans, information presumably communicated by them at some point in Spanish. To be sure, New Mexico's governors were never congratulated for their fluency in Puebloan languages, though some alcaldes mayores may have been bilingual. Bishop Tamarón opined that Puebloans and Spaniards seemed to communicate well when it came to matters of commerce and trade.

Indeed, that the Puebloan people partially defended themselves with a linguistic shield is likely a paramount reason why the Franciscans failed to establish fluent communications with them. It has already been noted that the major Puebloan tongues incorporated few cognates or loan words, despite the fact that the Spanish introduced them to many alien material items and intellectual concepts. Hence, an often helpful tool in mastering a new language was denied the mission priests. Certainly by the eighteenth century, the Puebloans would have learned that language was an effective weapon at keeping the Spanish, especially the missionaries, at arm's length. There was very little incentive, if any, for Puebloans to assist the Franciscans in their efforts to speak fluent Keres, Tano, or Zuñi, but there were many reasons to thwart the friars.[11]

The Puebloans had more incentives to learn the conquerors' language. The Spanish population grew steadily in the 1700s and settled over a broader region than before 1680. Interactions between Puebloans and government officials became more common as civil authority expanded in the colony, and Puebloans served as auxiliaries in Spanish military forces. Commercial ties also increased between Spaniards and Puebloans. These developments in eighteenth-century New Mexico provided concrete incentives for the Puebloans to learn Spanish, even if only as acknowledgment of the adage, "know thine enemy." Whether or when Puebloans chose to speak Spanish was likely determined by circumstances that would redound in the Puebloans' favor.

This study has focused on the breakdown of Franciscan power and influence in Spanish New Mexico within the context of significant developments throughout the frontier region, New Spain, and Spain. Over two centuries later the effects of this historical process linger. Certainly it is easy to find Catholic influence in late twentieth-century New Mexico. Large cities, small communities, and Puebloan reservations all have their Catholic churches. What is often more surprising, to outsiders of the region, is the vibrancy of Native American culture. Nowhere within the continental boundaries of the United States have native people been better able to sustain their traditional lands, social structures, and cultural activities than have the Puebloan, Hopi, and Navajo peoples. The English-speaking, Protestant juggernaut, which obliterated innumerable indigenous societies from the Atlantic to the Pacific, did not destroy all of the native groups within the Custody of Saint Paul. Several factors explain this anomaly: historical timing, environmental conditions, Spanish policies, and the resiliency and resourcefulness of Southwestern native people. Yet another factor sets these inhabitants apart from other Native Americans: for almost three centuries they experienced European culture in a setting that inadvertently allowed native people time to adapt themselves to meet future challenges. Especially after 1680, the Hopi were able to retain their autonomy almost completely for over a century, the Navajo moved in and out of the Spanish world, and the Puebloans found that their cultural and social mores could coexist with the Spanish. A significant factor contributing to these developments was the accommodation the Franciscan missionaries practiced with native people after "the year eighty." To be sure, accommodation was not the Franciscans' stated goal. Had the friars' circumstances been different it is certainly likely that they would have been more demanding of native religious compliance and more aggressive in eradicating native culture. Yet, the unforeseen consequence is part of our fascination with human history. Due to the decline of Franciscan hegemony in New Mexico, our world today is enriched by the native cultures that outlasted the missions.

Appendix

The Franciscans of New Mexico, 1692–1776

The following presents information on the ordained Franciscan friars who served in the Santa Fe district of the New Mexico missions during the 1692–1776 period. Included are known dates that the friars were active with the Custody of Saint Paul, nationality, personal/family background data, date of profession of faith, and other pertinent material.

Abadiano, Manuel (1765–1777), criollo. Professed in 1727 at age 18. Died at San Juan in 1777 at age 68.

Acevedo, Antonio (1682–1702), criollo, native of Veracruz. Professed at San Francisco de Puebla in 1674.

Aguilar, Juan (1731–1765), criollo, native of Puebla. Father: Juan de Aguilar, criollo, described as an artisan. Mother: Gertrudis de Ledesma, criolla (deceased at time Juan entered Order). Paternal grandparents owned a starch shop in Puebla. Maternal grandparents were traders in Veracruz. Professed at San Francisco de Puebla in 1709 at age 18.

Alpuente, Juan (1693–1696).

Álvarez, Juan (1680–1708), criollo, native of Mexico City. Father: gachupín from Toledo, described as a captain in the royal army. Mother: criolla from Mexico City. Professed at the convento of San Diego in Mexico City in 1679 at age 16. Served at least two terms as custos.

Aparicio, Antonio (1714–1726), gachupín. Arrived in New Spain about 1706.

Arbizu (Arvisu), José de (1694–1696), criollo, orphan (Mexico City?). Professed at San Francisco de Puebla in 1679 at age 16. Killed during the 1696 Pueblo uprising.

Archundía, José de (1731–?), criollo, native of Toluca. Father: Antonio de Archundía, native of Toluca. Mother: Isabel Montes de Oca, native of Toluca. Paternal grandfather was described as an artisan. Maternal grandfather was described as a merchant and bookkeeper for the Order of Saint Francis in Puebla.

Professed at San Francisco de México in 1723 at age 24. A brother entered the Order at about the same time.

Arévalo, Lucas de (1709–1714), gachupín. Arrived in New Spain about 1706.

Arias de Espinosa, Diego (1723–1737), hijo de provincia, native of Galicia. Father: Don Francisco Arias de Espinosa, native of Galicia, described as an officer in the royal navy. Mother: Doña Thomasa Francesca de Herrera, native of Galicia. Both paternal and maternal grandparents referred to as Don and Doña, and both grandfathers were described as merchants in Galicia. Professed at San Francisco de Puebla in 1714.

Arranegui, José de (1700–1708), hijo de provincia, native of Vizcaya. Father: Santiago de Arranegui, described as a merchant. Mother: Magdalena de Meabe. Both parents native to Vizcaya and still resided there at the time their son professed. Professed at San Francisco de México in 1695. Listed as procurador general for Santo Evangelio in 1713.

Bahamonde (Baamonde), Antonio (1694–1696), gachupín. Arrived in New Spain in 1692 as part of the Propaganda Fide.

Barroso, Cristóbal Alonso (1691–1700), hijo de provincia, native of Lisbon, Portugal. Professed at San Francisco de México in 1685.

Benavides, Rafael (1771–1807), criollo. Professed at San Francisco de México in 1768 at age 20. After 1778, served primarily in the El Paso district where he died in 1807.

Bermejo, Manuel (1749–1755), gachupín. Arrived in New Spain in 1743.

Blanco, José (1743–1748), criollo, native of Mexico City. Father: Don José Blanco, native of Burgos, Spain. Mother: Doña Catharina Álvarez, native of Mexico City. Professed at San Francisco de México in 1728 at age 16.

Bravo Lerchundí, Francisco Manuel (1730–1735), criollo, native of Puebla. Father: Antonio Bravo de Laguna, native of Puebla, described as an *alférez* (junior officer) in the Spanish army. Mother: Doña Ana Muñoz de Ballesteros, native of Puebla. Paternal grandparents were both gachupines and described as merchants. Maternal grandparents were criollos who owned a commercial enterprise that dyed cloth. Professed at San Francisco de Puebla in 1700 at age 16.

Bretons (Brotons), Francisco (1707–1713), criollo. Died at Taos in 1713 of an illness.

Brizuela, Antonio (1761–?), criollo, native of Mexico City. Professed in Mexico City at age 19. Arrived in New Mexico at age 31.

Burgos, José de (1760–1788), criollo, native of Veracruz. Professed in Puebla in 1748 at age 16.

Camargo, Antonio (1699–1735?/1737?), hijo de provincia, native of Santander. Father: Juan de Camargo, native of Santander. Mother: María Galbán, native of Santander. Professed in 1697. Served at least one term as custos.

Campo Redondo, Francisco (1757–1765).

Campos, Miguel (1755–1757).

Carbonel, Antonio (1694–1696), gachupín, arrived in New Spain in 1687. Died in the Pueblo uprising in 1696.

Castro, Jacobo de (1752–1762), hijo de provincia, native of Galicia. Father: José Manuel de Castro, native of Galicia. Mother: Juana de Soto, native of the city of Córdoba. Professed at San Francisco de México in 1736 at age 16. Served as custos at least three terms. Previously assigned as a missionary in the Custody of Tampico, where he served at least once as custos for that Franciscan region.

Cayetano de Otero, Francisco Benito (1731–1768), hijo de provincia, native of Galicia. Father: Francisco de Otero y Lamas, native of Galicia. Mother: Doña Manuela de la Vega y Montenegro, native of Galicia. Parents were described as landowners in Galicia. A brother of Fray Francisco was said to be a priest, and a sister, a nun. Professed at San Francisco de Puebla in 1725 at age 24.

Ceballos (Zevallos), Andrés (1726–1749), gachupín. Professed at age 17. Served as a missionary near Zacatecas for at least two years prior to his arrival in New Mexico.

Cepeda y Arriola, Miguel Francisco (1709–1712), criollo, native of Puebla. Father: Agustín de Cepeda, native of Puebla, described as a carpenter. Mother: Josepha de Arriola, native of Puebla. (Both parents were deceased when Miguel entered the Order.) Paternal grandparents were criollos and he was described as a trader. Maternal grandparents were gachupines and he was described as a surgeon. Professed at San Francisco de Puebla in 1704 at age 32.

Chavarría, Diego de (1689–1701), criollo, native of Tacubaya. Father: Luís de Chavarría, native of Tacubaya. Mother: Clara de Sumaya, native of Tacubaya. Professed at San Francisco de México in 1679 at age 17.

Claramonte, Andrés de (1764–1779), criollo, native of Mexico City. Professed in Mexico City in 1758 at age 21. Later served as a missionary outside of New Mexico and died in 1800.

Colina, Agustín de (1689–1708). Served at least one term as custos. Colina had previously served as a missionary for an undetermined period near Zacatecas.

Concepción González, Francisco de la (1739–1750), hijo de provincia, native of Burgos. Father: Andrés González, native of Burgos. Mother: Francesca Ambosso, native of Burgos. Professed at San Francisco de México in 1727 at age 21.

Corral, Juan Antonio del (1694–1698).

Corvera (Corbera), Francisco de (1691–1696), criollo, native of Manila, Philippines. Professed in Mexico City in 1684. Died in the Pueblo uprising in 1696.

Cruz, Juan de la (1719–1746), gachupín. Arrived in New Spain in 1717.

Cruz Polanco (Pollanco), José Antonio de la (1762–1773), criollo. Professed in 1744 at age 17.

Dávila Saavedra, Francisco Xavier (1750–1777), criollo, native of Florida. Professed in Veracruz in 1739 at age 24.

Daza, Juan (1693–1698), criollo, native of Mexico City. Father: Cristóbal Daza,

native of Mexico City. Mother: Doña Ana de Medina y Castro, native of Mexico City. Professed at San Francisco de Puebla in 1662.

Delgado, Carlos José (1710–1749), gachupín, native of Andalucía. Born in 1677. Arrived in New Spain as a member of the Propaganda Fide in 1708, but left that Franciscan group for unspecified reasons. On the roster of the Order's Hospicio de Santa Barbara del Pueblo de Tlatelolco in 1750.

Díaz, Ignacio (1731–?), criollo, native of Mexico City. Father: Doctor Salvador Díaz, native of Mexico City. Mother: Doña María de las Rosas, native of Mexico City. Professed at San Francisco de México in 1718 at age 17.

Díaz de Aguilar, Pedro (1726–1743), criollo, native of Puebla. Professed at San Cosmé de México in 1713.

Díez, José (1694–1696), gachupín. Member of the Propaganda Fide. From 1716 to 1718 was the guardian of the Propaganda Fide's Colegio de Santa Cruz in Querétaro.

Duenas, Francisco (1772–1793), criollo. Professed in Mexico City in 1733 at age 17.

Eguía de Lumbre, José de (1732–1743).

Esparragoza y Adame, José (1763–1766).

Esquer, Antonio (1724–1749), hijo de provincia, native of Sevilla. Father: Don Balthasar de Esquer, native of Sevilla. Mother: Doña María de Aguilar y Cueva, native of Sevilla. Professed at San Francisco de México in 1711 at age 17. A brother (Salvador Antonio Esquer) professed on the same day.

Ezeiza, Juan Antonio (1730–1762), hijo de provincia, native of Vizcaya. Father: Domingo de Ezeiza, native of Vizcaya. Mother: Bernarda de Almasorrayon, native of Vizcaya. Professed at San Francisco de México in 1724 at age 22.

Farfán, Francisco (1678–1703), hijo de provincia, native of Cádiz. Father: Juan Farfán, native of Cádiz, described as a night watchman. Mother: Isabel García, native of Cádiz. Both parents were living in Mexico City at the time Juan professed. Professed at San Francisco de México in 1662 at age 18.

Fernández, Sebastián Angel (1772–1788), hijo de provincia, native of Galicia. Professed in Mexico City in 1758 at age 19.

Gabaldón, Antonio (1723–1760), criollo, native of Puebla. Father: Don Antonio Ruíz Gabaldón (deceased when Antonio entered the Order), gachupín (Castilla?). Mother: Doña Michaela Rendon de Córdova, native of Puebla. Paternal grandparents (both referred to as Don and Doña) were natives of Castilla, grandfather described as a former *regidor* and *alcalde ordinario*. Maternal grandparents (she was referred to as Doña) were natives of Puebla, and described as owners of a commercial pork operation. Professed at San Francisco de Puebla in 1717 at age 17.

Garaicoechea, Juan de (1699–1706). Died at Zuñi in 1706.

García, Angel (1743–1749), hijo de provincia, native of Murcia, Spain. Father: Benito García, native of Albareta, Spain. Mother: Ana (?) Delgada, native of Madrid. Professed at San Francisco de México in 1728 at age 24.

García de la Concepción, Andrés José (1746–1779), criollo, native of Puebla. Father: Miguel García, native of Puebla, described as a blacksmith. Mother: Michaela Palacios, native of Puebla. Both sets of grandparents were criollos. Professed at San Francisco de Puebla in 1736 at age 17. Died in Mexico City in 1779.

García de Noriega, José (1756–1775), criollo, native of Mexico City. Professed in Mexico City in 1745 at age 16.

García Marín, José (1694–1696), gachupín. Arrived in New Spain in 1692. Member of the Propaganda Fide.

Gómez Cayuela, Manuel/Miguel (1745–1769), gachupín, professed in Andalucía in 1725 at age 26. Arrived in New Spain in 1743.

González, Jacinto (1733–1769), hijo de provincia, native of Cádiz. Father: Don Francisco Manuel González, native of Cádiz, described as a lawyer. Mother: Doña Margarita Teresa Toscano, native of Cádiz. Both sets of grandparents were natives of Andalucía, and both were referred to as Don and Doña. Professed at San Francisco de Puebla in 1730 at age 43. Fray Jacinto had been a lawyer for about twenty years previously in Oaxaca.

Guerrero, Antonio (1700–1706), criollo, native of Mexico City. Professed at San Francisco de México in 1692. He was custos for one term.

Guerrero, José Antonio (1714–1743), criollo, native of Mexico City. Father: Juan Clemente Guerrero, native of Madrid. Mother: Doña Josefa Martínez de la Vega, native of Mexico City. No information was offered on paternal grandparents, but maternal grandparents were natives of Mexico City and he was described as being involved in mining. Professed at San Francisco de México in 1694 at age 16. He was custos for at least one term.

Guzmán, Francisco Javier (1743–1767), criollo, native of Puebla. Father: Don Francisco de Guzmán, gachupín, described as a merchant. Mother: Doña Michaela Moncayo, criolla. Both parents resided in Tlaxcala. Paternal grandparents were only noted to have been natives of Spain. The maternal grandfather was a gachupín, and described as a regidor of Puebla; the maternal grandmother was a criolla (both were referred to as Don and Doña). Professed at San Francisco de Puebla in 1735 at age 17.

Hermida, Buenaventura (1772–1780), hijo de provincia, native of Galicia. Professed in 1759 at age 21.

Hernández, Juan José (1741–1758), criollo, native of Tlaxcala. Professed at San Cosmé de México in 1730.

Hinojosa, Juan José de (1765–1781), criollo, native of Puebla. Professed in Puebla in 1742 at age 19. He was custos for three terms.

Hoyuela, Gabriel (1730–1743?/1745?), criollo, native of Mexico City. Professed at San Francisco de México in 1720. He was custos for at least one term.

Iniesta, Agustín de (1743–1770), criollo, native of Zinacantepec (near Toluca). Father: Juan de Iniesta, native of Toluca, described as a woodcarver. Mother: Luzarda de la Fuente, native of Toluca. Both sets of grandparents were natives of Toluca, and only the grandmothers were referred to as Doña. Professed at San

Francisco de Llagas in Puebla in 1734 at age 24. He had earlier been a novice at San Cosmé de México.

Irazábal, Francisco de (1707–1732).

Irigoyen, José de (1724–1760), criollo, native of Puebla. Father: Don Pedro de Irigoyen, a gachupín from Navarra. Mother: Doña Rosa Irrieta y Maulean, native of Puebla. Paternal grandparents were also from Navarra, and were described as "from noble descent." The maternal grandparents were from Vizcaya, but he was described as an alcalde ordinario of Puebla. Professed at San Francisco de Puebla in 1716 at age 17.

Jesús Cuellar, Patricio de (1766–1774), criollo, native of Tulantzingo. Professed in Puebla in 1749 at age 16.

Jesús María, Domingo de (1694–1696), gachupín. Arrived in New Spain in 1692. Member of the Propaganda Fide.

Jesús María Casañas, Francisco de (1694–1696), gachupín, native of Catalonia. Member of the Propaganda Fide and had previously served in their mission efforts in Texas. Killed during the Pueblo uprising in 1696.

Jiménez de Cisneros, Alonso (1694–1706), criollo.

Junco y Junquera, José (1762–1776), criollo. Professed in Mexico City in 1753 at age 16. He was serving later (1779) in the Custody of Tampico mission field.

Larias, Francisco (1731–?).

Lipianí (Lepiane), Francisco de (1724–1728). Served one term as custos.

Liñán, Jerónimo (1711–1718). Left New Mexico after being accused of solicitation in the confessional.

Llanos, Juan José (1771–1787), criollo, native of Toluca. Professed in Mexico City in 1754 at age 18. Died in El Paso in 1787.

López Tello, José (1707–1729), criollo, native of Mexico City. Professed at San Francisco de México in 1702. He was custos for one term.

Loreno, Miguel (1731–1749).

Marino, José Manuel (1771–1779), criollo, born in 1735. He was transferred to the Custody of Tampico mission field in 1779.

Martínez (Martín), José Damián (1774–1779), hijo de provincia. Professed in Mexico City in the 1740s. In 1792 he was listed as the guardian of San Francisco de México.

Martínez de Araoz, Domingo (1706–1731), hijo de provincia, native of Gamboa. Father: Juan Martínez de Araoz, native of the Azores Islands, described as a ranchero. Mother: Doña Augustina de Aspe, native of Spain. Both parents lived near Tlaxcala. Professed at San Francisco de Puebla in 1699. Died at Santa Ana in 1731, possibly poisoned.

Mariano de Marulanda, Estanislai (1759–1778), criollo, native of Ozumba (northern central valley of Mexico). Professed in Mexico City in 1750 at age 25. He was described as blind in 1777.

Matha, Pedro de (1694–?), hijo de provincia, native of Toledo. Professed at San Francisco de México in 1688.

Menchero, Juan Miguel (1729–1750), hijo de provincia, native of Villanueva de los Infantes (Castilla). Father: Don Pedro Sánchez, native of Castilla, described as a merchant. Mother: Doña Antonia Ibañez, native of Castilla. Both sets of grandparents were referred to as Don and Doña, and both grandfathers were described as merchants. Fray Juan took the Menchero from his paternal grandfather. Professed at San Francisco de Puebla in 1714 at age 19.

Medrano, José (1772–1784), criollo, native of Toluca. Professed in 1748 at age 20.

Miranda, Antonio de (1700–1737), criollo, native of Sombrerete. After leaving New Mexico he served as a notary at Santiago de Tlatelolco and as provincial secretary in Mexico City into the late 1740s.

Mingues, Juan (1706–1720), criollo, native of Mexico City. Father: Francisco Mingues, gachupín, described as an artisan. Mother: Juana de los Ríos, native of Mexico City. (Both parents were deceased when Juan entered the Order.) The maternal grandparents lived in Parral and he was described as a merchant. Professed at San Francisco de México in 1694. Juan was killed in 1720 when the Villasur party was massacred.

Montaño, Pedro (1728–1758), criollo, native of Zempuala. Father: Diego de la Cruz, native of Zempuala. Mother: María Isabel de Saldenno, native of Zempuala. Professed at San Francisco de México in 1703 at age 17. Pedro labored primarily in the El Paso district, with but a brief tenure in the Santa Fe district.

Moreno, Antonio (1694–1696), criollo, native of Mexico City. Father: Don Francisco Moreno, native of Madrid. Mother: Doña Theresa Zarate, native of Mexico City. Professed at San Francisco de México in 1682 at age 17. He was killed in the Pueblo uprising in 1696.

Muñiz de Luna, Miguel (1691–1718), criollo, native of Puebla. Father: Antonio Muñiz, native of Puebla. Mother: Gregoria de Luna, native of Puebla. Professed at San Francisco de Puebla in 1684 at age 18. He served as custos for one term.

Muñoz de Castro, Juan (1680–1698).

Murciano de la Cruz, Tomás (1752–1762).

Obregón, Antonio de (1693–1700), hijo de provincia, native of Burgos. Father: Don Domingo de Obregón, native of Burgos. Mother: Doña Ana de Almondraez, native of Burgos. The parents were described as *hidalgos*. Professed at San Francisco de Puebla in 1690. He arrived in New Spain in the 1670s, and lived in Veracruz for at least twelve years before making his profession of faith.

Olaeta, José de (1771–1785), criollo. Professed in 1751 at age 24. Died in Santa Fe.

Ordóñez y Machado, Félix (1754–1756). Died at Abiquiu.

Oronzoro, Juan Carlos de (1733–1752), criollo, native of Puebla. Father: Captain Don Pedro Oronzoro, native of Andalucía, described as an army officer and alcalde mayor in the Philippines before coming to New Spain. Mother: Doña María Martínez, native of Mexico City. Paternal grandparents were described as hidalgos, and he had been an officer in the military. The maternal grandparents were referred to as Don and Doña, and he was described as an official with the Real Hacienda. Professed at San Francisco de Puebla in 1717 at age 18. He served as custos for at least one term.

Padilla, Diego de (1693–1711), criollo, native of Mexico City. Professed in Mexico City in 1680.

Padilla, Juan José de (1733–1756). Died at either Isleta or Laguna after being beaten/stabbed.

Peña, Juan de la (1698–1710), hijo de provincia, native of Andalucía. Father: Mateo de la Peña, native of San Vincente (Andalucía). Mother: Francesca Díaz de la Barrera, native of Andalucía. Professed at San Francisco de México in 1693 at age 19. He was custos at the time of his death from an illness in 1710.

Pérez de Mirabal, Juan José (1722–1762), hijo de provincia, native of Antequerra, Malaga. Father: Don Juan Alonso Pérez Mirabal, native of Antequerra. Mother: Doña Angela Ramírez Portilla, native of Antequerra. Admitted to San Francisco de México as a novice, he was a graduate of a seminary in Antequerra. Fray Juan was custos for at least one term.

Pino, Juan Jorge del (1717–1753), criollo, native of Puebla. Father: Francisco Xavier del Pino, native of Puebla. Mother: Francesca de Villagre, native of Puebla. Professed at San Francisco de México in 1706 at age 17.

Pino, Pedro Ignacio (1741–1767), criollo, native of Mexico City. Father: Don Juan Baptista Pino, native of Mexico City. Mother: Doña Petra Teresa de la Calle, native of Mexico City. Professed at San Francisco de México in 1730, but had been previously a novice at San Cosmé de México. He died at Acoma in 1767.

Prieto, Gerónimo (1694–1696), gachupín. Member of the Propaganda Fide. He arrived in New Spain in 1692.

Quintana, José Gabriel de la (1760–1769), criollo. Professed in 1746 at age 16.

Ramírez, Diego de (1694–1695), criollo, native of Puebla. Father: Juan Ramírez, native of Puebla. Mother: Ana López, native of Puebla. Professed at San Francisco de Puebla in 1665 at age 16.

Rodríguez, Joaquín Ildefonso (1763–1773), criollo. Professed in 1730 at age 16. By the time he departed New Mexico in 1773, he was described as "demented."

Rodríguez de Jerez, Joaquín Mariano (1755–1772), criollo. Professed in 1730 at age 16.

Rodríguez de San Antonio, Salvador (1664–1677; 1692–1694), criollo, native of Puebla. Father: Antonio Rodríguez, criollo. Mother: María Sánchez, criolla. Professed at San Francisco de Puebla in 1655 at age 16. He was the custos at the time of the reconquest in 1694.

Rodríguez de la Torre, Mariano (1752–1776), criollo. Professed in 1741 at age 16.

Rojo (Roxo), Manuel José (1750–1779), criollo, native of Mexico City. Father: Manuel José de Rojo, native of Mexico City, described as a metalsmith. Mother: María Yñes de Salas, native of Mexico City. Paternal grandparents were criollos; she was referred to as Doña, and he was described as a trader. Maternal grandparents were criollos, and he was also described as a metalsmith. Professed at San Cosmé de México in 1736 at age 23, but only after two other novice periods failed at San Francisco de México. He may have died in New Mexico in 1779.

Ruíz, Joaquín de (1769–1779), criollo. Professed in 1741 at age 16. Died in New Mexico in 1779.

Salas, Ramón (1760–1776), hijo de provincia, native of Andalucía. Professed in Mexico City in 1748 at age 24.

Sáenz (Sanz, Saanz) de Lezáun, Juan (1748–1760), hijo de provincia, native of Cádiz. Father: Don Miguel Joaquín Lezáun, native of Navarra. Mother: Doña Sebastiana [illegible] y Vivero, native of Gibraltar. Professed at San Francisco de México in 1731 at age 28.

San Antonio Terrón, José de (ca. 1732–1754), criollo, native of Real del Monte. Father: Francisco Terrón, native of Sevilla. Mother: Jacinta de Arronis, native of Mexico City. Professed at San Francisco de México in 1717 at age 16.

Sánchez, Juan Antonio (1718–1743), criollo, native of Puebla. Father: Juan Sánchez de Astroga, native of Puebla, described as a metalsmith. Mother: Doña Antonia de Solís y Villalobos, native of Querétaro. The paternal grandfather was described as a miller; the maternal grandfather was a merchant. Professed at San Francisco de Puebla in 1713.

Santa Cruz y Burgoa, Manuel Antonio de (1767–1768), hijo de provincia, native of Vizcaya. Professed in Mexico City in 1751 at age 22.

Sopecho, Manuel (1731–1752).

Sopeña, Manuel José de (1749–1752), criollo, native of Mexico City. Father: Francisco de Sopeña, native of Vizcaya. Mother: Doña Francisca de Velarde, native of Mexico City. Professed at San Francisco de México in 1707 at age 20.

Sospreda, Pascual (1756–?).

Tagle, Juan de (1699–1726), hijo de provincia, native of San Vicente de Barquiera. Father: Don Juan Gómez de Tagle, native of San Vicente de Barquiera. Mother: Doña Francisca de la Arena, native of San Vicente de Barquiera. Professed at San Francisco de México in 1695 at age 20. He served at least three terms as custos.

Tejada, Juan (1738–1752), criollo, native of Mexico City. Father: Don Lucas Alonso de Tejada, a gachupín, described as a master tailor. Mother: Doña Gabriela de Rivera y Armata, native of Mexico City. (Both parents were deceased when Juan entered the Order.) The maternal grandparents were criollos, referred to as Don and Doña, and he was described as a merchant. Professed at San Francisco de Puebla in 1730 at age 16.

Toledo, Juan José (1743–1769), criollo, native of Mexico City. Father: Don

Manuel de Toledo, native of Sevilla. Mother: Doña Paula de Méxia, native of Mexico City. (Both parents were deceased when Juan José entered the Order.) Professed at San Francisco de México in 1732 at age 17.

Trigo, José Manuel (1743–1757), criollo, native of Toluca. Father: Don Pedro de Trigo, native of Sevilla. Mother: Doña Antonia Jiménez de la Parra, native of Mexico City. Professed at San Francisco de México in 1728 at age 28.

Trizio, Miguel de (1694–1698), gachupín. Arrived in New Spain in 1692. Member of the Propaganda Fide.

Urquijo, José (1747–1755?/1760s?), criollo, native of Mexico City. Professed in Mexico City in 1732.

Vargas, Francisco de (1683–1698), gachupín, arrived in New Spain in 1669. Professed in 1665. He was custos for at least three terms. After leaving New Mexico he later served in the Custody of Tampico, where he was listed as custos in 1720.

Varo, Andrés (1729–1769), gachupín, arrived in New Spain by 1717. He professed in 1709 at about age 26. He was custos for at least three terms.

Vega, José Manuel de la (1764–1788), criollo, native of Mexico City. Professed in Mexico City in 1752 at age 18.

Vélez de Escalante, Francisco Silvestre (1774–1780), hijo de provincia, native of Treceno. Professed at San Francisco de México in 1767 at age 17. He died in Parral in 1780.

Zabaleta (Zavaleta), Juan de (1678–1706), criollo. Professed at San Francisco de Puebla in 1645. He was custos for one term.

Zambrano, Manuel (1727–1762), criollo, native of Mexico City. Father: Manuel Zambrano, native of Andalucía, described as a trader. Mother: Doña Nicolara Pérez Arroya, native of Tulantzingo. Maternal grandparents were referred to as Don and Doña, and he was described as a merchant. Professed at San Francisco de Puebla in 1711 at age 18.

Zamora, Antonio (1740–1764), criollo, native of Mexico City. Father: Don Juan Pérez de Zamora, native of Mexico City. Mother: Doña Michaela Garzeran, native of Mexico City. Professed at San Francisco de México in 1714 at age 19. A younger brother (José) professed at the same convento in 1713. Antonio was on a Custody of Tampico roster in 1728.

Zarte, Francisco Ignacio (1774–1779), criollo. Professed at San Francisco de Puebla in 1760 at age 21.

Zeinos, Diego (1694–1695).

Notes

Abbreviations

AACD (Archivo Arquidiocesano de la Catedral de Durango)
AASF (Archives of the Archdiocese of Santa Fe)
AGI (Archivo General de las Indias)
AGN (Archivo General de la Nación)
BNM (Biblioteca Nacional de México)
BNMUNM (Biblioteca Nacional de México, University of New Mexico, Special Collection)
INAH (Instituto Nacional de Antropología e Historia, Fondo Franciscano)
PPA (Papeles de Puebla de los Angeles, Informaciones de novios)
SANM (Spanish Archives of New Mexico, Series I and II)
NMHR (New Mexico Historical Review)

Chapter 1

1. The following works contributed to my conception and interpretation of this project: Robert Archibald, "Acculturation and Assimilation in Colonial New Mexico," *NMHR* 53, 3 (July 1978): 205–18; Herbert Eugene Bolton, "The Mission as a Frontier Institution in the Spanish American Colonies," in *Bolton and the Spanish Borderlands,* ed. John Francis Bannon (Norman: University of Oklahoma Press, 1964), 187–211; John Augustine Donohue, *After Kino: Jesuit Missions in Northwest New Spain, 1711–1767* (St. Louis: Jesuit Historical Institute, 1969); Fray Fidel de Jesús Chauvet, *Los franciscanos en México* (Mexico: Provincia del Santo Evangelio de México, 1989); John Leddy Phelan, *The Millennial Kingdom of the Franciscans in the New World* (Berkeley: University of California Press, 1970); Edward H. Spicer, *Cycles of Conquest: The Impact of Spain, Mexico, and the United States on the Indians of the Southwest, 1533–1960* (Tucson: University of Arizona Press, 1962); and David J. Weber, *The Spanish Frontier in North America* (New Haven: Yale University Press, 1992).

2. The biographical data on Fray Antonio Gabaldón was compiled from PPA, Vol. 15, folio 734–39; John L. Kessell, *Kiva, Cross and Crown: The Pecos Indians and New Mexico, 1540–1840* (Washington, D.C.: National Park Service, 1979), 499; and Eleanor B. Adams and Fray Angelico Chavez, *The Missions of New Mexico, 1776* (Albuquerque: University of New Mexico Press, 1976), 333.

3. Fray Angelico Chavez, *Origins of New Mexico Families* (Santa Fe: Historical Society of New Mexico, 1954), 177–78. Fray Juan José Pérez de Mirabal was joined by his brother, Don Carlos José Pérez de Mirabal, and Fray Antonio de Miranda's brother, Matias de Miranda, came to settle in New Mexico as well (see Chavez, *Origins*, 231–32).

4. Kessell, *The Missions of New Mexico Since 1776* (Albuquerque: University of New Mexico Press, 1980), 82.

5. SANM, Series II (Reel 9), no. 554a.

6. BNMUNM, Legajo 9, Part 2, no. 38.

Chapter 2

1. John L. Kessell, *Kiva, Cross and Crown: The Pecos Indians and New Mexico, 1540–1840* (Washington, D.C.: National Park Service, 1979), 3–25, 37–43. Kessell's summary of the sixteenth and seventeenth centuries in New Mexico is one of the better histories of this part of the colonial epoch.

2. Ibid., 45, 71–76, and Robert Ricard, *The Spiritual Conquest of Mexico: An Essay on the Apostolate and the Evangelizing Methods of the Mendicant Orders in New Spain, 1523–1572*, trans. Lesley Byrd Simpson (Berkeley: University of California Press, 1974), 2–5.

3. Kessell, *Kiva*, 78–90.

4. Ibid., 92–93.

5. Ibid., 96–99; Ramón A. Gutiérrez, *When Jesus Came the Corn Mothers Went Away: Marriage, Sexuality, and Power in New Mexico, 1500–1846* (Stanford: Stanford University Press, 1991), 92; and J. Manuel Espinosa, *Crusaders of the Rio Grande: The Story of Don Diego de Vargas and the Reconquest and Refounding of New Mexico* (Chicago: Institute of Jesuit History, 1942), 9–12.

6. Gutiérrez, *When Jesus Came*, 55–98.

7. Kessell, *Kiva*, 150–62, 216, and Gutiérrez, *When Jesus Came*, 128.

8. Fray Lino Gómez Canedo, *Evangelización y conquista: Experiencia franciscana en Hispanoamerica* (Mexico: Editorial Porrua, S.A., 1988), 24–25, and John Moorman, *A History of the Franciscan Order: From Its Origins to the Year 1517* (Oxford: Clarendon Press, 1968), 369–585.

9. Gómez Canedo, *Evangelización*, 23–24.

10. Ibid., 24–26.

11. Marion A. Habig, "The Franciscan Provinces of Spanish North America," *The Americas* 1, no. 2 (October 1944): 215–30, and Gómez Canedo, *Evangelización*, 39–43.

12. France V. Scholes, "Problems in the Early Ecclesiastical History of New Mexico," *NMHR* 7, no. 1 (January 1932): 35–42. Previously, scholars had cited 1622 for the formation of the Custody of Saint Paul. Scholes discovered that the date was earlier, but was unable to pinpoint it to a precise year. The direct quotation is found on p. 35.

13. Ibid., 42–43.

14. Scholes, "The First Decade of the Inquisition in New Mexico," *NMHR* 10, no. 2 (April 1935): 196–201.

15. Ricard, *Spiritual Conquest*, 22, 109–10; John Frederick Schwaller, *The Church and Clergy in Sixteenth-Century Mexico* (Albuquerque: University of New Mexico Press,

1987), 1–5; and Schwaller, *Origins of Church Wealth in Mexico: Ecclesiastical Revenues and Church Finances, 1523–1600* (Albuquerque: University of New Mexico Press, 1985), 161–71.

16. Lansing B. Bloom and Lynn B. Mitchell, "The Chapter Elections in 1672," *NMHR* 13, no. 1 (January 1938): 111–19.

17. Guillermo Porras Muñoz, *Iglesia y estado en Nueva Vizcaya, 1562–1821* (Mexico: Universidad Nacional Autónoma de México, 1980), 63–68, and Charles Gibson, *Spain in America* (New York: Harper & Row, 1966), 76–77.

18. Gibson, *Spain in America*, 76–80.

19. Kessell, *Kiva*, 93–94, and Gutiérrez, *When Jesus Came*, 46.

20. Kessell, *Kiva*, 93–95.

21. Scholes, "Church and State in New Mexico, 1610–1650," *NMHR* 11 (January 1936): 9–26, and Lansing B. Bloom, "The Governors of New Mexico," *NMHR* 10, no. 2 (April 1935): 154–55. Oñate and Don Juan de Eulate were the most notable exceptions to the three-year term.

22. These struggles between Franciscans and local civil officials are the primary focus of Scholes in "Church and State in New Mexico," *NMHR* 11 (January 1936): 9–76, 145–78, 283–94, 297–349, and 12 (January 1937): 78–106, and in *Troublous Times in New Mexico, 1659–1670* (Albuquerque: Historical Society of New Mexico, 1942).

23. Scholes, "The Supply Service of the New Mexico Missions in the Seventeenth Century," part 2, *NMHR* 5, no. 3 (July 1931): 180–210, and Kessell, *Kiva*, 144–47.

24. Scholes, "The Supply Service," 187–89.

25. Gutiérrez, *When Jesus Came*, 157–59.

26. Henry Warner Bowden, "Spanish Missions, Cultural Conflict and the Pueblo Revolt of 1680," *Church History* 44, no. 2 (June 1975): 226–28; Kessell, *Kiva*, 222; and Scholes, *Troublous Times*, 252–53.

27. Scholes, *Troublous Times*, 255–56; Gutiérrez, *When Jesus Came*, 127–32; and Bowden, "Spanish Missions," 226–28.

28. Scholes, *Troublous Times*, 249–53.

29. Kessell, *Kiva*, 238–39, and Gutiérrez, *When Jesus Came*, 133–35.

30. Kessell, *Kiva*, 238–39; Gutiérrez, *When Jesus Came*, 133–35; and Espinosa, *Crusaders*, 19.

31. Espinosa, *Crusaders*, 27–43, and J. Charles Kelly, "The Historic Indian Pueblos of La Junta de los Rios," part 1, *NMHR* 27, no. 4 (October 1952): 266–68.

Chapter 3

1. All statistical data presented herein on the Franciscans in New Mexico, unless noted otherwise, was compiled from the following sources: INAH (Fondo Franciscano), Vols. 0–12, 22–29, and 80–84; PPA (*Informaciones de novios*), Vols. 11–17; *Prontuario general y específico y colectivo de nomenclaturas de todos los religiosos que ha habido en esta Santa Provincia del Santo Evangelio desde su fundación por Fray Francisco Antonio de la Rosa Figeruera*, Nettie Lee Benson Latin American Library, Manuscript Collection, University of Texas at Austin (hereafter *Rosa Figeruera*; Eleanor B. Adams and Fray Angelico Chavez, *The Missions of New Mexico, 1776* (Albuquerque: University of New

Mexico Press, 1976), 328–40; and John L. Kessell, *Kiva, Cross and Crown: The Pecos Indians and New Mexico, 1540–1840* (Washington, D.C.: National Park Service, 1979), 498–501.

2. Francisco Morales, *Ethnic and Social Background of the Franciscan Friars in Seventeenth-Century Mexico* (Washington, D.C.: Academy of American Franciscan History, 1973), 54–55.

3. For Corvera, see Adams and Chavez, *The Missions*, 331. For Dávila Saaverde, see Kessell, *Kiva*, 500.

4. Morales, *Ethnic and Social Background*, 73.

5. For Miranda, see Adams and Chavez, *The Missions*, 336. For Barroso, see *Rosa Figeruera*.

6. Morales, *Ethnic and Social Background*, 11–12, 130–31.

7. Ibid., 29–36, 129, and D. A. Brading, *Church and State in Bourbon Mexico: The Diocese of Michoacán, 1749–1810* (Cambridge: Cambridge University Press, 1994), 116–17.

8. For a discussion on the usage of titles of respect such as Don and Doña, see James Lockhart and Stuart B. Schwartz, *Early Latin America: A History of Colonial Spanish America and Brazil* (Cambridge and New York: Cambridge University Press, 1983), 317–18. On the orphan background of Arbizu, see PPA, Vol. 13, folio 109.

9. Morales, *Ethnic and Social Background*, 100–17.

10. Ibid., 8–9.

11. Ibid., 5–6. For Iniesta, see PPA, Vol. 17, folios 8–15, and INAH, Vol. 30, folio 42.

12. For Jacinto González see PPA, Vol. 16, folios 725–30, and Kessell, *Kiva*, 500. Apparently, González arrived in New Spain with his parents who were natives of Cádiz. His father was said to have been a lawyer employed by the Real Hacienda in New Spain.

13. Morales, *Ethnic and Social Background*, 26, 113–14, and Kessell, *Kiva*, 109.

14. For Rafael Benavides, see Kessell, *Kiva*, 500. For Juan Álvarez, see INAH, Vol. 3, folios 135–40, and BNM, Caja 12, 199.1, folios 1–7, and Caja 20, 432, folio 1.

15. Morales, *Ethnic and Social Background*, 113–14, and Fray Lino Gómez Canedo, *Evangelización y conquista: Experiencia franciscana en Hispanoamerica* (Mexico: Editorial Porrua, S.A., 1988), 156–59.

16. Michael B. McCloskey, *The Formative Years of the Missionary College of Santa Cruz of Querétaro, 1683–1733* (Washington, D.C.: Academy of American Franciscan History, 1955), 12–13, 1932.

17. Ibid., 76–99, and Fray José Antonio Alcocer, *Bosquejo de la historia del Colegio de Nuestra Señora de Guadalupe y sus misiones* (Mexico: Editorial Porrua, S.A., 1958), 65–77.

18. McCloskey, *The Formative Years*, 38–40. For Carlos José Delgado, see Kessell, *Kiva*, 499.

19. Manuel José de Sopeña was stated to be twenty years of age when he professed his faith in February 1707 at San Francisco de México; see INAH, Vol. 25, folio 138.

20. The rosters and documents contained within INAH and PPA include these references.

21. For Juan José Pérez de Mirabal's tenure in New Mexico, see Adams and Chavez, *The Missions*, 337. For Andrés Varo's tenure, see Adams and Chavez, *The Missions*, 339.

22. Jacinto González was born in 1687 and was in New Mexico as late as 1769; see PPA, Vol. 16, folios 725–30, and Kessell, *Kiva*, 500. Andrés Varo was born about 1683 and was still in New Mexico in 1769; see Adams and Chavez, *The Missions*, 339.

23. For Juan de Tagle's mission duty in New Mexico, see Adams and Chavez, *The Missions*, 339.

24. For Juan de Garaicoechea and Francisco de Irazábal's terms at Zuñi, see Adams and Chavez, *The Missions*, 333, 335.

25. For José de Arranegui as procurador general, see Adams and Chavez, *The Missions*, 329, and Guillermo Porras Muñoz, *Iglesia y estado en Nueva Vizcaya, 1562–1821* (Mexico: Universidad Nacional Autónoma de México, 1980), 299. For Antonio de Miranda as provincial secretary, see PPA, Vol. 17, numerous citations between folios 835 and 1029. For Jacobo de Castro as provincial secretary, see Adams and Chavez, *The Missions*, 330.

26. Morales, *Ethnic and Social Background*, 69–71, and Brading, *Church and State*, 27.

27. Jim Norris, "The Franciscans in New Mexico, 1692–1754: Toward a New Assessment," *The Americas* 51 (October 1994): 154–59.

28. Robert H. Jackson and Edward Castillo, *Indians, Franciscans and Spanish Colonization: The Impact of the Mission System on California Indians* (Albuquerque: University of New Mexico Press, 1995), 58.

29. Adriann C. Van Oss, *Catholic Colonialism: A Parish History of Guatemala, 1524–1821* (Cambridge: Cambridge University Press, 1986), 149–51, 167–72.

Chapter 4

1. Good summaries of the 1680–1691 period are found in John L. Kessell, *Kiva, Cross and Crown: The Pecos Indians and New Mexico, 1540–1840* (Washington, D.C.: National Park Service, 1979), 240–43, and J. Manuel Espinosa, *Crusaders of the Rio Grande: The Story of Don Diego de Vargas and the Reconquest and Refounding of New Mexico* (Chicago: Institute of Jesuit History, 1942), 20–25.

2. The most complete background on Don Diego de Vargas is in Kessell, *Remote Beyond Compare: Letters of Don Diego de Vargas to His Family from New Spain and New Mexico, 1675–1706* (Albuquerque: University of New Mexico Press, 1989), 3–48.

3. Ibid., 127–321, and Espinosa, *Crusaders*, 27. The quote is found in Kessell and Rick Hendricks, eds., *By Force of Arms: The Journals of Don Diego de Vargas, 1691–1693* (Albuquerque: University of New Mexico Press, 1992), 79.

4. Kessell and Hendricks, *By Force of Arms*, 249, 463.

5. Espinosa, *Crusaders*, 41–42, and Kessell and Hendricks, *By Force of Arms*, documents inclusive, 239–99.

6. Kessell and Hendricks, *By Force of Arms*, 307–18.

7. Espinosa, *Crusaders*, 50–111, and Kessell and Hendricks, *By Force of Arms*, documents inclusive, 357–462.

8. For Fray Cristóbal Alonso Barroso, see Eleanor B. Adams and Fray Angelico Chavez, *The Missions of New Mexico, 1776: A Description by Fray Francisco Atanasio Domínguez with Other Contemporary Documents* (Albuquerque: University of New Mexico Press, 1976), 330, and *Rosa Figeruera*. For Fray Francisco de Corvera, see Adams

and Chavez, *The Missions*, 331. For Fray Miguel Muñiz de Luna, see Kessell, *Kiva*, 498, and PPA, Vol. 13, folios 370–74. Muñiz was a criollo born in Puebla in 1666.

9. Kessell and Hendricks, *By Force of Arms*, 391–93, 607.

10. Espinosa, *Crusaders*, 112–18.

11. Fray Francisco Farfán was a native of Cádiz who came to Mexico City with his parents about 1651. He professed his faith at San Francisco de México at age eighteen in July 1662; see INAH, Vol. 0, folios 662–64. For Farfán's role in 1680, see Charles Wilson Hackett, ed., and Charmion Clair Shelby, trans., *Revolt of the Pueblo Indians of New Mexico and Otermín's Attempted Reconquest, 1680–1682, Vol. I* (1942; reprint, Albuquerque: University of New Mexico Press, 1970), xcvi, 11, 58–60. For additional data on Farfán, see Kessell and Hendricks, *By Force of Arms*, 225–29.

12. For the documents regarding the Farfán-Velasco colonists, see Kessell, Hendricks, and Meredith Dodge, eds., *To The Royal Crown Restored: The Journals of Don Diego de Vargas, 1691–1694* (Albuquerque: University of New Mexico Press, 1995), 223–314.

13. Espinosa, *Crusaders*, 129–40.

14. Fray Salvador Rodríguez de San Antonio was a criollo, native of Puebla, where he professed his faith at age sixteen in 1655. He served in New Mexico from about 1664 until about 1677. See PPA, Vol. 11, folios 344–48; Adams and Chavez, *The Missions*, 338, and Kessell, Hendricks, and Dodge, *To The Royal Crown*, 67–69. For the negotiations among Governor Vargas, the Franciscans, and the government in Mexico City concerning the number of missionaries to be sent for the reconquest, see Kessell and Hendricks, *By Force of Arms*, 463–76.

15. For background of the Propaganda Fide personnel, see Fray Isidro Félix de Espinosa, *Crónica de los Colegios de Propaganda Fide de la Nueva España* (Washington, D.C.: Academy of American Franciscan History, 1964), 163, 227, 527. For the episode of diabolism involving Fray José Díez and other Propaganda Fide friars, see Fernando Cervantes, *The Devil in the New World: The Impact of Diabolism in New Spain* (New Haven: Yale University Press, 1994), 129–37. Fray Francisco de Jesús María Casañas's role in the eastern Texas missions is related in F. Todd Smith, *The Caddo Indians: Tribes at the Convergence of Empires, 1542–1854* (College Station: Texas A & M University Press, 1995), 29–32.

16. Fray Juan de Zabaleta (Zavaleta) was a criollo who professed in Puebla in 1645. He had been posted to Isleta prior to the 1680 revolt (see *Rosa Figueroa*, and Hackett and Shelby, *Revolt of the Pueblo Indians, Vol. I*, 59). Fray Juan Daza was a criollo from Mexico City where he professed in 1662 (see PPA, Vol. 12, folios 204–06). Fray Antonio de Obregón was an hijo de provincia (born in Burgos, Spain) who professed in February 1689 (see PPA, Vol. 13, folios 619–33). For Fray Antonio Carbonel, see *Rosa Figueroa*.

17. The reconquest is well told in the documentary collection in Kessell, Hendricks, and Dodge, eds., *To the Royal Crown*, 374–507.

18. Kessell, *Kiva*, 259, and J. Manuel Espinosa, *The Pueblo Indian Revolt of 1696* (Norman: University of Oklahoma Press, 1988), document 3, 71.

19. Espinosa, *Pueblo Indian Revolt*, document 10, 86–87.

20. Kessell, *Kiva*, 271.

21. Espinosa, *Pueblo Indian Revolt*, document 10, 86–87.

22. Ibid.

23. Ibid., document 11, 91–105.

24. Fray Francisco de Vargas was a gachupín friar who professed in 1665 and came to New Spain in 1669. He first appeared in the Custody of Saint Paul at El Paso in 1683. He served as procurador there in 1685 and was elected custos first in 1688. After leaving New Mexico in 1698, Fray Francisco was active in the Tampico missions as late as 1720. (See Adams and Chavez, *The Missions*, 339, and BNM, Caja 21, 444.3, folio 7; Caja 12, 205.1, folios 1–2; Caja 22, 447.2, folios 2–3; Caja 42, 958.5, folio 6. See also Espinosa, *Pueblo Indian Revolt*, document 11, 105–13.)

25. Espinosa, *Pueblo Indian Revolt*, document 11, 91–113, and Ramón A. Gutiérrez, *When Jesus Came the Corn Mothers Went Away: Marriage, Sexuality, and Power in New Mexico, 1500–1846* (Stanford: Stanford University Press, 1991), 157–62.

26. Kessell, *Kiva*, 275–76. Fray Francisco's reference to Governor Vargas as another "Hernán Cortés" is in Kessell, Hendricks, and Dodge, eds., *To The Royal Crown*, 68.

27. Espinosa, *Pueblo Indian Revolt*, documents 12–22, 113–46.

28. Ibid., 41–47 and document 24, 155–56.

29. Kessell, *Remote*, 62–63.

30. Espinosa, *Pueblo Indian Revolt*, documents 24–25, 155–57.

31. Ibid., documents 28–29, 163–68.

32. Ibid., document 29, 165–68.

33. Ibid., documents 31–46, 170–86. Those who did not request soldiers were Zabaleta (Taos), Carbonel (Nambé), Ramírez (Bernalillo), and Cisneros (Cochití).

34. Ibid., documents 48–50, 186–94.

35. Ibid., documents 51–65, 195–204.

36. Ibid.

37. Kessell, *Kiva*, 287–93, and Espinosa, *Pueblo Indian Revolt*, 50–55.

38. Espinosa, *Pueblo Indian Revolt*, document 85, 243–46.

39. Ibid., document 88, 257–80.

40. Ibid., documents 92–93, 291–94.

41. For García Marín, Navarro, and Trizio, see Feliz de Espinosa, *Crónica*, 227, 527. For Arbizu, see Adams and Chavez, *The Missions*, 329, and PPA, Vol. 13, folio 109. Chavarría was a criollo from Tacubaya who professed at San Francisco de México (see INAH, Vol. 24, folio 121, and Adams and Chavez, *The Missions*, 331). Matha was from Toledo and professed in Mexico City (see *Rosa Figeruera*). Moreno, a criollo from Mexico City, was seventeen when he professed at San Francisco de México (see INAH, Vol. 25, folio 10). Ramírez was a criollo from Puebla who was sixteen when he professed in April 1658 at San Francisco de Puebla (see PPA, Vol. 12, folios 25–28).

Chapter 5

1. Rick Hendricks, "Pedro Rodríguez Cubero: New Mexico's Reluctant Governor, 1697–1703," *NMHR* 68, no. 1 (January 1993): 13–23; John L. Kessell, *Remote Beyond Compare: Letters of Don Diego de Vargas to His Family from New Spain and New Mexico, 1675–1706* (Albuquerque: University of New Mexico Press, 1989), 60–66; and J.

Manuel Espinosa, *Crusaders of the Rio Grande: The Story of Don Diego de Vargas and the Reconquest and Refounding of New Mexico* (Chicago: Institute of Jesuit History, 1942), 308–10.

2. Hendricks, "Pedro Rodríguez Cubero," 27–28; and Kessell, *Remote Beyond Compare*, 66–67; Espinosa, *Crusaders*, 311–55.

3. Kessell, *Remote*, 187, and Eleanor B. Adams and Fray Angelico Chavez, *The Missions of New Mexico, 1776: A Description by Fray Francisco Atanasio Domínguez with Other Contemporary Documents* (Albuquerque: University of New Mexico Press, 1976), 339.

4. Espinosa, *Crusaders*, 342–43, and Richard E. Greenleaf, "The Inquisition in Eighteenth-Century New Mexico," *NMHR* 60, no. 1 (January 1985): 30.

5. Hendricks, "Pedro Rodríguez Cubero," 29–31; Kessell, *Kiva, Cross and Crown: The Pecos Indians and New Mexico, 1540–1840* (Washington, D.C.: National Park Service, 1979), 293–94; and Ramón A. Gutiérrez, *When Jesus Came the Corn Mothers Went Away: Marriage, Sexuality, and Power in New Mexico, 1500–1846* (Stanford: Stanford University Press, 1991), 157. In *Crusaders* (pp. 342–42), Espinosa characterizes the Rodríguez administration as stagnant, although that hardly seems to be the case in light of the more recent scholarship.

6. Charles W. Hackett, *Historical Documents Relating to New Mexico, Nueva Vizcaya, and Approaches Thereto, to 1773*, collected by Adolph A. F. Bandelier and Fanny R. Bandelier (Washington, D.C.: Carnegie Institute of History, 1937), 385–86.

7. AASF (Reel 51), 1701, No. 2 and 1703, No. 3.

8. SANM (Reel 3), Nos. 84–85; Hendricks, "Pedro Rodríguez Cubero," 30–31; and Espinosa, *Crusaders*, 347–52.

9. AASF (Reel 51), 1703, No. 4.

10. Hendricks, "Pedro Rodríguez Cubero," 33–35.

11. Kessell, *Remote*, 85–87.

12. AASF (Reel 51), 1704, No. 1.

13. SANM (Reel 3), No. 104.

14. Edward K. Flagler, "From Asturias to New Mexico: Don Francisco Cuervo y Valdés," *NMHR* 69, no. 3 (July 1994): 249–55.

15. Frederic James Athearn, "Life and Society in Eighteenth-Century New Mexico, 1692–1776" (Ph.D. diss., University of Texas at Austin, 1974), 53–62.

16. Oakah L. Jones, Jr., *Pueblo Warriors and Spanish Conquest* (Norman: University of Oklahoma Press, 1966), 71–79.

17. AGI, Audiencia de México, Legajo 701, titles 246–47.

18. SANM (Reel 3), No. 121; Hackett, *Historical Documents*, 381–83; Athearn, "Life and Society," 59–60; and Flagler, "From Asturias to New Mexico," 258–59.

19. Charles R. Cutter, *The "Protector de Indios" in Colonial New Mexico, 1659–1821* (Albuquerque: University of New Mexico Press, 1986), 2–50.

20. Ibid., 35–50, and Jones, *Pueblo Warriors*, 77–78.

21. Cutter, *"Protector de Indios,"* 56–57, 77–79.

22. Data drawn from sources cited earlier in chapter 3, note 1.

23. Hackett, *Historical Documents*, 373–76, and Adams and Chavez, *The Missions*, 333.

24. For Fray Domingo Martínez de Araoz, see PPA, Vol. 14, folios 503–07. For Fray José de Arranegui, see INAH, Vol. 5, folios 722–26 and Vol. 25, folio 71. For Fray Antonio Camargo, see INAH, Vol. 25, folio 86. For Fray Juan de Tagle, see INAH, Vol. 25, folio 70. For Fray Juan de la Peña, see INAH, Vol. 25, folio 60. For Fray José Guerrero, see INAH, Vol. 5, folios 641–47 and Vol. 80, folios 271–82.

25. For Fray Agustín Colina, see Adams and Chavez, *The Missions*, 329.

26. Hackett, *Historical Documents*, 369–71.

27. Ibid., 373–76.

Chapter 6

1. Edward K. Flagler, "Governor José Chacón, Marqués de la Peñuela: An Andalusian Nobleman on the New Mexico Frontier," *NMHR* 65, no. 4 (October 1990): 455–64.

2. Ibid., 456, 462.

3. Ibid., 464–65, and Frederic James Athearn, "Life and Society in Eighteenth-Century New Mexico, 1692–1776" (Ph.D. diss., University of Texas at Austin, 1974), 73–74.

4. Flagler, "Governor José Chacón," 465–66, and Athearn, "Life and Society," 67–68.

5. Flagler, "Governor José Chacón," 472–74, and Oakah L. Jones, *Pueblo Warriors and Spanish Conquest* (Norman: University of Oklahoma Press, 1966), 79–86.

6. John L. Kessell, *Kiva, Cross and Crown: The Pecos Indians and New Mexico, 1540–1840* (Washington, D.C.: National Park Service, 1979), 310–12.

7. Jones, *Pueblo Warriors*, 36, 61–62.

8. France V. Scholes, "The First Decade of the Inquisition in New Mexico," *NMHR* 10, no. 2 (April 1935): 201, and Marc Simmons, *Witchcraft in the Southwest: Spanish and Indian Supernaturalism on the Rio Grande* (Lincoln: University of Nebraska Press, 1974), 18–28.

9. Simmons, *Witchcraft*, 28–30; Richard E. Greenleaf, "The Inquisition in Eighteenth-Century New Mexico," *NMHR* 60, no. 1 (January 1985): 34–35; and Athearn, "Life and Society," 68–69; SANM (Reel 4), No. 137b.

10. Richard L. Greenleaf, "The Inquisition in Eighteenth-Century New Mexico," *NMHR* 60 (January 1985): 29–35. In addition, the Franciscans in New Mexico received instructions in 1715 from the Holy Office that urged them to use prudence in involving the Inquisition in any matters dealing with the local native population (see AASF (Reel 51), 1715, No. 2).

11. Kessell, *Kiva*, 312–15, and BNMUNM, Legajo 6, Part 1, No. 3.

12. INAH, Vol. 25, folio 70; Eleanor B. Adams and Fray Angelico Chavez, *The Missions of New Mexico, 1776: A Description by Fray Francisco Atanasio Domínguez with Other Contemporary Documents* (Albuquerque: University of New Mexico Press, 1976), 339; and Athearn, "Life and Society," 73–74.

13. AASF (Reel 51), 1710, Nos. 2, 3, 6, and SANM (Reel 4), No. 163.

14. SANM (Reel 4), Nos. 136, 165.

15. SANM (Reel 3), No. 122.

16. Max L. Moorhead, "The Presidio Supply Problem of New Mexico in the Eighteenth Century," *NMHR* 36, no. 3 (July 1961): 211, and BNMUNM, Legajo 6, Part 1, No. 3.

17. Marc Simmons, *Spanish Government in New Mexico* (Albuquerque: University of New Mexico Press, 1990), 58–59, and BNMUNM, Legajo 6, Part 1, No. 3.

18. BNMUNM, Legajo 6, Part 1, No. 3 (specifically, see Chacón to Tagle, 12 May 1711).

19. BNMUNM, Legajo 6, Part 1, No. 3 (specifically, see Bretons to Tagle and Bretons's testimony, both dated 19 May 1711); Adams and Chavez, *The Missions*, 330; and Kessell, *Kiva*, 311.

20. BNMUNM, Legajo 6, Part 1, No. 3 (specifically, see Chacón to Tagle, 18 and 20 May 1711), and Adams and Chavez, *The Missions*, 202–08.

21. BNMUNM, Legajo 6, Part 1, No. 3 (specifically, see López to Tagle, 11 May 1712).

22. Ibid. (specifically, see Tagle to López, 11 May 1712 and López to Morrote, 20 May 1712).

23. Ibid. (specifically, see Chacón to Tagle, 27 April and 2 May 1712).

24. Kessell, 312, and Flagler, 475.

25. BNMUNM, Legajo 6, Part 1, No. 3 (specifically, see Morrote to Flores, 12 October 1712).

26. Greenleaf, "The Inquisition," 35.

27. AGN, Inquisición, 758. Morrote likely traveled with Chacón from New Mexico and quite possibly first received the allegations against Bretons from Chacón.

28. Jones, *Pueblo Warriors*, 86–93.

29. Kessell, *Kiva*, 312–19, and Jones, *Pueblo Warriors*, 86–93.

30. Kessell, *Kiva*, 313–19, and Jones, *Pueblo Warriors*, 87–90.

31. SANM (Reel 5), No. 233.

32. SANM (Reel 4), Nos. 205, 212.

33. AASF (Reel 51), 1715, No. 2.

34. Ted J. Warner, "Don Félix Martínez and the Santa Fe Presidio, 1693–1730," *NMHR* 45, no. 4 (October 1970): 274–83.

35. Adams and Chavez, *The Missions*, 329–40, and Kessell, *Kiva*, 498–500.

36. AASF (Reel 51), 1708, No. 1, and BNMUNM, Legajo 6, Part 1, No. 3.

37. For Cepeda y Arriola, see Kessell, *Kiva*, 499, and PPA, Vol. 14, folios 796–801. For Delgado, see Kessell, *Kiva*, 499. For Guerrero, see INAH, Vol. 80, folios 271–82.

38. Francisco Morales, *Ethnic and Social Background of the Franciscan Friars in Seventeenth-Century Mexico* (Washington, D.C.: Academy of Franciscan History, 1973), 73. For Aparicio and Arévalo, see Kessell, *Kiva*, 499.

39. Adams and Chavez, *The Missions*, 329–40.

Chapter 7

1. The issue of episcopal authority in New Spain is a complex and often contradictory affair. Essentially, Exponi nobis fecisti, the 1522 papal bull, granted the regular clergy broad powers to perform the sacraments, assign missionaries, collect the tithe from non–native people, and receive fees for religious services. These rights were revoked by the Council of Trent, and the Council's decision was confirmed in the Mexican Council of 1565. Pope Pius V, however, in his bull Exponi nobis (1567) restored the right to perform sacraments to the regular clergy in the absence of secular clergy or if bishops were great distances away (generally more than two days' ride). The Crown's Ordenanza del Patronazgo (1574) upheld the episcopal jurisdiction over tithes and fees for services, as did the Mexican Council of 1585, but neither addressed specifically the problem posed by the unavailability of secular priests or a bishop's remoteness from a region. It was this ambiguity that the Franciscans exploited in New Mexico. See John Frederick Schwaller, *The Church and Clergy in Sixteenth-Century Mexico* (Albuquerque: University of New Mexico Press, 1987), 1–5, and *Origins of Church Wealth in Mexico: Ecclesiastical Revenues and Church Finances, 1523–1600* (Albuquerque: University of New Mexico Press, 1985), 161–71.

2. Guillermo Porras Muñoz, *Iglesia y estado en Nueva Vizcaya, 1562–1821* (Mexico: Universidad Nacional Autónoma de México, 1980), 20–26.

3. Ibid., 7–8.

4. Eleanor B. Adams, ed., *Bishop Tamarón's Visitation of New Mexico, 1760* (Albuquerque: University of New Mexico Press, 1954), 2–3, and Porras Muñoz, *Iglesia y estado*, 27–28. The Spanish referred to the Atlantic Ocean as the "North Sea." Obviously, a line drawn north from the Río Grande would not intersect with that body of water.

5. In regard to the tithe being remitted to the archbishop of Mexico, see Porras Muñoz, *Iglesia y estado*, 37, and AASF (Reel 51), 1730, No. 4. While there are no specific statements concerning fees for services, money was always scarce in New Mexico. Services were often paid for in produce, livestock, and labor, which were therefore consumed locally.

6. Adams, *Bishop Tamarón*, 4–5, and Porras Muñoz, *Iglesia y estado*, 36.

7. Adams, *Bishop Tamarón*, 7–9. The dates of tenure for the various Durango prelates in this chapter are sometimes different from those offered by Adams. I have chosen to use the dates in AACD, Libros I, II, XLIX.

8. Adams, *Bishop Tamarón*, 9–10, and France V. Scholes, *Troublous Times in New Mexico, 1659–1670* (Albuquerque: Historical Society of New Mexico, 1942), 249.

9. Adams, *Bishop Tamarón*, 10–12, and Porras Muñoz, *Iglesia y estado*, 38.

10. Adams, *Bishop Tamarón*, 13.

11. Ibid., 3, and Porras Muñoz, *Iglesia y estado*, 428.

12. Porras Muñoz, *Iglesia y estado*, 129–37, 170–75, 288.

13. Ibid., 129–37.

14. AGI, Guadalajara, Legajo 206, Title 320, and Porras Muñoz, *Iglesia y estado*, 459.

15. Ibid.

16. Bishop Tapiz to Philip V in AGI, Guadalajara, Legajo 206, Title 322.

17. Council of the Indies to Viceroy Casafuerte in AGI, Guadalajara, Legajo 206, Title 322 and Legajo 77, Title 179. A copy of the 7 December 1722 cédula is in BN-MUNM, Legajo 7, Part 4, No. 20.

18. Adams, *Bishop Tamarón*, 14–15, and BNMUNM, Legajo 7, Part 4, No. 21.

19. AGI, Guadalajara, Legajo 78, Title 180; BNMUNM, Legajo 7, Part 4, No. 20; and Adams, *Bishop Tamarón*, 14–15.

20. AGI, Guadalajara, Legajo 209, Title 334, and BNMUNM, Legajo 7, Part 4, Nos. 18, 20.

21. Adams, *Bishop Tamarón*, 15. Crespo began a visita of the entire diocese the previous year in the region west of Durango. He returned to that city by mid-February 1730 and remained there until his departure for New Mexico in April. He inspected numerous missions and parish churches while en route to New Mexico, generally along a northerly direction through Parral and Chihuahua. He completed inspecting the diocese in 1731–1732 (see AACD, Libro XLV, folios 32–35).

22. Eleanor B. Adams and Fray Angelico Chavez, *The Missions of New Mexico, 1776: A Description by Fray Francisco Atanasio Domínguez with Other Contemporary Documents* (Albuquerque: University of New Mexico Press, 1976), 339–40.

23. Varo to Crespo, 19 June 1730 and 8 and 10 July 1730, Crespo to Varo, 10 July 1730, in BNMUNM, Legajo 7, Part 4, No. 24. A copy of Varo's diary/report of the visita is in BNMUNM, Legajo 7, Part 4, No. 24.

24. Quote from Varo entry 6 July 1730 in BNMUNM, Legajo 7, Part 4, No. 24. Crespo's quote is in Adams, *Bishop Tamarón*, 100. Crespo's logbook is in AACD, Libro XLV.

25. Entries from Varo 23–26 July 1730, in BNMUNM, Legajo 7, Part 4, No. 24. Crespo performed the sacrament of confirmation for 204 individuals at Isleta and 454 in Albuquerque (see AACD, Libro XLV, folios 52–53).

26. Entry from Varo, 28 July 1730, BNMUNM, Legajo 7, Part 4, No. 24.

27. Varo to Crespo, 16 August 1730; Varo to missionaries, 11 August 1730; and Varo to Governor Bustamante, 18 August 1730, in BNMUNM, Legajo 7, Part 4, No. 20. See Varo entries through 18 August 1730 in BNMUNM, Legajo 7, Part 4, No. 24.

28. Adams, *Bishop Tamarón*, 95–99, and Varo entries for 19–28 August 1730, BNMUNM, Legajo 7, Part 4, No. 24. According to Crespo's logbook, north of Santa Fe he confirmed 281 at Picurís, 432 at Taos, 296 at San Ildefonso, 229 at San Juan, and 250 combined from Nambé, Tesuque, and Pojoaque. There is no mention of confirmations at Santa Clara or Santa Cruz de la Cañada (see AACD, Libro XLV, folios 52–53).

29. Adams, *Bishop Tamarón*, 104, and Varo entry for 31 August 1730, BNMUNM, Legajo 7, Part 4, No. 24. A copy of Crespo's arancel is in AASF (Reel 51), 1730, No. 4. Roybal was from New Mexico, educated in Mexico City, recently ordained, and just ordered by Crespo to Santa Fe. See Fray Angelico Chavez, *Origins of New Mexico Families in the Spanish Colonial Period* (Santa Fe: Historical Society of New Mexico, 1975), 275. Interestingly, Crespo licensed Roybal to hear confessions on 18 August (prior to the inspection north of Santa Fe). Varo made no note of that, although the custos would have vehemently opposed that move. Thus, Crespo probably kept that information from Varo (see AACD, Libro XLV, folios 3, 8).

30. Adams, *Bishop Tamarón*, 98–99, and Varo entries through 2 October 1730, BN-

MUNM, Legajo 7, Part 4, No. 24. Crespo's logbook notes 821 confirmed at Pecos, 188 at Galisteo, 360 at Cochití, 281 at Santo Domingo, 234 at San Felipe, 307 at Jémez, 203 at Zía, and 318 at Santa Ana. Altogether, Crespo claimed to confirm 4,404 individuals north of El Paso (see AACD, Libro XLV, folios 52–53).

31. Adams, *Bishop Tamarón*, 96–99.

32. Ibid., 102–03.

33. Affidavits of 3 and 10 February and 22 March 1731 in BNMUNM, Legajo 7, Part 4, No. 24.

34. AACD, Libro XLV, folios 3, 21, 27.

35. A copy of Fray Francisco Seco's Memorial is found in BNMUNM, Legajo 7, Part 5, No. 36.

36. Adams, *Bishop Tamarón*, 16, and AGI, Guadalajara, Legajo 79, Titles 194, 196.

37. Adams, *Bishop Tamarón*, 16, and Porras Muñoz, *Iglesia y estado*, 119–20. Roybal was confirmed in his positions by 1733. He was posted to El Paso (1733–1736) before returning to Santa Fe. Also in 1733, Crespo appointed José de Bustamante, another secular priest, as a vicar for New Mexico. José was a relative of Governor Bustamante, although by 1733 Juan Domingo de Bustamante was no longer governor. No records exist of any Franciscan response to this appointment and after 1736 there is no mention of José Bustamante in church or government records (see Chavez, *Origins*, 275). For Elizacoechea as bishop of Michoacán, see D. A. Brading, *Church and State in Bourbon Mexico: The Diocese of Michoacán, 1749–1810* (Cambridge: Cambridge University Press, 1994), 45, 72, 88, 150, 176.

38. Varo to Elizacoechea, 23 July 1737, BNMUNM, Legajo 7, Part 6, No. 62. See also BNMUNM, Legajo 7, Part 6, No. 69.

39. The other friar cited as fluent was Fray Juan José de Padilla, BNMUNM, Legajo 7, Part 6, No. 69.

40. AGI, Escribanía de Cámara, Legajo 960, Title 3, and Guadalajara, Legajo 80, Title 205.

41. Elizacoechea visited two missions at Junta de los Ríos in November 1742. On 17 November he confirmed fifty-six individuals at San Francisco de la Junta de los Ríos. Two days later he confirmed forty-five at Nuestra Señora de Guadalupe de la Junta de los Ríos (see AACD, Libro XLVIII, folios 88, 124).

Chapter 8

1. Ted J. Warner, "Don Félix Martínez and the Santa Fe Presidio, 1693–1730," *NMHR* 45, no. 4 (October 1970): 274–83, and Fray Angelico Chavez, *Origins of New Mexico Families* (Santa Fe: Historical Society of New Mexico, 1975), 226.

2. Warner, "Don Félix Martínez," 284–88.

3. SANM (Reel 5), Nos. 251, 269a.

4. Lansing B. Bloom, "A Campaign Against the Moqui Pueblos," *NMHR* 6, no. 2 (April 1931): 158–226, and Charles W. Hackett, *Historical Documents Relating to New Mexico, Nueva Vizcaya, and Approaches Thereto, to 1773*, collected by Adolph A. F. Bandelier and Fanny R. Bandelier (Washington, D.C.: Carnegie Institute of History, 1937), 385–87.

5. AASF (Reel 51), 1716, Nos. 2–3, and 1717, Nos. 2–3 and SANM (Reel 5), No. 285.

6. SANM (Reel 5), No. 280 and Chavez, *Origins*, 304.

7. Elizabeth Howard West, "The Right of Asylum in New Mexico in the Seventeenth and Eighteenth Centuries," *NMHR* 41, no. 2 (April 1966): 130–31.

8. Warner, "Don Félix Martínez," 290–91; John L. Kessell, *Kiva, Cross and Crown: The Pecos Indians and New Mexico, 1540–1840* (Washington, D.C.: National Park Service, 1979), 321; and Chavez, *Origins*, 226.

9. Warner, "Don Félix Martínez," 292–301, and Kessell, *Kiva*, 324.

10. Henri Folmer, "Contraband Trade Between Louisiana and New Mexico in the Eighteenth Century," *NMHR* 16, no. 3 (July 1941): 249–56, and Elizabeth A. H. John, *Storms Brewed in Other Men's Worlds: The Confrontation of Indians, Spanish and French in the Southwest, 1540–1795* (Lincoln: University of Nebraska Press, 1975), 230–46.

11. John, *Storms*, 248–49, and Alfred Barnaby Thomas, *After Coronado: Spanish Exploration Northeast of New Mexico, 1692–1727. Documents from the Archives of Spain, Mexico, and New Mexico* (Norman: University of Oklahoma Press, 1935), 33–39, 137–219.

12. BNMUNM, Legajo 6, Part 4, No. 22, and J. Charles Kelly, "The Historic Indian Pueblos of Junta de los Rios," part 1, *NMHR* 27, no. 4 (October 1952): 267–68.

13. Kessell, *Kiva*, 324–25, and Chavez, *Origins*, 150–51.

14. Frederic James Athearn, "Life and Society in Eighteenth-Century New Mexico, 1692–1776" (Ph.D. diss., University of Texas at Austin, 1974), 99–100.

15. It should be noted that the Reglamento de 1729 was not so different from Spain's official policy toward native people along the northern frontier since the last quarter of the sixteenth century. It is significant that governmental interest in the region was obviously growing; see Oakah L. Jones, Jr., *Pueblo Warriors and Spanish Conquest* (Norman: University of Oklahoma Press, 1966), 103–07, and Max L. Moorhead, *The Apache Frontier: Jacobo Ugarte and Spanish–Indian Relations in Northern New Spain, 1769–1791* (Norman: University of Oklahoma Press, 1968), 15–16.

16. Marc Simmons, *Spanish Government in New Mexico* (Albuquerque: University of New Mexico, 1968), 170–71, and Athearn, "Life and Society," 104–05.

17. Kessell, *Kiva*, 324–25; Jones, *Pueblo Warriors*, 102–03; and Athearn, "Life and Society," 101.

18. Hackett, *Historical Documents*, 387, and Kessell, *Kiva*, 368.

19. SANM, Series II (Reel 6), No. 343a. In fairness to Bustamante, at least early in his administration, he cannot be accused of being as fiercely anti–Catholic as some other governors had been. Indeed, Bustamante spent his own funds for a new mission church that was constructed at Nambé in 1725; see Eleanor B. Adams and Fray Angelico Chavez, *The Missions of New Mexico, 1776: A Description by Fray Francisco Atanasio Domínguez with Other Contemporary Documents* (Albuquerque: University of New Mexico Press, 1976), 52.

20. AASF, (Reel 51), 1727, No. 1.

21. BNMUNM, Legajo 7, Part 5, No. 31, and Kessell, *Kiva*, 325–26.

22. BNMUNM, Legajo 7, Part 5, Nos. 33, 45, and Athearn, "Life and Society," 114.

23. SANM, Series II (Reel 7), No. 382a, and Chavez, *Origins*, 197.

24. SANM, Series II (Reel 7), No. 382a. Perhaps Montaño's zeal played a role in this affair. Shortly after Fray Pedro came to New Mexico, he was involved in an Inquisition case involving a Spaniard of some stature by the name of Pedro de Chavez. Montaño brought a variety of charges against Chavez including blasphemy, grave robbing, and incest; see Richard E. Greenleaf, "The Inquisition in Eighteenth-Century New Mexico," *NMHR* 60, no. 1 (January 1985): 35–38.

25. SANM, Series II (Reel 7), No. 389.

26. Jones, *Pueblo Warriors*, 111, and Athearn, "Life and Society," 122–24.

27. Pino arrived by 1717, Sánchez by 1718, and Cruz by 1719; see Adams and Chavez, *The Missions*, 328–40. Fray Jerónimo Liñán left under a cloud after being accused of soliciting women in the confessional; see Kessell, *Kiva*, 499.

28. Pérez de Mirabal arrived by 1722, Arias de Espinosa and Gabaldón by 1723, Esquer and Irigoyen by 1724, Díaz de Aguilar and Ceballos by 1726, Zambrano by 1727, Montaño by 1728, and Varo, as noted previously, in 1729. Tagle left by 1726 and López by 1729; see Adams and Chavez, *The Missions*, 328–40, and Kessell, *Kiva*, 496–503. Bustamante's 1727 roster is in BNMUNM, Legajo 7, Part 4, No. 20, as "Report on the Missions of New Mexico."

29. Adams and Chavez, *The Missions*, 328–40; Kessell, *Kiva*, 496–503; and Adams, *Bishop Tamarón's Visitation of New Mexico, 1760* (Albuquerque: University of New Mexico Press, 1954), 95.

30. Bravo Lerchundí and Hoyuela arrived by 1730, Menchero by 1730, González, Oronzoro, and Padilla by 1733, and Tejada and Terrón by 1736; see Adams and Chavez, *The Missions*, 328–40, and Kessell, *Kiva*, 496–503.

31. There was speculation at the time of Araoz's death that he was poisoned by natives at Santa Ana; see BNM, Caja 28, 524.3, folio 3.

32. For Cruz, see Adams and Chavez, *The Missions*, 331 and Kessell, *Kiva*, 499. For Gabaldón, see PPA, Vol. 15, folios 734–39, and Kessell, *Kiva*, 499. For Irigoyen, see PPA, Vol. 15, folios 623–30, and Kessell, *Kiva*, 499. For Pino, see INAH, Vol. 25, folio 138. For Sánchez, see PPA, Vol. 15, folios 364–68. For Ceballos, see INAH, Vol. 134, folios 199–204. For Montaño, see INAH, Vol. 25, folio 116. For Varo, see Adams and Chavez, *The Missions*, 339.

33. For Aguilar, see PPA, Vol. 15, folios 204–12. For Archundía, see PPA, Vol. 16, folios 285–90, and INAH, Vol. 27, folio 105. For Díaz, see INAH, Vol. 26, folio 80. For Otero, see PPA, Vol. 16, folios 254–58, and Kessell, *Kiva*, 500. For Menchero, see PPA, Vol. 15, folios 526–30, and BNMUNM, Legajo 7, Part 6, No. 75. For Oronzoro, see PPA, Vol. 15, folios 725–33. For Terrón, see INAH, Vol. 26, folio 71.

34. Casafuerte to Navarrete, AGI, Guadalajara, Legajo 722, Title 250. On the matter of sending a large contingent of gachupín friars to New Mexico, see AGI, Guadalajara, Legajo 722, Titles 251–53, 401.

35. The hijos de provincia were Arias de Espinosa, Esquer, González, Menchero, Otero, and Pérez de Mirabal. The fifteen criollos were Archundía, Aguilar, Bravo Lerchundí, Díaz, Díaz de Aguilar, Gabaldón, Hoyuela, Irigoyen, Montaño, Oronzoro, Pino, Sánchez, Tejada, Terrón, and Zambrano; see previous citations, especially notes 32 and 33.

36. Adams, *Bishop Tamarón*, 97, and John, *Storms*, 254–55.

Chapter 9

1. AASF (Reel 51), 1727, No. 1. For background information on Camargo, see INAH, Vol. 25, folio 86.

2. Virve Piho, *La secularización de las parroquias en la Nueva España y su reper-cusión en San Andrés Calpán* (Mexico: Instituto Nacional de Antropología e Historia, 1981), 128–42.

3. Jim Norris, "The Franciscans in New Mexico, 1692–1754: Toward a New Assess-ment," *The Americas* 51, no. 2 (October 1994): 165, and Edward P. Dozier, *The Pueblo In-dians of North America* (Prospect Heights, Illinois: Waveland Press, 1983), 181–82.

4. Norris, 166.

5. Ibid., 166–67.

6. Ibid., 167.

7. AASF (Reel 51), 1731, No. 1, and John L. Kessell, *Kiva, Cross and Crown: The Pecos Indians and New Mexico, 1540–1840* (Washington, D.C.: National Park Service, 1979), 329–30.

8. Menchero's parents were Don Pedro Sánchez and Doña Antonia Ibañez who were both said to be from Villanueva de los Infantes (Castilla). Fray Juan took the name Menchero from his paternal grandparents. For this and other background on Menchero and his early career, see PPA, Vol. 15, folios 526–30, and Vol. 16, folios 628–33, 687–91. See also BNMUNM, Legajo 7, Part 6, No. 5 and BNM, Caja 28, 539.3, folio 3.

9. These instructions are complete in AASF (Reel 51), 1731, Nos. 1, 2. See also Kessell, *Kiva,* 329–33.

10. Menchero's original report and recommendations have not been discovered. The provincial orders, related reports, and accompanying letters found in this citation leave little doubt as to Menchero's assessment and critique of Santiago de Tlatelolco's mis-sionary training; see INAH, Vol. 99 *(Asuntos de conventos y colegios),* folios 55–64.

11. AASF (Reel 51), 1734, No. 1.

12. AASF (Reel 51), 1738, Nos. 1–3.

13. BNMUNM, Legajo 7, Part 6, No. 75. The testimonies of these three friars further included the assertion that Santiago Roybal, the secular clergyman appointed by Bishop Crespo, was also unable to speak any Puebloan languages.

14. "Testimony, Reports and Orders Regarding Accusations Against Fray Francisco de la Concepción González for Public Scandals and Disturbances, 1743–1748," in BN-MUNM, Legajo 8, Part 1, No. 38.

15. The statistical data on the friars' average years in missions is calculated from the same sources cited in chapter 3.

16. For Miranda's appointment to Santiago de Tlatelolco, see BNM, Caja 28, 527.1, folios 1–6v. Miranda is noted as provincial secretary for Santo Evangelio in numerous documents in PPA, Vol. 17, folio 835 (November 1745) through folio 1039 (October 1748).

17. Kessell, *Kiva,* 365–67.

18. Henry W. Kelly, "Franciscan Missions in New Mexico, 1740–1760," part 2, *NMHR* 16, no. 1 (January 1941): 68–69.

19. AGI, Guadalajara, Legajo 81, Titles 213–14.

20. Background on Delgado is found in Eleanor B. Adams and Fray Angelico Chavez, *The Missions of New Mexico, 1776: A Description by Fray Francisco Atanasio Domínguez with Other Contemporary Documents* (Albuquerque: University of New Mexico Press, 1976), 331–32; Kessell, *Kiva*, 499; and BNM, Caja 28, 525.3, folios 53–54.

21. Kelly, "Franciscan Missions," 45–46. Background information on Pino is in INAH, Vol. 27, folio 43 and Vol. 30, folio 32, and Adams and Chavez, *The Missions*, 337.

22. Kelly, "Franciscan Missions," 45–46, and Charles W. Hackett, *Historical Documents Relating to New Mexico, Nueva Vizcaya, and Approaches Thereto, to 1773*, collected by Adolph A. F. Bandelier and Fanny R. Bandelier (Washington, D.C.: Carnegie Institute of History, 1937), 388–90.

23. Hackett, *Historical Documents*, 388–90.

24. Kelly, "Franciscan Missions," 45–46, and Hackett, *Historical Documents*, 414–15. Background information on Irigoyen is found in PPA, Vol. 15, folios 623–30; Adams and Chavez, *The Missions*, 335; and Kessell, *Kiva*, 499. For Toledo, see INAH, Vol. 27, folio 68, and Adams and Chavez, *The Missions*, 339.

25. Kelly, "Franciscan Missions," 51–54, and Hackett, *Historical Documents*, 417–20.

26. SANM, Series I (Reel 3), No. 531 and Series I (Reel 5), No. 848, and Frederic James Athearn, "Life and Society in Eighteenth-Century New Mexico, 1692–1776" (Ph.D. diss., University of Texas at Austin, 1974), 134. For background information on Hernández, see Kessell, *Kiva*, 500.

27. Kelly, "Franciscan Missions," 51–54.

28. Ibid., 56–59, and Hackett, *Historical Documents*, 393–95.

29. Hackett, *Historical Documents*, 416.

30. Kelly, "Franciscan Missions," 59, and SANM, Series II (Reel 6), No. 1187.

31. Kelly, "Franciscan Missions," 60, and Hackett, *Historical Documents*, 420–32.

32. Kelly, "Franciscan Missions," 60–61. For background information on Bermejo, see Adams and Chavez, *The Missions*, 330. For Sáenz, see INAH, Vol. 27, folio 61, and Adams and Chavez, *The Missions*, 339. For Trigo, see INAH, Vol. 27, folio 17. For Andrés García de la Concepción, see PPA, Vol. 17, folios 303–11, and Adams and Chavez, *The Missions*, 333. For Gómez, see Adams and Chavez, *The Missions*, 334.

33. Menchero's visita report is in Hackett, *Historical Documents*, 388–406. Statistical data are the same as noted in chapter 3.

34. For background information on Blanco, see INAH, Vol. 27, folio 19. For Angel García, see INAH, Vol. 27, folio 16, and Adams and Chavez, *The Missions*, 333. For Iniesta, see INAH, Vol. 30, folio 42; PPA, Vol. 17, folios 8–15; and Adams and Chavez, *The Missions*, 334–35. For Zamora, see INAH, Vol. 26, folio 53, and Adams and Chavez, *The Missions*, 340. Background information for Gómez, Sáenz, and Concepción González is cited above.

35. Bermejo, Gómez, Sáenz, and Concepción González's backgrounds are all cited previously in this chapter.

36. Adams and Chavez, *The Missions*, 329–40, and Kessell, *Kiva*, 499–500.

37. Hackett, *Historical Documents*, 391–95, 414–16. Statistical data are the same as cited in chapter 3.

Chapter 10

1. Elizabeth A. H. John, *Storms Brewed in Other Men's Worlds: The Confrontation of Indians, Spanish and French in the Southwest, 1540–1795* (Lincoln: University of Nebraska Press, 1975), 315–19; Oakah L. Jones, Jr., *Pueblo Warriors and Spanish Conquest* (Norman: University of Oklahoma Press, 1966), 111–16; and John L. Kessell, *Kiva, Cross and Crown: The Pecos Indians and New Mexico, 1540–1840* (Washington, D.C.: National Park Service, 1979), 372–85.

2. Henri Folmer, "Contraband Trade Between Louisiana and New Mexico in the Eighteenth Century," *NMHR* 16, no. 3 (July 1941): 262–63, and Jones, *Pueblo Warriors*, 116.

3. Charles W. Hackett, *Historical Documents Relating to New Mexico, Nueva Vizcaya, and Approaches Thereto, to 1773*, collected by Adolph A. F. Bandelier and Fanny R. Bandelier (Washington, D.C.: Carnegie Institute of History, 1937), 389–90.

4. Frederic James Athearn, "Life and Society in Eighteenth-Century New Mexico, 1692–1776" (Ph.D. diss., University of Texas at Austin, 1974), 158–59.

5. Hackett, *Historical Documents*, 390–91, and Kessell, *Kiva*, 334–35, 387.

6. Kessell, *Kiva*, 372–78, 335. A description of the attack on Abiquiu is found in Varo's *Informe* of 1749, BNMUNM, Legajo 8, Part 1, No. 38.

7. Kessell, *Kiva*, 387–89.

8. Hackett, *Historical Documents*, 392.

9. BNMUNM, Legajo 8, Part 1, No. 10.

10. For Concepción González, see INAH, Vol. 27, folio 7. The investigation in the Concepción González matter is in BNMUNM, Legajo 8, Part 1, No. 38. See also Kessell, *Kiva*, 335.

11. BNMUNM, Legajo 8, Part 1, No. 38; Athearn, "Life and Society," 171; and Fray Angelico Chavez, *Origins of New Mexico Families in the Spanish Colonial Period* (Santa Fe: Historical Society of New Mexico, 1975), 150, 192–93.

12. BNMUNM, Legajo 8, Part 2, No. 52, and SANM, Series I (Reel 5), No. 848, and (Reel 3), No. 531.

13. SANM, Series I (Reel 6), No. 1257 and Peter Gerhard, *The North Frontier of New Spain*, rev. ed. (Norman: University of Oklahoma Press, 1993), 196–99.

14. AASF (Reel 52), 1747, No. 1.

15. Athearn, "Life and Society," 172.

16. The complete Informe is in BNMUNM, Legajo 8, Part 2, No. 57.

17. Kessell, *Kiva*, 344, 378–85 (quote is on p. 378); Jones, *Pueblo Warriors*, 121–26; and Alfred Barnaby Thomas, *The Plains Indians and New Mexico, 1751–1778: A Collection of Documents Illustrative of the Eastern Frontier of New Mexico* (Albuquerque: University of New Mexico Press, 1940), 63.

18. John, *Storms*, 321–27, and Kessell, *Kiva*, 382–91.

19. SANM, Series I (Reel 1), No. 186.

20. BNMUNM, Legajo 8, Part 2, No. 54.

21. Henry W. Kelly, "Franciscan Missions of New Mexico, 1740–1760," part 3, *NMHR* 16, no. 2 (April 1941): 149, and Kessell, *Kiva*, 334. BNMUNM, Legajo 8, Part 2, No. 62 establishes the dates that Ornedal was in New Mexico. Ornedal's official titles and duties are described in Archivo Hidalgo del Parral (Reel 1749), frames 13–14.

22. In "Franciscan Missions" (pp. 151–54), Kelly effectively covers most of Ornedal's report. A copy of Ornedal's Informe in BNMUNM, Legajo 8, Part 2, No. 56, provides additional points and the quote.

23. Ornedal's *Informe*, BNMUNM, Legajo 8, Part 2, No. 56.

24. Ibid.

25. Ferdinand VI in 1749 decreed that regular clergy serving as parish priests be replaced by secular clergymen. Viceroy Conde de Revillagigedo was in favor of accelerating the pace of secularization in New Spain, though that aim was hampered by a severe shortage of secular clergy. Perhaps these factors are part of what motivated Ornedal, although there are no documents from the viceroy that attest to such stipulations. See Fray Diego Miguel Bringas de Manzaneda y Encinas, *Friar Bringas Reports to the King: Methods of Indoctrination on the Frontier of New Spain, 1796–1797*, ed. and trans. Daniel S. Matson and Bernard L. Fontana (Tucson: University of Arizona Press, 1977), 15–17.

26. Kelly, "Franciscan Missions," part 2, 16, no. 1, 61–63.

27. Hackett, *Historical Documents*, 432–38.

28. Kelly, "Franciscan Missions," part 2, 16, no. 1, 65–67.

29. John Francis Bannon, *Spanish Borderlands Frontier* (Albuquerque: University of New Mexico Press, 1979), 150–51, and Russell C. Ewing, "The Pima Outbreak in November, 1751," *NMHR* 13, no. 4 (October 1938): 338–47. A copy of Sedelmayr's Relación is found in BNMUNM, Legajo 8, Part 2, No. 65.

30. BNMUNM, Legajo 8, Part 3, Nos. 67, 74, 75, and Hackett, *Historical Documents*, 425–30, 479–501.

31. Hackett, *Historical Documents*, 438–57.

32. Ibid., 455.

33. BNMUNM, Legajo 8, Part 3, No. 76, and Chavez, *Origins*, 145, 183–84.

34. BNMUNM, Legajo 8, Part 3, No. 76. A similar series of certifications were made for the El Paso missionaries by officials and prominent citizens there; see BNMUNM, Legajo 9, Part 1, No. 12.

35. Hackett, *Historical Documents*, 496–98, and Kelly, "Franciscan Missions," part 2, 16, no. 1, 61–63.

36. Eleanor Adams and Fray Angelico Chavez, *The Missions of New Mexico, 1776: A Description by Fray Francisco Atanasio Domínguez with Other Contemporary Documents* (Albuquerque: University of New Mexico Press, 1976), 85–87, and Hackett, *Historical Documents*, 493–98. Varo's report was the last such known document out of New Mexico until 1758, according to Provincial Fray Pedro Serrano in Hackett, *Historical Documents*, 496–97.

37. Richard E. Greenleaf, "The Inquisition in Eighteenth-Century New Mexico," *NMHR* 60, no. 1 (January 1985): 43–44. For background on Montaño, see INAH, Vol. 25, folio 116.

38. Greenleaf, "The Inquisition," 44–45.

39. Thomas, *The Plains Indians*, 65–67.

40. Robert Ryal Miller, "New Mexico in the Mid-Eighteenth Century," *Southwest Historical Quarterly* 79, no. 2 (October 1975): 169–81. The quotes are on pp. 174 and 181.

41. Elizabeth A. H. John, *Storms Brewed in Other Men's Worlds: The Confrontation of Indians, Spanish and French in the Southwest, 1540–1795* (Lincoln: University of Nebraska Press, 1975), 329–30, and Thomas, *The Plains Indians*, 33–34.

42. Hackett, *Historical Documents*, 473–74, 496–500, and Adams and Chavez, *The Missions*, 246–47.

43. The 1752 roster is in BNMUNM, Legajo 9, Part 2, No. 21; Castro's 1755 visita report, BNMUNM, Legajo 9, Part 2, No. 31; and the 1757/1759 roster, BNMUNM, Legajo 9, Part 2, No. 38.

44. BNMUNM, Legajo 9, Part 2, No. 21.

45. BNMUNM, Legajo 9, Part 2, No. 31.

46. BNMUNM, Legajo 9, Part 2, No. 38.

47. Background on Castro is drawn from Adams and Chavez, *The Missions*, 330; INAH, Vol. 27, folio 84; and BNM, Caja 43, 978.1, folios 1–4v and 979.1, folios 1–11.

48. BNMUNM, Legajo 9, Part 2, No. 31.

Chapter 11

1. Eleanor B. Adams, *Bishop Tamarón's Visitation of New Mexico, 1760* (Albuquerque: University of New Mexico Press, 1954), 19–20.

2. Ibid., 21, 27.

3. Ibid., 34–43.

4. Ibid., 78.

5. Ibid., 25–26, and Charles W. Hackett, *Historical Documents Relating to New Mexico, Nueva Vizcaya, and Approaches Thereto, to 1773*, collected by Adolph A. F. Bandelier and Fanny R. Bandelier (Washington, D.C.: Carnegie Institute of History, 1937), 468–79.

6. Adams, *Bishop Tamarón*, 43–48.

7. Ibid., 48–71.

8. Ibid., 53–54, 64–65, 67–68.

9. Ibid., 76–77.

10. Ibid., 74, 48 (quote).

11. Ibid., 48–49.

12. AASF (Reel 52), 1762, No. 1; 1765, No. 2; 1767, Nos. 1, 2 (expulsion of the Jesuits), 3. See also Adams, *Bishop Tamarón*, 81–85.

13. Adams, *Bishop Tamarón*, 77–81, and BNMUNM, Legajo 9, Part 2, No. 59.

14. BNMUNM, Legajo 10, Part 1, No. 11.

15. BNMUNM, Legajo 10, Part 1, No. 1.

16. BNMUNM, Legajo 10, Part 1, No. 3, and AASF (Reel 52), 1768, No. 1.

17. For the eventual secularization of those four Spanish communities, see Lawrence Kinnaird and Lucia Kinnaird, "Secularization of Four New Mexico Missions," *NMHR* 54, no. 1 (January 1979): 35–41. The Diocese of Durango entered a chaotic period with Tamarón's death. Fray José Vicente Díaz Bravo of the Carmelite Order and a theologian at the University of Pamplona was appointed bishop in 1769. Díaz Bravo arrived in Durango late during the following year, but apparently suffered a mental breakdown by January 1771. He died in April 1772 but his successor, Don Antonio Macarulla Minguilla y Aguilanin (formerly bishop of Comayagua), did not arrive in Durango until the autumn of 1773. Thus, the bishopric of Durango was not effectively directed for about five years; see Guillermo Porras Muñoz, *Iglesia y estado en Nueva Vizcaya, 1562–1821* (Mexico: Universidad Nacional Autónoma de México, 1980), 124–29.

18. Adams, *Bishop Tamarón*, 30, 45–47, and John, *Storms*, 329–30.

19. Adams, *Bishop Tamarón*, 30, and John, *Storms*, 330–31.

20. John, *Storms*, 331–34, and John L. Kessell, *Kiva, Cross and Crown: The Pecos Indians and New Mexico, 1540–1840* (Washington, D.C.: National Park Service, 1979), 392–93.

21. BNMUNM, Legajo 9, Part 3, No. 54.

22. Ibid.

23. Ibid. For Junta de los Ríos, see J. Charles Kelly, "The Historic Indian Pueblos of Junta de los Rios," part 1, *NMHR* 27, no. 4 (October 1952): 257–95.

24. Kelly, "The Historic Indian Pueblos," 257–95, and part 2, 28, no. 1 (January 1953): 21–51, and Kessell, *Kiva*, 301–02.

25. Richard E. Greenleaf, "The Inquisition in Eighteenth-Century New Mexico," *NMHR* 60, no. 1 (January 1985): 47–48.

26. Marc Simmons, *Witchcraft in the Southwest: Spanish and Indian Supernaturalism on the Rio Grande* (Lincoln: University of Nebraska Press, 1974), 32, and Eleanor Adams and Fray Angelico Chavez, *The Missions of New Mexico, 1776: A Description by Fray Francisco Atanasio Domínguez with Other Contemporary Documents* (Albuquerque: University of New Mexico Press, 1976), 336. For Ordóñez at Abiquiu during these dates, see Franciscan rosters in BNMUNM, Legajo 9, Part 2, Nos. 31, 38.

27. John, *Storms*, 432–41.

28. Alfred Barnaby Thomas, "Governor Mendinueta's Proposals for the Defense of New Mexico," *NMHR* 6, no. 1 (January 1931): 24–25.

29. John, *Storms*, 468–71, and Kessell, *Kiva*, 394–97. John blames Mendinueta for the renewal of hostilities between the Spanish and Comanches (see pp. 466–68). On the other hand, Simmons believes Mendinueta to have been a vigorous and able governor; see *Spanish Government in New Mexico* (Albuquerque: University of New Mexico Press, 1968), 53.

30. John, *Storms*, 474–84.

31. Ibid., 441–45, 472–73, and Simmons, *Spanish Government*, 115–16.

32. SANM, Series II (Reel 10), No. 634.

33. Simmons, *Coronado's Land: Essays on Daily Life in Colonial New Mexico* (Albuquerque: University of New Mexico Press, 1991), 118–26.

34. BNMUNM, Legajo 10, Part 1, No. 4.

35. BNMUNM, Legajo 10, Part 1, No. 5.

36. AASF (Reel 52), 1772, No. 2.

37. Greenleaf, "The Inquisition," 48, and Adams and Chavez, *The Missions*, 273, 337.

38. AASF (Reel 52), 1772, No. 2; BNMUNM, Legajo 10, Part 1, No. 18; and SANM, Series II (Reel 10), Nos. 680, 683, 685.

39. For background on Vélez de Escalante, see Eleanor B. Adams, "Fray Silvestre and the Obstinate Hopi," *NMHR* 38, no. 2 (April 1963): 97–98, 115–18.

40. Adams and Chavez, *The Missions*, xiv–xxi (quotes are on p. xx).

41. Adams, "Fray Silvestre," 105–38, and Thomas, *Forgotten Frontiers: A Study of the Spanish Indian Policy of Don Juan Bautista de Anza, Governor of New Mexico, 1777–1787* (Norman: University of Oklahoma Press, 1962), 152–65.

42. Adams and Chavez, *The Missions*, xv, 270–73.

43. Ibid., 277–78, and Adams, "Fray Silvestre," 101–02.

44. Adams and Chavez, *The Missions*, 68, 86, 210.

45. Ibid., 115, 75, 138, 215, 86, 167.

46. Ibid., 179, 193, 88, 98, 207.

47. Ibid., 107, 94–95.

48. Ibid., 81–84, 126, 147–48, 31, 39–40.

49. Ibid., 81–82, 151, 169, 174, 158.

50. Ibid., 80, 96–97, 123–25, 193, 180–81. Ruíz's evangelical methods are found on pp. 308–15.

51. Ibid., 289–96.

52. Ibid., 300, 291–92.

53. Ibid., 205–06, 86, 164, 291–92.

54. Ibid., 300.

55. Ibid., 296, 300.

56. Adams, "Fray Silvestre Vélez de Escalante's Letter to the Missionaries of New Mexico," *NMHR* 40, no. 4 (October 1965): 321–31.

Chapter 12

1. Eleanor Adams and Fray Angelico Chavez, *The Missions of New Mexico: A Description by Fray Francisco Atanasio Domínguez with Other Contemporary Documents*, 1776 (Albuquerque: University of New Mexico Press, 1976), xvii–xviii, 301–02.

2. John L. Kessell, *Kiva, Cross and Crown: The Pecos Indians and New Mexico, 1540–1840* (Washington, D.C.: National Park Service, 1979), 348–49, and Adams and Chavez, *The Missions*, 301, 328–40.

3. Kessell, *Kiva*, 348–49, and Kessell, *The Missions of New Mexico Since 1776* (Albuquerque: University of New Mexico Press, 1980), 14.

4. Kessell, *Kiva*, 352–53; Kessell, *The Missions of New Mexico*, 44–45; and Peter Gerhard, *The North Frontier of New Spain*, rev. ed. (Norman: University of Oklahoma Press, 1993), 198–99. J. Charles Kelly found that the Junta de los Ríos missions had probably stopped operating by the end of the 1770s; see "The Historic Indian Pueblos of Junta de los Rios," part 2, *NMHR* 28, no. 1 (January 1953): 21–51. See also Ramón A. Gutiérrez, *When Jesus Came the Corn Mothers Went Away: Marriage, Sexuality, and Power in New Mexico, 1500–1846* (Stanford: Stanford University Press, 1991), 167, 311.

5. Alfred Barnaby Thomas, ed. and trans., *Teodoro de Croix and the Northern Frontier of New Spain, 1776–1783: From the Original Document in the Archives of the Indies, Seville* (Norman: University of Oklahoma Press, 1941), 105–14; Marc Simmons, *Coronado's Land: Essays on Daily Life in Colonial New Mexico* (Albuquerque: University of New Mexico Press, 1991), 162–72; and Pedro Baptista Pino, *The Exposition on the Province of New Mexico, 1812*, ed. and trans. Adrian Bustamante and Marc Simmons (Santa Fe: Rancho de Golondrinas; Albuquerque: University of New Mexico Press, 1995), 9, 30–32.

6. The Bourbon policies toward the Church are best seen in Nancy M. Farriss, *Crown and Clergy in Colonial Mexico, 1759–1812: The Crisis of Ecclesiastical Privilege* (London: The Athlone Press, 1968), especially pp. 1–196.

7. Gutiérrez, *When Jesus Came*, 46, 66, 92, 145.

8. Kessell, *Kiva*, 78–90; France V. Scholes, "Church and State in New Mexico, 1610–1650," *NMHR* 11 (1936): 20–31, 85–90; and Scholes, *Troublous Times in New Mexico, 1659–1670* (Albuquerque: Historical Society of New Mexico, 1942), 3–5, 20, 71–74.

9. Jim Norris, "The Franciscans in New Mexico, 1692–1754: Toward a New Assessment," *The Americas* 54, no. 2 (October 1994): 153–59.

10. Ibid., 165–68.

11. Ibid., 168.

Bibliography

Archival Sources

Archivo Franciscano, Biblioteca Nacional de México (BNM), México, D.F.

Archivo Arquidiocesano de la Catedral de Durango (AACD), New Mexico State Library, Southwest Collection (microfilm holdings), Las Cruces, New Mexico

Archives of the Archdiocese of Santa Fe (AASF); Archivo General de las Indias, Spain (AGI); Audiencia de México; Archivo General de la Nación, Mexico (AGN); Inquisición; Archivo de Hidalgo del Parral, Mexico (AHP); Biblioteca Nacional de México, Mexico (BNMUNM); Archivo Franciscano; Spanish Archives of New Mexico, Series I and II (SANM), Center for Southwest Research, University of New Mexico, Albuquerque, New Mexico

Fondo Franciscano, Instituto Nacional de Antropología e Historia (INAH), México, D.F.

Papeles de Puebla de los Angeles (PPA), John Carter Brown Library, Brown University, Providence, Rhode Island

Prontuario general y específico y colectivo de nomenclaturas de todos los religiosos que ha habido en esta Santa Provincia del Santo Evangelio desde su fundación por Fray Francisco Antonio de la Rosa Figueruela, Nettie Lee Benson Latin American Library, Manuscript Collection, University of Texas at Austin

Theses and Published Sources

Adams, Eleanor B. *Bishop Tamarón's Visitation of New Mexico, 1760*. Albuquerque: University of New Mexico Press, 1954.

———. "Fray Silvestre and the Obstinate Hopi." *New Mexico Historical Review* (*NMHR*) 38, no. 2 (April 1963): 97–138.

———. "Fray Silvestre Vélez de Escalante's Letter to the Missionaries of New Mexico." *NMHR* 40, no. 4 (October 1965): 318–32.

———and Fray Angelico Chavez. *The Missions of New Mexico, 1776: A Description by Fray Francisco Atanasio Domínguez with Other Contemporary Documents*. Albuquerque: University of New Mexico Press, 1976.

Alcocer, Fray José Antonio. *Bosquejo de la historia del Colegio de Nuestra Señora de Guadalupe y sus misiones.* 1788. Reprint, Mexico: Editorial Porrua, S.A., 1958.

Archibald, Robert. "Acculturation and Assimilation in Colonial New Mexico." *NMHR* 53, no. 3 (July 1978): 205–18.

Athearn, Frederic James. "Life and Society in Eighteenth–Century New Mexico, 1692–1776." Ph.D. diss., University of Texas at Austin, 1974.

Bannon, John Francis. *The Spanish Borderlands Frontier, 1531–1821.* New York: Holt, Rinehart and Winston, 1963.

Bloom, Lansing B. "A Campaign Against the Moqui Pueblos Under Governor Phélix Martínez, 1716." *NMHR* 6, no. 2 (April 1931): 158–226.

————. "The Governors of New Mexico." *NMHR* 10, no. 2 (April 1935): 152–57.

————and Lynn B. Mitchell. "The Chapter Elections in 1672." *NMHR* 13, no. 1 (January 1938): 85–119.

Bolton, Herbert Eugene. "The Mission as a Frontier Institution in the Spanish American Colonies." In *Bolton and the Spanish Borderlands*, edited by John Francis Bannon, 187–211. Norman: University of Oklahoma Press, 1964.

Bowden, Henry Warner. "Spanish Missions, Cultural Conflict and the Pueblo Revolt of 1680." *Church History* 44, no. 2 (July 1975): 217–28.

Brading, D. A. *Church and State in Bourbon Mexico: The Diocese of Michoacán, 1749–1810.* Cambridge: Cambridge University Press, 1994.

Bringas de Manzaneda y Encinas, Fray Diego Miguel. *Friar Bringas Reports to the King: Methods of Indoctrination on the Frontier of New Spain, 1796–1797.* Translated and edited by Daniel S. Matson and Bernard L. Fontana. Tucson: University of Arizona Press, 1977.

Cervantes, Fernando. *The Devil in the New World: The Impact of Diabolism in New Spain.* New Haven: Yale University Press, 1994.

Chavez, Fray Angelico. *Origins of New Mexico Families in the Spanish Colonial Period.* Santa Fe: Historical Society of New Mexico, 1975.

Cutter, Donald R. *The "Protector de Indios" in Colonial New Mexico, 1659–1821.* Albuquerque: University of New Mexico Press, 1986.

Donohue, John Augustine. *After Kino: Jesuit Missions in Northwest New Spain, 1711–1767.* St. Louis: Jesuit Historical Institute, 1969.

Dozier, Edward P. *The Pueblo Indians of North America.* Prospect Heights, Illinois: Waveland Press, 1983.

Espinosa, Fray Isidro Félix de. *Crónica de los colegios de Propaganda Fide de la Nueva España.* 1746. Reprint, Washington, D.C.: Academy of American Franciscan History, 1964.

Espinosa, J. Manuel. *Crusaders of the Rio Grande: The Story of Don Diego de Vargas and the Reconquest and Refounding of New Mexico.* Chicago: Institute of Jesuit History, 1942.

————. *The Pueblo Indian Revolt of 1696 and the Franciscan Missions in New Mexico: Letters of the Missionaries and Related Documents.* Norman: University of Oklahoma Press, 1988.

Ewing, Russell C. "The Pima Outbreak in November, 1751." *NMHR* 13, no. 4 (October, 1938): 337–47.

Farriss, Nancy. *Crown and Clergy in Colonial Mexico, 1759–1812: The Crisis of Ecclesiastical Privilege.* London: The Athlone Press, 1968.

Flagler, Edward K. "Governor José Chacón, Marqués de la Peñuela: An Andalusian Nobleman on the New Mexico Frontier." *NMHR* 65, no. 4 (October 1990): 455–75.

————. "From Asturias to New Mexico: Don Francisco Cuervo y Valdés." *NMHR* 69, no. 3 (July 1994): 249–61.

Folmer, Henri. "Contraband Trade Between Louisiana and New Mexico in the Eighteenth Century." *NMHR* 16, no. 3 (July 1941): 249–74.

Gerhard, Peter. *The North Frontier of New Spain.* Rev. ed. Norman: University of Oklahoma Press, 1993.

Gibson, Charles. *Spain in America.* New York: Harper & Row, 1966.

Gómez Canedo, Fray Lino. *Evangelización y conquista: Experiencia franciscana en Hispanoamerica.* Mexico: Editorial Porrua, S.A., 1988.

Greenleaf, Richard E. "The Inquisition in Eighteenth-Century New Mexico." *NMHR* 60, no. 1 (January 1985): 29–60.

Gutiérrez, Ramón A. *When Jesus Came the Corn Mothers Went Away: Marriage, Sexuality, and Power in New Mexico, 1500–1846.* Stanford: Stanford University Press, 1991.

Habig, Marion A., O.F.M. "The Franciscan Provinces of Spanish North America." *The Americas* 1, no. 2 (October 1944): 215–30.

Hackett, Charles W. *Historical Documents Relating to New Mexico, Nueva Vizcaya, and Approaches Thereto, to 1773.* Collected by Adolph A. F. Bandelier and Fanny R. Bandelier. Washington, D.C.: Carnegie Institute of History, 1937.

————, ed. and Charmion Clair Shelby, trans. *Revolt of the Pueblo Indians of New Mexico and Otermín's Attempted Reconquest, 1680–1682.* 2 vols. 1942. Reprint, Albuquerque: University of New Mexico Press, 1970.

Hendricks, Rick. "Pedro Rodríguez Cubero: New Mexico's Reluctant Governor, 1697–1703." *NMHR* 68, no. 1 (January 1993): 13–39.

Jackson, Robert H. and Edward Castillo. *Indians, Franciscans and Spanish Colonization: The Impact of the Mission System on California Indians.* Albuquerque: University of New Mexico Press, 1995.

Jesús Chauvet, Fray Fidel de. *Los franciscanos en México.* Mexico: Provincia del Santo Evangelio de México, 1989.

John, Elizabeth A. H. *Storms Brewed in Other Men's Worlds: The Confrontation of Indians, Spanish and French in the Southwest, 1540–1795.* Lincoln: University of Nebraska Press, 1975.

Jones Jr., Oakah L. *Pueblo Warriors and Spanish Conquest*. Norman: University of Oklahoma Press, 1966.

Kelly, Henry W. "Franciscan Missions of New Mexico, 1740–1760." Parts 1–3. *NMHR* 15, no. 4 (October 1940): 345–68; 16, no. 1 (January 1941): 41–69; 16, no. 2 (April 1941), 148–83.

Kelly, J. Charles. "The Historic Indian Pueblos of Junta de los Rios," parts 1 and 2. *NMHR* 27, no. 4 (October 1952): 257–95; 28, no. 1 (January 1953): 21–51.

Kessell, John L. *Kiva, Cross and Crown: The Pecos Indians and New Mexico, 1540–1840*. Washington, D.C.: National Park Service, 1979.

———. *The Missions of New Mexico Since 1776*. Albuquerque: University of New Mexico Press, 1980.

———. *Remote Beyond Compare: Letters of Don Diego de Vargas to His Family from New Spain and New Mexico, 1675–1706*. Albuquerque: University of New Mexico Press, 1989.

———and Rick Hendricks, eds. *By Force of Arms: The Journals of Don Diego de Vargas, 1691–1693*. Albuquerque: University of New Mexico Press, 1992.

———, Rick Hendricks, and Meredith Dodge, eds. *To The Royal Crown Restored: The Journals of Don Diego de Vargas, 1692–1694*. Albuquerque: University of New Mexico Press, 1995.

Kinnaird, Lawrence and Lucia Kinnaird. "Secularization of Four New Mexico Missions." *NMHR* 54, no. 1 (January 1979): 35–41.

Lockhart, James and Stuart B. Schwartz. *Early Latin America: A History of Colonial Spanish America and Brazil*. Cambridge and New York: Cambridge University Press, 1983.

McCloskey, Michael B. *The Formative Years of the Missionary College of Santa Cruz of Querétaro, 1683–1733*. Washington, D.C.: Academy of American Franciscan History, 1955.

Miller, Robert Ryal. "New Mexico in the Mid-Eighteenth Century: A Report Based on Governor Vélez Cachupín's Inspection." *Southwest Historical Quarterly* 79, no. 2 (October 1975): 166–81.

Moorhead, Max L. *The Apache Frontier: Jacobo Ugarte and Spanish-Indian Relations in Northern New Spain, 1769–1791*. Norman: University of Oklahoma Press, 1968.

———. "The Presidio Supply Problem of New Mexico in the Eighteenth Century." *NMHR* 36, no. 3 (July 1961): 210–29.

Moorman, John. *A History of the Franciscan Order: From Its Origins to the Year 1517*. Oxford: Clarendon Press, 1968.

Morales, Fray Francisco. *Ethnic and Social Background of the Franciscan Friars in Seventeenth-Century Mexico*. Washington, D.C.: The Academy of American Franciscan History, 1973.

Norris, Jim. "The Franciscans in New Mexico, 1692–1754: Toward a New Assessment." *The Americas* 51, 2 (October 1994): 151–71.

Oss, Adriann C. Van. *Catholic Colonialism: A Parish History of Guatemala, 1524–1821*. Cambridge: Cambridge University Press, 1986.

Phelan, John Leddy. *The Millennial Kingdom of the Franciscans in the New World*. Berkeley: University of California Press, 1970.

Piho, Virve. *La secularización de las parroquias en la Nueva España y su repercusión en San Andrés Calpán*. Mexico: Instituto Nacional de Antropología e Historia, 1981.

Pino, Pedro Baptista. *The Exposition on the Province of New Mexico, 1812*. Translated and edited by Adrian Bustamante and Marc Simmons. Santa Fe: Rancho de Golondrinas; Albuquerque: University of New Mexico Press, 1995.

Porras Muñoz, Guillermo. *Iglesia y estado en Nueva Vizcaya, 1562–1821*. Mexico: Universidad Nacional Autónoma de México, 1980.

Ricard, Robert. *The Spiritual Conquest of Mexico: An Essay on the Apostolate and the Evangelizing Methods of the Mendicant Orders in New Spain, 1523–1572*. Translated by Lesley Byrd Simpson. Berkeley: University of California Press, 1974.

Scholes, France V. "The Supply Service of the New Mexico Missions in the Seventeenth Century," part 2. *NMHR* 5, no. 3 (July 1931): 180–210.

———. "Problems in the Early Ecclesiastical History of New Mexico." *NMHR* 7, no. 1 (January 1932): 32–74.

———. "The First Decade of the Inquisition in New Mexico." *NMHR* 10, no. 2 (April 1935): 195–241.

———. "Church and State in New Mexico, 1610–1650," parts 1–5. *NMHR* 11, no. 1 (January 1936): 9–76; 11, no. 2 (April 1936): 145–78; 11, no. 3 (July 1936): 283–94; 11, no. 4 (October 1936): 297–349; 12, no. 1 (January 1937): 78–106.

———. *Troublous Times in New Mexico, 1659–1670*. Albuquerque: Historical Society of New Mexico, 1942.

Schwaller, John Frederick. *Origins of Church Wealth in Mexico: Ecclesiastical Revenues and Church Finances, 1523–1600*. Albuquerque: University of New Mexico Press, 1985.

———. *The Church and Clergy in Sixteenth-Century Mexico*. Albuquerque: University of New Mexico Press, 1987.

Simmons, Marc. *Spanish Government in New Mexico*. Albuquerque: University of New Mexico Press, 1990.

———. *Witchcraft in the Southwest: Spanish and Indian Supernaturalism on the Rio Grande*. Lincoln: University of Nebraska Press, 1974.

———. *Coronado's Land: Essays on Daily Life in Colonial New Mexico*. Albuquerque: University of New Mexico Press, 1991.

Smith, F. Todd. *The Caddo Indians: Tribes at the Convergence of Empires, 1542–1854*. College Station: Texas A & M University Press, 1995.

Spicer, Edward H. *Cycles of Conquest: The Impact of Spain, Mexico, and the United States on the Indians of the Southwest, 1533–1960*. Tucson: University of Arizona Press, 1962.

Thomas, Alfred Barnaby. "Governor Mendinueta's Proposals for the Defense of New Mexico, 1772–1778." *NMHR* 6, no. 1 (January 1931): 21–39.

———. *Forgotten Frontiers: A Study of the Spanish Indian Policy of Don Juan Bautista de Anza, Governor of New Mexico, 1777–1787.* Norman: University of Oklahoma Press, 1932.

———. *After Coronado: Spanish Exploration Northeast of New Mexico, 1692–1727: Documents from the Archives of Spain, Mexico, and New Mexico.* Norman: University of Oklahoma Press, 1935.

———. *The Plains Indians and New Mexico, 1751–1778: A Collection of Documents Illustrative of the Eastern Frontier of New Mexico.* Albuquerque: University of New Mexico Press, 1940.

———, ed. and trans. *Teodoro de Croix and the Northern Frontier of New Spain, 1776–1783: From the Original Document in the Archives of the Indies, Seville.* Norman: University of Oklahoma Press, 1941.

Warner, Ted J. "Don Félix Martínez and the Santa Fe Presidio, 1693–1730." *NMHR* 45, no. 4 (October 1970): 269–310.

Weber, David J. *The Spanish Frontier in North America.* New Haven: Yale University Press, 1992.

West, Elizabeth Howard. "The Right of Asylum in New Mexico in the Seventeenth and Eighteenth Centuries." *NMHR* 41, no. 2 (April 1966): 115–53.

Index

Abadiano, Manuel, 151
Abiquiu, 104, 114, 141–42, 143, 150, 151
Acoma mission, 35, 45, 51, 130, 135, 148, 149
Adrian VI, Pope, 11
Aguilar, Juan, 93, 94
Albuquerque, Duke of, 55, 59
Albuquerque: and Crespo's *visita*, 77, 186n25; establishment of, 49; raids against, 143; residents, Dominguez's view of, 150; secularization of, 79, 137–38, 157, 194n17; staffing of, 118, 129, 134
alcaldes mayores: as an entrenched bureaucracy, 88; and Indian witchcraft cases, 57; and kivas, destruction of, 56, 64; language proficiency of, 163; removal of, 13, 88; support the Franciscans, 13, 102, 125, 141
Alonso Barroso, Cristóbal, 18
Alpuente, Juan, 34, 35, 40, 41
Alta California missions, 26
alternativa system, 25
Álvarez, Juan: background of, 21; on Cuervo, 48–49; as ecclesiastical judge, El Paso, 71–72; orders friars out of civil disputes, 46, 47; regains commissary of the Inquisition, 46; report of 1706, 50, 51–52
el año ochenta, legacy of, 5, 16, 42
Anza, Juan Bautista de, 157
Apaches: arms sold to, 56; Jicarilla mission, 95; Menchero's entrada to, 116; prisoners and slaves of, 65; raiding by, 48, 56, 64, 88, 91, 139, 143
Aparicio, Antonio, 67
arancels, 74, 75, 78, 117, 145. *See also* fees for religious services
Archundía, José de, 89, 93, 94
Arévalo, Lucas de, 67
Arias de Espinosa, Diego, 92
Arranegui, José, 24, 51
Arvisu (Arbizu) José de, 19, 41, 42
asylum, right of, 85, 146
Awátovi, 45

Baamonde (Bahamonde) Antonio, 33
Baca (Vaca), Bernabé, 125
Baptista Pino, Pedro, 158
Barroso, Cristóbal Alonso, 31, 51
Benavides, Rafael, 21
Bermejo, Manuel, 108, 109
Bernalillo, 38
Blanco, José, 108
Bourbon family, rule of. *See* Spanish Crown
Bravo Lerchundí, Francisco Manuel, 93
Bretons (Brotons), Francisco, 60–61, 63–64, 67, 184n27
Bucareli y Ursua, Antonio, 144, 146
Burgos, José de, 151, 153
Bustamante, Bernardo de, 116
Bustamante, José Perea, 79, 187n37
Bustamante, Juan Domingo de, 77, 78, 79, 87–90, 188n19

Camargo, Antonio, 51, 84–85, 89–90, 97, 109
La Cañada. *See* Santa Cruz de la Cañada
Carbonel, Antonio, 33, 40, 41, 181n33
Carrizal, 133, 135, 144
Casafuerte, Marqués de, 75, 76, 87, 94
Castro, Jacobo de, 24–25, 129–31, 133
Cayetano de Otero, Francisco Benito, 91, 93, 94, 115
Ceballos (Zevallos), Andrés, 92, 109
La Cebolleta mission, 107, 122–23
Cepeda y Arriola, Miguel Francisco, 66
Chacón, Fernando de, 157–58
Chacón Medina Salazar y Villaseñor, José: appointment of, 54–55, 68; and Cuervo, 55; and Fr. López's transfer, 61–62; and Inquisition cases, 57–58; and kivas, destruction of, 56–57; military defense concerns of, 55–56; and missionary trading, 59–60; and the Tiwa controversy, 60–61
Chama, 119
Charles III, 132
Chavarría, Diego de, 39, 42, 181n41